FAITH AND FREEDOM

FAITH AND FREEDOM

A Complete Handbook for
Defending Your Religious Rights

Mathew D. Staver

CROSSWAY BOOKS • WHEATON, ILLINOIS
A DIVISION OF GOOD NEWS PUBLISHERS

Faith and Freedom:
A Complete Handbook for Defending Your Religious Rights

Copyright © 1995 by Mathew D. Staver

Published by Crossway Books
   a division of Good News Publishers
   1300 Crescent Street
   Wheaton, Illinois 60187

Cover photos: Jim Whitmer Photography, Wheaton, Illinois

Cover Design: Cindy Kiple

First printing, 1995

Printed in the United States of America

Library of Congress Cataloging-in-Publication Data
Staver, Mathew D., 1956–
 Faith and freedom : a complete handbook for defending your
religious rights / Mathew D. Staver.
   p. cm.
 Includes bibliographical references and index.
 1. Church and state—United States. 2. Freedom of religion—
United States. 3. Religion in the public schools—Law and
legislation—United States. I. Title.
KF4865.S73 1995   342.73'0852—dc20   94-37644
ISBN 0-89107-835-5

05	04	03	02	01	00	99	98	97	96	95
15	14	13	12	11	10	9	8	7	6	5	4	3	2	1

Contents

92218

Acknowledgments

As with most projects of any magnitude, many people are responsible for the finished product. The team of people who assisted me is exceptional. They, like me, have put their heart and soul in this project. The contents of this book arise out of personal experience, numerous telephone calls answering people's questions, attendance at numerous commission and board meetings, hours and hours of research, and litigation in the courtroom.

Susan Engel has been faithful in answering thousands of telephone calls from people across the country inquiring regarding religious liberty. She has also dutifully worked on typing, editing, and indexing. Peggy Bush and Barbara Broley have been with me through the stressful days and have also diligently typed and proofed this book. Rick Nelson has undertaken the painstaking task of grammatical revisions and the laborious task of checking each one of the footnotes. Rick and Jeff Kipi have labored with me in the courtroom and have drafted legal memoranda in preparation for our litigated cases out of which part of this research is based. Through all these hectic times, Georgean Himes has been a constant reminder that God is still in control. While being president and founder of Liberty Counsel and working on religious liberty issues full-time, I also manage a multiple office law practice and a governmental consulting corporation full-time. My friends and colleagues have stood beside me daily. They have shared in the joys, and they have shared in the sorrows we have encountered along the way. Michael Rouse and Pamela Cox have always been faithful in holding down the fort when I was gone from the law practice. Pamela Freeman has tried to juggle many activities simultaneously. My daughter, Meredith, has been understanding of my work load and has been of great assistance in working on the index. Without the prayers and assistance of my colleagues and friends whom I work with every day, this book would clearly not be possible. I could speak about each one individually, but that would require volumes. Knowing my space is limited, I wish to give my gratitude and heartfelt thanks to Anita Beach, Venetia Bennett, Robin Browning, Carla

Camelin, Stuart Christmas, Amy Creamer, Jane Cunningham, Ralph Douglas, Donna Early, Melinda Fernbach, Timothy Garland, Melanie Hall, Joan Kettlehut, GiGi Killian, Jill Larson, Kymberly Lyons, Jon Johnson, Nicole Arfaras, Candy McGuire, Loretta Overton, Flo Shetterly, Shelley Spadafore, Laura Tolley, Laura Turco, Kimberly Welker, and Rhonda White.

The one whom I wish to thank the most is my best friend and wife, Anita L. Staver. She has been my faithful companion, my counselor, and my encourager. She has given me comfort through the hard times, and she has laughed with me through the joyous times. She has been through the stress, and she has been through the calm. She has been understanding when I regularly work fourteen hour days, day after day after day. Without her, this book clearly would not be possible. She has been able to maintain her sense of sanity and a sense of humor, and she has always kept me pointed in the right direction.

Foreword

ity the public school principal in December," began the *New York Times* summary. "Between Hanukkah, Christmas and Kwanzaa (a Black-American holiday that celebrates family and community and is based on African harvest festivals), this long last month lays a minefield of grand proportions for educators trying to acknowledge the holidays without bridging the separation of church and state." The object, said one A.C.L.U. official, is "to treat all religions and atheism equally." As one school district framed its policy: "Trees are allowed; religious decorations and Nativity scenes are not. Menorahs are allowed, but there is no daily lighting of candles. Concerts and parties are prefaced with the words holiday or winter instead of Christmas."[1]

One might fairly ask how such distinctions follow from the simple words of the religion clauses of the First Amendment: "Congress shall make no law respecting an establishment of religion, or prohibiting the free exercise thereof. . . ." The short answer is that they don't. The current interpretations of the religion clauses are the product not of constitutional intent but of a bewildering array of Supreme Court decisions, the inventiveness of which is exceeded only by their tendency to secularize the public life of the nation and to work a restrained but taxing persecution on Christian and other religious parents who want to integrate their faith with that public life.

The Supreme Court's erroneous interpretations of the Establishment Clause have institutionalized agnostic secularism as the official national creed. This error has been compounded by the Supreme Court's misinterpretation of the Fourteenth Amendment so as to bind the state and local governments strictly by the Court's interpretation of the Bill of Rights. Through its application of the Bill of Rights strictly against the states, the Supreme Court has claimed for itself the power to determine the meaning and application of virtually all personal and civil rights. The effect of this

---

[1]*New York Times*, Dec. 16, 1993, p. B1.

inventive jurisprudence is nowhere more evident than with respect to the religion clauses of the First Amendment.

Professor Edward S. Corwin accurately summarized the original intent of the Establishment Clause of the First Amendment, that "Congress should not prescribe a national faith, a possibility which those states with establishments of their own—Massachusetts, New Hampshire, Connecticut, Maryland, and South Carolina—probably regarded with fully as much concern as those which had gotten rid of their establishment."[2] Justice Joseph Story, who served on the Supreme Court from 1811 to 1845 and who himself was a Unitarian, said:

> Probably, at the time of the adoption of the Constitution, and of the [First] Amendment to it, . . . the general, if not the universal sentiment in America was, that Christianity ought to receive encouragement from the State, so far as such encouragement was not incompatible with the private rights of conscience, and the freedom of religious worship. An attempt to level all religions, and to make it a matter of state policy to hold all in utter indifference, would have created universal disapprobation, if not universal indignation. . . . The real object of the amendment was, not to countenance, much less to advance Mohammedanism, or Judaism, or infidelity, by prostrating Christianity; but to exclude all rivalry among Christian sects, and to prevent any national ecclesiastical establishment which should give to a hierarchy the exclusive patronage of the national government.[3]

The framers of the First Amendment would have rejected the view of today's Supreme Court, which excludes prayer from public life and forbids even the posting of the Ten Commandments in public schools. The Northwest Ordinance, adopted by the Continental Congress in 1787, provided public support for religious education: "Religion, morality, and knowledge, being necessary to good government and the happiness of mankind, schools and the means of education, shall forever be encouraged." This enactment was reaffirmed by the First Congress in 1789. After the new Constitution was ratified, the Congress on September 24-26, 1789, did two things. They approved and sent to the states for ratification the First Amendment. And they called on President Washington to "recommend to the people of the United States a day of public thanksgiving and prayer, to be observed by acknowledging, with grateful hearts, the many signal favors of Almighty God." Can you believe that the Congress intended the First Amendment to forbid the sort of prayer it recommended on the same day? Nor was this a result of inadvertence. Representative Thomas Tucker of South Carolina objected that the call for a day of prayer "is a religious matter, and, as such, is proscribed to us." Congress passed the resolution, deliberately overriding the argument the Supreme Court has adopted as doctrine today.[4]

---

[2]Edward Samuel Corwin, *The Powers in a Secular State* (1951), pp. 102, 106.
[3]Joseph Story, *Commentaries on the Constitution of the United States* (3rd ed., Boston: Hilliard, Gray, 1858), 2 Secs. 1874, 1877.
[4]Annals of Congress 915 (1789).

In *The Church of the Holy Trinity v. United States*, in 1892, the Supreme Court unanimously held that a Congressional statute forbidding the immigration of persons under contract to perform labor did not apply to an English minister who entered this country under a contract to preach at a New York church. After reciting the legislative history of the act, the Court said,

> But beyond all these matters no purpose of action against religion can be imputed to any legislation, state or national, because this is a religious people. This is historically true. From the discovery of this content to the present hour, there is a single voice making this affirmation. . . . If we pass beyond these matters to a view of American life as expressed by its laws, its business, its customs and its society, we find everywhere a clear recognition of the same truth. . . . These, and many other matters which might be noticed, add a volume of unofficial declarations to the mass of organic utterances that this is a Christian nation.[5]

The American religious consensus, however, eroded. The Supreme Court in recent years has reflected as well as encouraged that erosion by interpreting the Establishment Clause to require not merely neutrality on the part of government among Christian and other theistic sects, but neutrality between theism and nontheism. It is impossible, however, for government to maintain neutrality on the existence of God. To affirm God is a preference for theism, to deny Him a preference for atheism, and to suspend judgment a preference for agnosticism which is itself a religion.

The Court, nevertheless, requires government at all levels to maintain a neutrality between theism and nontheism. Justice William Brennan argued in his concurrence in the 1963 school prayer case that the words "under God" could still be kept in the Pledge of Allegiance only because they "no longer have a religious purpose or meaning." Instead, according to Brennan, they "may merely recognize the historical fact that our Nation was believed to have been founded 'under god'."[6] This false neutrality would logically prevent an assertion by any government official, whether president or school teacher, that the Declaration of Independence—the first of the Organic Laws of the United States printed at the head of the United States Code—is, in fact, true when it asserts that men are endowed "by their Creator" with certain unalienable rights and when it affirms "the Laws of Nature and of Nature's God," a "Supreme Judge of the world" and "Divine Providence." The result, in practical effect, is a governmental preference for the religion of agnostic secularism.

Generations of public school children have passed through the system in the past three decades without ever seeing the state, in the persons of their teachers, acknowledge that there is a standard of right and wrong higher

---

[5]143 U.S. 457, 470-71 (1892).
[6]*School District of Abington Township v. Schempp*, 374 U.S. 203, 304 (1963).

than the state and that "the Laws of Nature and of Nature's God" are in fact a limit on the power of the state. Moreover, the false rule of neutrality requires that public schools must treat sensitive moral issues such as homosexual activity, promiscuity, abortion, etc., in a "nonjudgmental" manner that cannot help but indoctrinate a relativistic attitude in the students. One result is a potential abridgment of the free exercise of religion of students who do not subscribe to the secular orthodoxy. And the process tends to wean the students away from their belief in God. As one writer in *The American Atheist* put it:

> And how does a god die? Quite simply because all his religionists have been converted to another religion, and there is no one left to make children believe they need him.
>
> Finally, it is irresistible—we must ask how we can kill the god of Christianity. We need only insure that our schools teach only secular knowledge; that they teach children to constantly examine and question all theories and truths put before them in any form; and that they teach nothing is proven by the number of persons who believe a thing to be true. If we could achieve this, god would indeed be shortly due for a funeral service.[7]

What are parents to do in the face of the immersion of public institutions by aggressive secularism? Fortunately, they are not without remedy. Legal avenues remain through which they can fight back in the education of their children and even in the introduction of Christian principle into the public order itself. This book by Mathew D. Staver is a powerful weapon in this fight. Mr. Staver is an expert, perceptive, and properly inventive advocate who is not afraid of a fight. He has provided here a clear and understandable guidebook for all of us who would otherwise be lost in the legalistic maze. More important, he treats the law of the state in proper context. In truth, life and the law come ultimately from God, rather than the state, and they are subject to His dominion. Nor is this a time for pessimism. God is not dead. He is not even tired. We are on the winning side. It is time for us to fight back. Mathew Staver's important book will help mightily in that fight.

—Professor Charles E. Rice
Notre Dame Law School

---

[7]Bozarth, "On Keeping God Alive," *American Atheist,* Nov. 1977, 7-8.

PREFACE

Prior to entering law school, I was in the pastoral ministry. During my days as a pastor, I was continually confronted with the interaction between church and state. At one time I was invited to a pastors' meeting where a film on abortion was shown. I had no position on the issue but presumed that I favored abortion. After viewing this video about the development of the unborn child, I changed my views and became pro-life. Thereupon I began reading the United States Supreme court opinion of *Roe v. Wade*,[1] and the more I learned about the abortion issue, the more I was led to legal issues.

While pastoring, I also became frustrated every year during the Christmas season when one nativity scene after another was challenged in court. These events, among others, formed the background to my law school education. After entering law school and studying constitutional law, I began to realize that there is a great deal of misinformation on religious liberty issues.

In 1989, I founded Liberty Counsel in order to provide education and legal defense on religious liberty matters. I have learned that we lose our religious liberties for three primary reasons: (1) ignorance of the law, (2) hostility toward religion, and (3) apathy. Most of the cases in which Liberty Counsel is involved resolve through education. A minority of cases involve someone who is actually hostile toward religion. In this battle over religious liberty, I frequently encounter a great deal of apathy among Christians and other religious people. Most people would rather run than fight and lose their rights rather than struggle for them. The issue of religious liberty is not simply a legal right—it is the ability to continue to spread the gospel in a free nation. The intent of this book is to provide sufficient education in areas of free speech and religious rights, and it is hoped that this book will play a small part in continuing the free channels of religious liberty.

---

[1]410 U.S. 113 (1973).

1

Religion: An Endangered Species

An objective observer cannot escape the conclusion that this country was founded upon Judeo-Christian principles. During his travels in this country in the 1830s, Alexis de Tocqueville stated, "On my arrival in the United States the religious aspect of the country was the first thing that struck my attention."[1] The early founders of this country came here not so much to flee religious persecution but to evangelize a new continent. The first colonial grant from Queen Elizabeth to Sir Walter Raleigh in 1584 was to enact laws provided "they be not against the true Christian faith."[2] The first charter of Virginia by King James in 1606 was to propagate the "Christian religion to such people, [who] as yet live in darkness."[3] The Mayflower Compact of 1620 was for the "advancement of the Christian Faith."[4]

The signers of the Declaration of Independence in 1776 clearly acknowledged that they were "endowed by their Creator with certain unalienable Rights." In the same year, the Delaware Constitution required an oath from all officers as follows: "[I] profess faith in God the Father, and in Jesus Christ His only Son, and in the Holy Ghost, one God, blessed forevermore: and I do acknowledge the Holy Scriptures of the Old and New Testament to be given by divine inspiration."[5] The Massachusetts Constitution of 1780 spoke of the "right" and "duty" of all citizens to "worship the Supreme Being."[6] The Maryland Constitution of 1807 spoke of the "duty of every man to worship God," noting that no person could be a witness unless he or she "believes in the existence of God."[7] Likewise, the Mississippi Constitution of 1832 stated that one could not hold state office and deny the "being of God, or a future state of rewards and pun-

---

[1]Alexis de Tocqueville, *Democracy in America* (New York: Vintage Books, 1945) 1:319.
[2]*The Church of the Holy Trinity v. United States*, 143 U.S. 457, 466 (1892).
[3]*Id.*
[4]*Id.*
[5]*Id.* at 468.
[6]*Id.*
[7]*Id.*

ishment."[8] Indeed, John Adams once said, "Our Constitution was made only for a moral and religious people. It is wholly inadequate for the government of any other."[9]

Reviewing this history, the United States Supreme Court stated in 1892 that "this is a religious nation . . . we are a Christian people," and concluded, "this is a Christian nation."[10] Benjamin Franklin served as one of this country's early founders. As an ambassador to France, he once stated that "[w]hoever will introduce into public affairs the principles of Christianity will change the face of the world." When the Constitutional Convention was about to fall apart, Benjamin Franklin stood up and uttered his famous words: "If a sparrow cannot fall without [God's] notice, is it probable that an empire can rise without His aid?"[11]

George Washington distinguished himself as a great general, representative of Virginia, and the first president of the United States. He did not mince words with his convictions regarding religion when he stated: "Do not let anyone claim to be a true American if they ever attempt to remove religion from politics. Anyone who does this cannot be called American." George Washington also once stated that "reason and experience both forbid us to expect that the national morality can prevail in exclusion of religious principles. Take away religion, and the country will fail."[12]

Patrick Henry recognized the Judeo-Christian foundation of this country when he stated: "It cannot be emphasized too strongly or too often that this great nation was founded not by religionists, but by Christians, not on religions, but on the Gospel of Jesus Christ." John Quincy Adams once declared that the "highest glory of the American Revolution was this: It connected in one indissoluble bond, the principles of civil government with the principles of Christianity." Interestingly, a House Judiciary report of March 27, 1854, issued the following statement in response to a petition to separate Christian principles from government: "In this age there is no substitute for Christianity: that was the religion of the Founders of the Republic and they expected it to remain the religion of their descendants. . . . The great vital and conservative element in our system is the belief of our people in the pure doctrine and Divine truths of the Gospel of Jesus Christ."

Without question, the early founders did not separate their political beliefs from their religious beliefs. Indeed, this country was based upon Judeo-Christian principles that permeated society. A burning desire of many early pioneers was to develop a society in which religion could flourish. Many sacrificed everything they accumulated, and some even forfeited their lives. Once the pioneers arrived on this continent, they staked out

---

[8]*Id.*
[9]John Adams, 1789, *quoted in War in Religious Freedom* 1.
[10]*The Church of the Holy Trinity*, 113 U.S. at 471.
[11]Benjamin Franklin, June 28, 1787, *quoted by* Smyth, *Writings*, IX:600; *quoted by* Alison et al., *The Real Benjamin Franklin* 258-59.
[12]Washington, Farewell Address, September 17, 1796; *quoted by* Johnson, *George Washington the Christian* 217-18.

crosses and penned in their original charters their conviction that God had led them to a new country to spread the gospel of Jesus Christ.

Society has changed since those early days. After becoming comfortable with their new freedom, many mainline religions became infected by liberal theology. Many churches forsook the gospel and searched for a historical Jesus whom they could not find. These churches became socially-oriented and neglected the very heart of the gospel. They had actually lost the gospel through their liberal interpretation of the Bible, no longer believing in the resurrection of Jesus Christ, in miracles, or in the changing power of the gospel other than through psychology. In response to this liberal trend, many reformers emphasized a purity from within and became repulsed at the liberal agendas of many mainline churches. This backlash resulted in pietism wherein the individual relationship with God was emphasized to the neglect of society. The pendulum swung to the opposite end of extremism.

During this age of pietism, many Christians, fed up with liberal denominations, withdrew from society and public influence, believing association with any social agenda was dirty. As these Christians abandoned society, what remained were nonreligious persons in places of public influence or those so-called religious persons who had forgotten their religious roots. The pietistic Christians and the liberal secularists were content to stuff God in a box. God had His own corner reserved within the church; He was hidden within the communion chalice.

This country moves toward secularism at its peril. We have come to accept the standard that where government increases, religion must decrease. We have also come to accept the presumption that government and religion mix like oil and water, that where government treads, religion must flee.

Paul Blanshard, a secular humanist writing in *The Humanist* magazine, once noted that the first seventy-five years of the twentieth century have been "a good seventy-five years, full of rebellion against religious superstition, inspired by developing science, and increasingly open to religious realism."[13] He also stated, "I doubt that any span in human history has carried the world farther along the road to honest doubt."[14] Mr. Blanshard noted that his "primary hero" in moving this nation to a secular society was the United States Supreme Court.

Reviewing the first seventy-five years of the twentieth century, and the United States Supreme Court's impact on public education, Mr. Blanshard concluded:

> I think the most important factor moving us toward a secular society has been the educational factor. Our schools may not teach Johnny to read properly, but the fact that Johnny is in school until he is sixteen tends to lead toward the elimination of religious superstition. The average

---

[13]Paul Blanshard, "Three Cheers for Our Secular State," *The Humanist*, March/April 1976, p. 17.
[14]*Id.*

American child now acquires a high school education, and this militates against Adam and Eve and all other myths of alleged history. . . . I am convinced that religious belief of millions of Americans is only nominal. It is warm-hearted service religion, not creedal religion. When I was one of the editors of *The Nation* in the twenties, I wrote an editorial explaining that golf and intelligence were the two primary reasons that men did not attend church. Perhaps I would now say golf and a high school diploma.[15]

Indeed, one of the factors moving this country toward a secularist society is the combination of the United States Supreme Court and public schools. Originally the United States Supreme Court had no jurisdiction over First Amendment issues because the First Amendment only applied to restrict the activities of the federal government. The First Amendment was not applicable to the individual states until the 1940s when the Supreme Court said it was applicable to the states.[16] In the early 1960s, the Supreme Court, utilizing the First Amendment, struck down prayer[17] and Bible readings[18] within the public school system. In fact, testimony before the Supreme Court at that time suggested that Bible reading could have been psychologically harmful to the child.[19] In 1980, the Supreme Court pulled the Ten Commandments from a classroom bulletin board in the state of Kentucky and thus from all bulletin boards in all public schools throughout the nation.[20] One state court addressing the issue of prayers in public schools lamented that

an unacceptably high number of citizens who are undergoing difficult times in this country are children and young people. School-sponsored prayer might provide hope to sustain them and principles to guide them in the difficult choices they confront today. But the Constitution as the Supreme Court views it does not permit it. Choices are made in order to protect the interest of all citizens. Unfortunately, in this instance there is no satisfactory middle ground. . . . Those who are anti-prayer thus have been deemed the victors. This is the difficult but obligatory choice this court makes today.[21]

Not only has prayer been struck down in public school classrooms, but one federal court even ruled that invocations delivered before public high school football games violated the Constitution.[22]

---

[15]*Id.*
[16]*Cantwell v. Connecticut*, 310 U.S. 296 (1940) (Free Exercise Clause); *Everson v. Board of Education*, 330 U.S. 1 (1947) (Establishment Clause); *Illinois ex rel. McCollum v. Board of Education*, 333 U.S. 203 (1948) (same).
[17]*Engel v. Vitale*, 370 U.S. 421 (1962).
[18]*School District of Abington Township v. Schempp*, 374 U.S. 203 (1963).
[19]*Id.*
[20]*Stone v. Graham*, 449 U.S. 39 (1980).
[21]*Bennett v. Livermore Unified School District*, 238 Cal. Rpt. 819 (1987).
[22]*Jager v. Douglas County School District*, 862 F.2d 824 (11th Cir. 1989), *cert. denied*, 490 U.S. 1090 (1989).

Not all prayer has been removed from the public setting. Interestingly, the United States Supreme Court has ruled that state legislatures are permitted to select and compensate legislative chaplains to open the sessions with prayer.[23] Other federal courts have approved congressional chaplains[24] and the practice of opening county board meetings with prayer.[25]

Nevertheless, significant restrictions have been placed upon religious liberty. While federal courts have increasingly removed religion from public places, at the same time, the United States Supreme Court has weakened the First Amendment Free Exercise Clause.[26] This strengthening of the Establishment Clause and concurrent weakening of the Free Exercise Clause has resulted in the rapid loss of First Amendment religious liberty. Notwithstanding, there are many religious freedoms that can still be exercised vigorously. If they are not, the freedoms that remain today will not remain tomorrow.

The Supreme Court tends to wax and wane from generation to generation. The Supreme Court will probably never return to the state of interpretation prior to 1940 when the First Amendment applied only to restrict the federal government. Part of the problem in moving away from the original intent of the First Amendment is that there has been no consistent jurisprudential approach to interpreting the Constitution. This is because under the present system the Supreme Court's interpretation changes from generation to generation instead of remaining consistent and absolute. Within this myriad of varying Supreme Court interpretations, many religious liberty rights still remain. This book is intended to be a guide to those religious liberty rights. It is important that this country continue to remain free and continue to recognize the importance of religion. Once religion is suffocated or stuffed in a box, this country, as President Washington once said, will certainly fail.

The history of the Soviet Union should teach the United States a lesson. For many years, religion was found mostly in churches turned into museums. However, religious belief and practice continued to operate underground. When the Soviet Communist government failed, the faithful rebounded and now religion flourishes within Russia. At one time, Madalyn Murray O'Hair, the atheist who removed Bible readings from school, wanted to defect to the Soviet Union so that she could live in a country run by atheistic principles. Today she no longer wants to defect because the United States has certainly changed over the years and, to some extent, is trading places with the former Soviet Union in matters regarding religion. Freedom in this country was bought by sacrifice, and it might just be time for those who want religious freedom to consider the same sacrifices.

---

[23]*Marsh v. Chambers*, 463 U.S. 783 (1983).
[24]*Murray v. Buchanan*, 720 F.2d 689 (D.C. Cir. 1983).
[25]*Bogen v. Doty*, 598 F.2d 1110 (8th Cir. 1979).
[26]*Employment Division v. Smith*, 494 U.S. 872 (1990).

2

General Constitutional Principles

THE HISTORY OF THE FIRST AMENDMENT

In order to adequately understand the purpose of the First Amendment, an overview of American history is essential. At one time, I detested history because it did not appear to affect my present day life. History, to me, was made up of names, dates, and facts. However, I entered college and began to view history as His Story, that is God's story of Himself acting within history. Now history has taken on an entirely new meaning for me. In looking back over time, I can see more clearly God's divine will throughout history. Anyone who ignores history is doomed to repeat its mistakes, so it's no wonder American history has been so drastically altered in our public schools. We are now suffering the consequences of that revised history, and we will continue to do so as the school age children of today become adults and leaders of the country.

History was extremely important for the Israelite nation. To this day, the famous Shema from Deuteronomy 6:4 is still repeated in Jewish synagogues, "Hear, O Israel, the Lord our God is one." The Book of Deuteronomy represents the rehearsing of the law surrounding the birth of the nation of Israel. Moses knew the importance of history, which is why he recounted God's historical intervention in the nation's past as the new generation was about to enter the promised land. This new generation was not a part of the old history, so Moses wanted what God had done for their ancestors to be fresh in their minds. The Shema begins the famous section where Moses commands the parents to diligently teach their children about God and His intervention in history.

We have strayed from the correct interpretation of the First Amendment because we have ignored its historical purpose. Looking back into our nation's history, we find Christopher Columbus came to this continent not to flee persecution or for mere exploration, but because he felt God was leading him to spread the gospel in a new land. Later, the Puritans left England because they were impressed that God was leading them to establish the gospel in foreign lands. Public schools were developed in order to teach children how to read the Bible.

After the original thirteen colonies declared independence from Great Britain in 1776, they considerd forming a limited federal government for the primary purpose of national security. In order to "secure the blessings of liberty" for future generations, the colonies adopted the Constitution of the United States in 1787. The Constitution established a federal government with a very limited and prescribed authority. It set forth three branches of government: the Executive (to carry out the laws), the Legislative (to enact the laws and be accountable to the people) and the Judicial (to interpret the laws). At that time, the Judicial was the weakest of the three branches.

After forming the federal government, the thirteen colonies were concerned that the new government would infringe upon the authority of the individual states by imposing federal bureaucracy into the state system. The colonies wanted to create a limited power that would serve the will of the individual sovereign states. They did not want to lose their identity to a national-based government. To accomplish this goal, the first ten amendments, known as the Bill of Rights, were drafted in 1789 and adopted by the colonies on December 15, 1791. The First Amendment, which pertains to religious liberty, states, "Congress shall make no law respecting an establishment of religion, or prohibiting the free exercise thereof. . . ." These amendments were written for the express purpose of limiting the authority of the federal government. The Tenth Amendment reaffirms this when it states that any authority not specifically granted to the federal government was reserved solely for the individual states.

The First Amendment explicitly prohibited the federal government from establishing a national-based church and from prohibiting the free exercise of religion within the states.[1] The federal government had absolutely no jurisdiction over religious matters within the states. If a state established a national church or religion, the federal government had no authority to promote or inhibit the practice of religion within the state. Indeed, as late as the Revolutionary War, there were established churches in at least eight of the thirteen colonies and established religions in at least four of the other five.[2] The individual states were regulated by their own individual constitutions or by their own legislative actions, not by the federal government, and certainly not by the United States Supreme Court.

Supreme Court Justice Joseph Story, who died in 1845, wrote that "at the time of the adoption of the Constitution, . . . the general, if not the universal, sentiment in America was, that Christianity ought to receive encouragement from the State so far as such encouragement was not incompatible with the private rights of conscience and the freedom of religious worship."[3]

---

[1]John Eidsmoe, *The Christian Legal Advisor* (Milford, MI: Mott Media) 1984, pp. 97-164.
[2]*Engel v. Vitale*, 370 U.S. 421, 427-48 (1962).
[3]Joseph Story, 2 *Commentaries on the Constitution of the United States* 593 (Boston, 1833).

In 1875, Senator James Blaine, later a Republican candidate for president in 1884, introduced a resolution for a constitutional amendment that read as follows:

> No State shall make any law respecting an establishment of religion or prohibiting the free exercise thereof; and no money raised by taxation in any state for the support of public school or derived from any public fund therefor, nor any public land devoted thereto, shall ever be under the control of any religious sect or denomination; nor shall any money so raised or lands so devoted be divided between religious sects or denominations.

This amendment was never added to the Constitution because it did not receive two-thirds majority vote of the Senate.[4]

The first part of the Blaine Amendment is identical to the present First Amendment except that it replaces the word "Congress" with "State." The debates indicate that this amendment would, for the first time, limit the authority of the states in religious matters, whereas previously, only the federal government had been prohibited from acting in religious matters. Senator Stevenson stated during these debates,

> Friend as he was of religious freedom, he [Thomas Jefferson] would never have consented that the states, which brought the Constitution into existence, upon whose sovereignty this instrument rests, which keep it within its expressly limited powers, could be degraded in that the government of the United States, a government of limited authority, the mere agent of the state with prescribed powers, should undertake to take possession of their schools and of their religion.[5]

The issue did not die with the failure of the Blaine Amendment. Again in 1937, Senator Borah attempted a similar amendment which also failed for lack of two-thirds vote.[6]

However, what the legislature failed to do for lack of support, and what the thirteen colonies specifically feared, eventually came to pass in 1940. The year 1940 marks a drastic departure from the intent and purpose of the First Amendment and begins a totally new era in our history. Until 1940, the First Amendment had been specifically written, and properly interpreted, to keep the federal government's hands off religious issues within the states. In other words, since the federal government only had authority to act where the colonies so granted, and since the colonies had stated specifically that the federal government had no authority in matters of religion, the federal government had no jurisdiction to act on religious matters within the states.

---

[4]Alfred W. Meyer, "The Blaine Amendment and the Bill of Rights," *Harvard Law Review* 939 (1951).
[5]Cong. Rec. 5589 (1876).
[6]S.J. Res. 92, 75th Cong., 1st Sess. (1937).

Writing for *The Humanist*, Paul Blanshard stated that his primary hero toward changing this country into a secular society was the United States Supreme Court.[7] I agree with Blanshard when he states that the turning point of American history occurred in 1940.

In 1940, the United States Supreme Court ignored the historical context of the First Amendment and applied the First Amendment Free Exercise Clause to the states in the case of *Cantwell v. Connecticut*.[8] Then, in 1947, the Supreme Court applied the First Amendment Establishment Clause to the states in *Everson v. Board of Education*.[9] In my view, the Court has incorrectly applied the First Amendment to the states by application of the Fourteenth Amendment.[10] Now, instead of the First Amendment erecting a barrier against the federal government at the state border, it has been interpreted to create a bridge to allow the federal government to intrude on state matters pertaining to religion.

Even more amazing than the United States Supreme Court misinterpreting the First Amendment is the fact that there was very little public outcry denouncing its action. Since 1940, the Supreme Court has prohibited schools from composing a prayer to recite before class,[11] prohibited the use of the Lord's Prayer in public schools,[12] and stripped the Ten Commandments from the classroom bulletin board.[13] The Court has also struck down an Arkansas statute that restricted the teaching of evolution by reasoning that the statute had a religious purpose.[14]

Since the Court ignored the clear meaning of the First Amendment and failed to appreciate the Judeo-Christian foundation of the Constitution, the Court has been forced to invent minute distinctions in order to rationalize its unpredictable rulings. For example, in 1989 the Court ruled that a nativity scene was unconstitutional but that a Jewish menorah was constitutional.[15] Though the Court has upheld the constitutionality of other nativity scenes, the Court reasoned in the *County of Allegheny* case that the nativity scene there violated the First Amendment because it was at the dominant entrance to the county courthouse. The menorah was held constitutional because it was placed at a different location on the city property and was closer to the other secular symbols of Christmas such as a Christmas tree. The Court suggested that if the nativity scene had been closer in proximity to the Christmas tree, then it would have been held constitutional. This nit-picking has no legal basis in the Constitution, because

[7]Paul Blanshard, "Three Cheers for Our Secular State," *The Humanist*, March/April 1976, p. 17.
[8]310 U.S. 296 (1940).
[9]330 U.S. 1 (1947).
[10]The Fourteenth Amendment was adopted in 1868. Congressional debates on the Blaine Amendment in 1875 reveal that the intent of the Fourteenth Amendment was not to incorporate application of the First Amendment to the individual states.
[11]*Engel v. Vitale*, 370 U.S. 421 (1962).
[12]*School District of Abington Township v. Schempp*, 374 U.S. 203 (1963).
[13]*Stone v. Graham*, 449 U.S. 39 (1980).
[14]*Epperson v. Arkansas*, 393 U.S. 97 (1968).
[15]*County of Allegheny v. American Civil Liberties Union*, 492 U.S. 573 (1989).

the Court had no jurisdiction interpreting religious matters pertaining to the states. The Court has created its own authority and its own quagmire; unfortunately, religious freedom suffers as a result.

The document that was intended to secure religious freedom, in the hands of decision-makers devoid of absolutes, has become the document that often restricts religious freedom. Though history clearly indicates that the First Amendment was never meant to be applicable to the states, the Supreme Court's interpretation since 1940 applying the First Amendment to the states is not likely to change. One federal judge in Alabama ruled that he was unable to decide a First Amendment case because federal courts had no jurisdiction over state religious matters in that the First Amendment was never meant to be applicable to the states.[16] According to Judge Hand, since the First Amendment did not apply to the individual states, the states were free to establish their own religion as they chose and the federal government could not prevent this practice.[17] Judge Hand's decision was quickly and succinctly overruled by the court of appeals in Atlanta, stating that it did not matter what the judge's feeling was regarding the history of the First Amendment, the First Amendment was applicable to the states because the Supreme Court said it was, and federal courts must follow court precedent.[18] The federal appeals court indicated that federal "district courts and circuit courts are bound to adhere to the controlling decisions of the Supreme Court."[19] The appeals court also noted that if the federal courts did not follow the precedent of the United States Supreme Court, anarchy would occur, and therefore, the United States Supreme Court's decisions "must be followed by the lower federal courts no matter how misguided the judges of those courts may think it to be."[20] Once the case made its way to the United States Supreme Court, the Court ruled that the states "have no greater power to restrain the individual freedoms protected by the First Amendment than does the Congress of the United States."[21] The Supreme Court then reiterated that it believed the First Amendment became applicable to the individual states after the adoption of the Fourteenth Amendment to the United States Constitution in 1868.[22]

Therefore, it is now assumed without critical analysis that the First Amendment is applicable to the individual states through the Fourteenth Amendment to the United States Constitution. Notwithstanding this presumption, Supreme Court decisions have invented various tests only to expand or ignore these tests when interpreting First Amendment cases. Clearly the Court's attitude toward religion has changed, even to the point

---

[16]*Jaffree v. Board of School Commissioners*, 554 F. Supp. 1104, 1128 (S.D. Ala. 1983).
[17]*Id.*
[18]*Jaffree v. Board of School Commissioners*, 705 F.2d 1526, 1535-36 (11th Cir. 1983).
[19]*Id.* at 1533 (citing *Hutto v. Davis*, 454 U.S. 370, 375 (1982)).
[20]*Id.* at 1533-34 (citing *Davis*, 454 U.S. at 375).
[21]*Wallace v. Jaffree*, 472 U.S. 38, 48-49 (1985).
[22]*Id.* at 48-56.

of calling the free exercise of religion embodied in the First Amendment a "luxury" which cannot always be accommodated.[23]

When interpreting the First Amendment, the statement of Oliver Wendell Holmes is apropos: "A page of history is worth a volume of logic."[24] The best interpretation of the First Amendment is one that is "illuminated by history."[25] The United States Supreme Court has noted the following in this respect:

> In applying the First Amendment to the states through the Fourteenth Amendment . . . it would be incongruous to interpret that clause as imposing more stringent First Amendment limits on the states than the draftsmen imposed upon the Federal Government.[26]

Therefore, the historical context of the First Amendment is crucial to a proper resolution of any case.

A review of the history surrounding the First Amendment indicates that as the first act of the Continental Congress in 1774, the Reverend Mister Duche opened with prayer and read from Psalm 31.[27] From inception Congress and state legislatures have opened their sessions with an invocation by a paid chaplain.[28] Courts have historically opened their daily proceedings with the invocation "God save the United States and this Honorable Court."[29] The Supreme Court of the United States itself has the Ten Commandments inscribed above the bench recognizing the biblical foundations of our legal heritage.[30]

George Washington began the tradition of taking the Presidential oath of office upon the Bible. When he assumed office in 1789, he stated, "It would be peculiarly improper to omit of this first official act my fervent supplications to that Almighty Being who rules over the Universe. . . ."[31] Indeed, Washington added the phrase at the end of the Presidential oath, "So help me God." An impressive list of presidents subsequent to Washington have invoked the protection and help of Almighty God.[32]

---

[23]*Employment Division v. Smith*, 494 U.S. 872 (1990).

[24]*New York Trust Company v. Eisner*, 256 U.S. 345, 349 (1921).

[25]*Lynch v. Donnelly*, 465 U.S. 668, 678 (1984) (citing *Walz v. Tax Commission*, 397 U.S. 664, 671 (1970)).

[26]*Marsh v. Chambers*, 463 U.S. 783, 790-91 (1983).

[27]Mr. Duche's prayer was as follows: "Be thou present oh God of wisdom and direct the counsel of this honorable assembly; enable them to settle all things on the best and surest foundation; that the scene of blood may be speedily closed; that order, harmony, and peace may be effectually restored, and truth and justice, religion and piety, prevail and flourish among the people. Preserve the health of their bodies and the vigor of their minds, shower down on them, and the millions they represent, such temporal blessings as Thou seest expedient for them in this world, and crown them with everlasting glory in the world to come. All this we ask in the name and through the merits of Jesus Christ Thy Son and our Savior. Amen."

[28]*Marsh*, 463 U.S. at 787-89. *See Lynch*, 465 U.S. at 673-74.

[29]*Marsh*, 463 U.S. at 786.

[30]*Lynch*, 465 U.S. at 677.

[31]*Engel*, 370 U.S. at 466 (Stewart, J., dissenting).

[32]*Id.* at 446-49.

James Madison, the father of the Bill of Rights, was a member of the Congressional Committee that recommended the chaplaincy system.[33] Madison voted for the bill authorizing payment of chaplains.[34] Reverend William Lynn was elected chaplain of the House of Representatives and paid $500 from the federal treasury.

On September 25, 1789, the day the final agreement was made on the Bill of Rights, the House requested President Washington to proclaim a Day of Thanksgiving to acknowledge "the many signal favors of Almighty God."[35] He proclaimed November 26, 1789, a Day of Thanksgiving to offer "our prayers and thanksgiving to the great Lord and Ruler of nations, and beseech Him to pardon our national and other transgressions."[36] Later, President Madison issued four Thanksgiving Day proclamations: July 9, 1812; July 23, 1813; November 16, 1814; and March 4, 1815.[37] Successive presidents have continued this tradition.

A correct interpretation of the First Amendment must be in accord "with what history reveals was the contemporaneous understanding of its guarantees."[38] The Supreme Court recognizes "that religion has been closely identified with our history and our government."[39] The history of this country "is inseparable from the history of religion."[40] "The line we must draw between the permissible and impermissible is one which accords with history and faithfully reflects the understanding of the Founding Fathers."[41] The historical setting of the First Amendment should often be reviewed to insure that the court interpretations "comport with what history reveals was the contemporaneous understanding of its guarantees."[42] When adopted, the First Amendment prohibited the federal government from coercively intruding into religion. "Government policies of accommodation, acknowledgment, and support for religion are an accepted part of our political and cultural heritage."[43] Interpreting the First Amendment consistent with history would certainly do a great deal to bring uniformity and reason back to constitutional jurisprudence. On occasion, the courts use history as part of their interpretation, and on other occasions, the courts simply ignore history. Despite these inconsistencies, there still remains clear constitutional decisions by which to guide religious liberty. The twentieth century certainly poses a real challenge to religious liberty.

---

[33]H.R. Rp. No. 124, 33rd Cong., 1st Sess. (1789), *reprinted in* 2 No. 2 *Reports of Committees of the House of Representatives* 4 (1854).
[34]1 Annals of Cong. 891 (J. Gales, ed. 1834).
[35]H.R. Jour., 1st Cong., 1st Sess., 123 (1826 ed.); S. Jour., 1st Cong., 1st Sess., 88 (1820 ed.); *Lynch*, 465 U.S. at 674 n.2.
[36]*Lynch*, 465 U.S. at 674 n.2.
[37]R. Cord, *Separation of Church and State*, 31 (1982).
[38]*Lynch*, 465 U.S. at 673.
[39]*Abington Township*, 374 U.S. at 212.
[40]*Engel*, 370 U.S. at 434 (1962).
[41]*Abington Township*, 374 U.S. at 294 (Brennan, J., concurring).
[42]*Lynch*, 465 U.S. at 673. *See also Committee for Public Education and Religious Liberty v. Nyquist*, 413 U.S. 756 (1973); *Walz*, 397 U.S. at 664; *Marsh*, 463 U.S. at 783.
[43]*County of Allegheny*, 492 U.S. at 657 (Kennedy, J., concurring in part and dissenting in part).

We have in many ways moved from the First Amendment's intent to create religious prosperity and freedom to the allegation that the First Amendment is to mandate "that the government remain secular."[44] History certainly does not bear out the statement that the First Amendment was to make government secular, but rather supports a conclusion that the First Amendment was meant to create religious prosperity, prohibiting government from intruding in religion but allowing religion to interact within the public square. Indeed, former Supreme Court Justice Joseph Story noted the following about the First Amendment:

> Probably, at the time of the adoption of the Constitution, and of the amendment to it, now under consideration, the general, if not the universal, sentiment in America was, that Christianity ought to receive encouragement from the State, so far as such encouragement was not incompatible with the private rights of conscience, and the freedom of religious worship.[45]

The often quoted expression of Thomas Jefferson regarding the "wall of separation between church and state"[46] has become so popular that many people believe the words are in the Constitution. However, this phrase is not in the Constitution. In fact, Thomas Jefferson was in France at the time the First Amendment was drafted and adopted. Jefferson did not believe that there should be no interaction between church and state. On three occasions, President Jefferson signed into law federal land grants specifically to promote proselytizing among native American Indians.[47] In 1803, President Jefferson proposed to the United States Senate a treaty with the Kaskaskia Indians in which the federal government was to "give annually for seven years one hundred dollars towards the support of a priest" and "further give the sum of three dollars to assist the said tribe in the erection of a church."[48] The treaty was ratified on December 23, 1803, and at Jefferson's request, it included an appropriation for a Catholic Mission.

Moreover, Thomas Jefferson was the first president of the School Board for the District of Columbia. There the Bible and the Watts Hymnal were used as primary textbooks.[49] As the founder of the University of Virginia, Jefferson believed that religious instruction was important to a proper education. In fact, he stated: "The want of instruction in the various creeds of religious faith existing among our citizens presents, therefore, a chasm in the general institution of the useful sciences."[50]

---

[44]*Id.* at 574.
[45]Joseph Story, 2 *Commentaries on the Constitution of the United States* 593 (Boston, 1833).
[46]8 *Works of Thomas Jefferson* 113.
[47]R. Cord, *Separation of Church and State*, 41-46 (1982).
[48]*A Treaty Between the United States of America in the Kaskaskia Tribe of Indians*, 7 Stat. 78-79 (Peter's ed. 1846).
[49]J. Wilson, *Public Schools of Washington* 1 Records of the Columbia Historical Society 4 (1897).
[50]*Illinois ex rel. McCollum v. Board of Education*, 333 U.S. 203, 245-46 (1948) (Reed, J., dissenting), (citing 19 *The Writings of Thomas Jefferson* 414-17 (memorial edition 1904)).

On July 13, 1787, the Continental Congress enacted the Northwest Ordinance which provided that "Religion, morality, and knowledge being essential to good government and the happiness of mankind, schools and the means of education shall be forever encouraged."[51] On August 7, 1789, after the final agreement on the wording of the Bill of Rights, the newly formed Congress re-enacted the Northwest Ordinance.[52]

History is clearly a good teacher in determining the intent of the First Amendment. The amendment was not intended to erect an impregnable wall between church and state. Indeed, our national motto declares, "In God We Trust."[53] Not only our currency but also our national anthem contains the national motto.[54] Since 1954, the Pledge of Allegiance has contained the words "One nation *under God* with liberty and justice for all."[55] Clearly, an objective observer "cannot look at even this brief resumé without finding that our history is pervaded by expressions of religious beliefs."[56] As the United States Supreme Court has recognized, the "real object" of the First Amendment was "to prevent any national ecclesiastical establishment, which should give to an hierarchy the exclusive patronage of the national government."[57]

APPLICATION OF THE FIRST AMENDMENT

When determining whether an individual has a constitutional right under the First Amendment or any other provision in the Bill of Rights, it is important to note how these constitutional provisions are to be applied. The First Amendment has two religion clauses. The first clause is known as the Establishment Clause and states as follows: "Congress shall make no law respecting the establishment of religion. . . ." The remaining part of the First Amendment dealing with religion has been termed the Free Exercise Clause and states as follows: ". . . or prohibit the free exercise thereof. . . ." The entire First Amendment states as follows:

> Congress shall make no law respecting an establishment of religion, or prohibiting the free exercise thereof, or abridging the freedom of speech, or of the press, or the right of the people peacefully to assemble, and to petition the Government for a redress of grievances.[58]

---

[51]Ord. of 1787, July 13, 1787, Art. III, *reprinted in Documents Illustrative of the Formation of the Union of American States* 52 (1927).

[52]An Act to provide for the Government of the Territory Northwest of the river Ohio (Northwest Ordinance), Ch. 8, 1 Stat. 50-51 (Peter's ed. 1845).

[53]Joint Resolution to establish a National Motto of the United States, Ch. 795, Pub. L. No. 84-851, 70 Stat. 732 (1957).

[54]*Engel,* 370 U.S. at 440, 449.

[55]Joint Resolution, etc., Pub. L. No. 94-344, § 1 (19), 90 Stat. 810, 813 (1978), codified, as amended, at 36 U.S.C. § 172 (1978).

[56]*Lynch,* 465 U.S. at 677.

[57]Id. at 678, *quoting* J. Story 2, *Commentaries on the Constitution of the United States* 593 (1833).

[58]U.S. Const. amend. I.

The First Amendment is meant to protect individuals from government intrusion. Therefore, it provides liberty to individuals and restraint on the government. In order for the First Amendment to be applicable to any situation, two factors must be involved: (1) a person[59] and (2) some form of governmental action. Only a governmental entity is prohibited from establishing a religion and only a governmental entity is prohibited from restricting the free exercise of religion. A private entity can establish a religion, and a private individual can restrict the free exercise of anyone else's religion.

A classic example of how the Constitution works is to compare the difference between a public and a private school. A public school is a governmental entity and therefore is prohibited by the Establishment Clause from establishing a religion. As a governmental entity, the public school is also prohibited from restricting the free exercise of religion. On the other hand, a private school can promote or proselytize in religious matters without any governmental interference, and no matter how offensive the promotion or establishment of a religion may be to an individual, the Constitution through the Establishment Clause has no application to a private school. Of course, there might be some form of application if the private school were to have some form of governmental funding or other governmental connection, but again, it is the governmental action which is being restrained, not the private action. A private Christian school which receives no federal funds can require mandatory chapel every day and may also prohibit the distribution of religious literature. However, a public school would violate the Establishment Clause by requiring mandatory chapel every day and would violate the Free Exercise and Free Speech Clause by prohibiting the distribution of religious literature.[60] A public school could not compel a Jehovah's Witness to salute the flag because to do so would violate the student's free exercise of religion.[61] A private Christian school receiving no federal funds could compel a student to salute the flag.

In summary, there must be some form of governmental action for the Establishment Clause, the Free Speech Clause, or the Free Exercise Clause to apply in any given situation. Without governmental action, there is no application of the First Amendment.

PUBLIC FORUM DOCTRINE

Throughout this book the reader will be confronted by the terms "traditional public forum," "limited or designated public forum," and "nonpublic forum." These terms are important in order to determine First Amendment free speech rights. In order to ascertain what limits, if any, may

---

[59]Since corporations are considered legal persons, in some cases corporations can bring First Amendment claims.
[60]Nowak, Rotunda, and Young, *Constitutional Law*, 3d Ed. (St. Paul, MN: West Publishing Co.) 1986 pp. 421-48.
[61]*Murdock v. Pennsylvania*, 319 U.S. 105 (1943).

be imposed on free speech rights, the United States Supreme Court has "often focused on the place of that speech, considering the nature of the forum the speaker seeks to employ."[62] The United States Supreme Court has recently stated that

> Public places are of necessity the locus for discussion of public issues, as well as protest against arbitrary government action. At the heart of our jurisprudence lies the principle that in a free nation citizens must have the right to gather and speak with other persons in public places. The recognition that certain government-owned property is a public forum provides open notice to citizens that their freedoms may be exercised there without fear of a censorial government, adding tangible reinforcement to the idea that we are a free people.[63]

The "public forum doctrine is to give effect to the broad command of the First Amendment to protect speech from governmental interference."[64] There are three categories of public forums best described as follows: (1) traditional—defined as parks, streets, or sidewalks that have been held in trust for the use of the public and for purposes of assembly, communicating thoughts between citizens, and discussing public questions; (2) designated or limited—which is created when the state intentionally opens public property for use by the public for assembly, speech or other expressive activities; and (3) nonpublic—which exists when the state does not designate public property for indiscriminate expression by the public at large, by certain speakers, or by certain subjects. Generally the standard for review for a traditional, limited, or designated public forum is a strict or intermediate scrutiny test; whereas, under the nonpublic forum the rational basis or reasonable nexus test is used. For the government to limit the content of speech under the former it must show a compelling interest, and any restriction must be narrowly tailored to achieve that interest; while under the latter, the government must show a reasonable basis for the restriction. Time, place, and manner restrictions are permissible only if content neutral, narrowly tailored to serve a significant government interest, and such restrictions leave open ample alternative channels of expression.[65] A classic example of a time restriction is one that frequently occurs for parade permits. A governmental entity may limit parade permits to a certain time in order to avoid rush hour traffic. This time restriction would be permissible so long as it was content neutral and, therefore, applicable to all permits. However, time, place, and manner restrictions may not be so stringent so as to effectively preclude use of the forum. For example, it would be impermissible to allow a parade permit only at midnight.

---

[62]*Frisby v. Schultz*, 487 U.S. 474, 479 (1988). *See also Heffron v. ISKCON*, 452 U.S. 640 (1981).
[63]*ISKCON v. Lee*, 112 S. Ct. 2711, 2716-17 (1992).
[64]*Id.* at 2717.
[65]*See, e.g., Perry Education Ass'n v. Perry Local Educators' Ass'n*, 460 U.S. 37 (1983).

Traditional public forums are essentially a closed class consisting of public parks, streets, and sidewalks. These types of public property have immemorially been left open for expressive activity allowing citizens to assemble and communicate with other citizens. By nature of the property, the location is considered a traditional public forum and cannot be closed to public use. A designated or limited public forum is one where the government intentionally opens up the public facility for use by the community. Examples include a public library where outside organizations can meet in various rooms, public school facilities used after hours by outside community organizations, or any other facility open to the public. Once the designated or limited public forum is open to the public, the same strict scrutiny standard that is used for the traditional public forum is applied. The main difference between this classification and a traditional public forum is that a traditional public forum by the nature of the property is always open to the public. A designated public forum need not be open, and at any time can be closed so long as the closure of the facility is done in a nondiscriminatory basis. For example, a public school could close its facilities to all groups in the community. A public library could prohibit all outside users from using the facilities other than for checking out and reading books. However, a public school or public library cannot close its facilities only to religious but not secular organizations because to do so would discriminate on the content of the speech and would violate the First Amendment. Finally, an example of a nonpublic forum would be an airport, but even in a public airport, all First Amendment activity cannot be prohibited.

Commenting on the traditional and designated or limited public forums, the Supreme Court stated the following:

> In these quintessential public [forums], the government may not prohibit all communicative activity. For the State to enforce a content-based exclusion it must show that its regulation is necessary to serve a compelling state interest and that it is narrowly drawn to achieve that end. . . . The State may also enforce regulations of the time, place, and manner of expression which are content neutral, and are narrowly tailored to serve a significant government interest, and leave open ample alternative channels of communication.[66]

As noted above, the government may place reasonable time, place, and manner restrictions on expression so long as these restrictions are content neutral. Content neutral regulations are those that are "justified without reference to the content of the regulated speech"[67] A time, place, and manner restriction must not be based upon the content of the speech. In other words, the government would violate the First Amendment if, because of the content of the speech being religious, it decided to restrict the time,

---

[66]*Frisby*, 487 U.S. at 481 (quoting *Perry Education Ass'n*, 460 U.S. at 45).
[67]*Virginia State Board of Pharmacy v. Virginia Citizens Consumer Council*, 425 U.S. 748, 771 (1976).

place, or manner of the religious speech. A neutral regulation would be one that is done in a nondiscriminatory manner regardless of the content of speech. A reasonable time regulation in a traditional public forum would be one that permitted use of a street for a parade during hours other than rush hour traffic. Some government facilities try to regulate the place of the speech, yet in doing so, the government must leave open ample alternative channels of communication. The Supreme Court has held that "one is not to have the exercise of his liberty of expression in appropriate places abridged on the plea that it may be exercised in some other place."[68]

The Supreme Court has clearly expressed its disdain for content-based restrictions on free speech. "The First Amendment generally prevents government from proscribing free speech, or even expressive conduct because of disapproval of the ideas expressed. Content-based regulations are presumptively invalid."[69] Undoubtedly, the "First Amendment does not permit [government] to impose special prohibitions to those speakers who express views on disfavored subjects."[70]

Moreover, within a public forum, the government cannot prohibit expressive activity on the basis that the speaker is associated with some other radical or disruptive group. The First Amendment protects freedom of speech and freedom of association. The Supreme Court has noted the following:

> Among the rights protected by the First Amendment is the right of individuals to associate to further their personal beliefs. While the freedom of association is not explicitly set out in the Amendment, it has long been held to be implicit in the freedoms of speech, assembly, and petition.[71]

The interrelationship between free speech and group activity was reaffirmed by the Supreme Court when it stated:

> It should be obvious that the exclusion of any person or group—all-Negro, all-Oriental, or all-white—from public facilities infringes upon the freedom of the individual to associate as he chooses. . . . "The associational rights which our system honors permit all white, all black, all brown, all yellow clubs to be formed. They also permit all Catholic, all Jewish, or all agnostic clubs to be established. Government may not tell a man or woman who his or her associates must be." . . . The freedom to associate applies to the beliefs we share, and to those we consider reprehensible. It tends to produce the diversity of opinion that oils the machinery of democratic government and insures peaceful, orderly change.[72]

[68]*Schneider v. New Jersey,* 308 U.S. 147, 151-52 (1939).
[69]*R.A.V. v. City of St. Paul,* 112 S. Ct. 2538, 2542 (1992).
[70]*Id.* at 2547.
[71]*Healy v. James,* 408 U.S. 169, 181 (1972).
[72]*Gilmore v. City of Montgomery,* 417 U.S. 556, 575 (1974).

In one case, a school attempted to prohibit the formation of a student club on a university campus because its national parent or affiliate organization had been shown to be disruptive and violent in nature. Thus, the associational free speech rights of the individual club were violated by the school because the university lumped that particular student group in with other individuals simply because of their relationship to the other individuals. To do so violated the First Amendment according to the United States Supreme Court.[73] Consequently, a governmental entity cannot prohibit free speech expressive activities within a public forum on the basis that another individual or group with which the speaker is affiliated has been shown to be violent or disruptive in nature.[74] The Supreme Court has amply noted that an "individual's freedom to speak, to worship, and to petition the government for the redresses of grievances could not be vigorously protected from interference by the state [if] our correlative freedom to engage in group effort toward those ends were not also guaranteed."[75]

Though the Supreme Court may be tending to move away from the public forum doctrine to some extent,[76] the public forum doctrine is still well-embedded in constitutional interpretation. It is important to know the difference between a traditional public forum, a designated or limited public forum, and a nonpublic forum. In summary, traditional public forums are public parks, streets, and sidewalks. Such public forums are always open to the public. Designated or limited public forums are those public facilities intentionally open to public use by the government. A nonpublic forum is neither a traditional public forum, nor has it been intentionally opened to outside use. However, not all free speech activities can be excluded from a nonpublic forum. Of course, in speaking about public forums, we are always considering government action and control of the public forum to which the citizen seeks access for First Amendment expressive purposes.

---

[73]*Healy*, 408 U.S. at 169.
[74]*NAACP v. Claiborne Hardware Co.*, 458 U.S. 886 (1982).
[75]*Roberts v. United States Jaycees*, 468 U.S. 609 (1984).
[76]R.A.V., 112 S. Ct. at 2538 (Not using the public forum analysis in a free speech case); *ISKCON v. Lee*, 112 S. Ct. at 2711 (Not using a public forum analysis in a free speech case involving an international airport and discussing whether international airports should be considered as traditional public forums because of the nature of the airport being similar to such forums).

3

Students' Rights on Public School Campuses

FREEDOM OF SPEECH

Students on public school campuses enjoy constitutional protection of free speech and free exercise of religion. Student speech can be prohibited only when speech activities "substantially interfere with the work of the school, or impinge upon the rights of other students."[1] In *Tinker v. Des Moines Independent School District*, the United States Supreme Court stated:

> In our system, state-operated schools may not be enclaves of totalitarianism. School officials do not possess absolute authority over their students. Students in schools as well as out of school are 'persons' under our Constitution. They are possessed of fundamental rights which the State must respect, just as they themselves must respect their obligations to the State. In our system, students may not be regarded as closed-circuit recipients of only that which the State chooses to communicate. They may not be confined to the expression of those sentiments that are officially approved. In the absence of a specific showing of constitutionally valid reasons to regulate their speech, students are entitled to freedom of expression of their views.[2]

The Supreme Court further stated, "It can hardly be argued that either students or teachers shed their constitutional rights to freedom of speech or expression at the schoolhouse gate."[3] While students should not disrupt class by speaking out on issues unrelated to the curriculum, they may express their views during class time on the topic being studied.

The Court recognized that when a student is "in the cafeteria, or on the

---

[1]*Tinker v. Des Moines Independent School District*, 393 U.S. 503, 509 (1969).
[2]*Id.* at 511.
[3]*Id.* at 506.

playing field, or on the campus during the authorized hours, he may express his opinions."[4] Therefore, students have a guaranteed right to free speech on public school campuses. When students walk on the premises of any public school, kindergarten through college, they carry with them the First Amendment protection of free speech and free exercise of religion.[5] These students do not shed their Constitutional rights when they enter the schoolhouse gate.[6] Federal courts have the duty "to apply the First Amendment mandates in our educational system" in order "to safeguard the fundamental values of freedom of speech and inquiry."[7] Indeed, the Supreme Court has specifically stated that students may express themselves all the way "from kindergarten through high school."[8] This statement was made prior to the Supreme Court's decisions dealing with colleges, and thus, it can rightfully be said that students have free speech rights from kindergarten through college.

Some opponents of student free speech have attempted to restrict student rights by arguing that public schools are closed, limited, or designated public forums. In using this terminology, opponents of student free speech argue that student speech activities are limited to that type of speech condoned by the school. Some erroneously argue that schools may allow secular speech but prohibit all religious speech so long as the prohibition on speech is applied against all religious speech. Others argue that student speech can be prohibited so long as it is equally prohibited across the board, both secular and religious. This is the same kind of argument that is used regarding student-initiated clubs. However, the analysis for student-initiated clubs is different than the analysis for student speech where students are not requesting use of school facilities. As for student-initiated clubs, schools can prohibit all student clubs so long as the prohibition applies equally to secular and religious clubs. However, this is in the context where students are requesting the use of school facilities.[9] In the context of free speech, students are not requesting use of school facilities. To the contrary, they are commanded by law to be on the public school campus, and once there under mandate of law, schools cannot flatly prohibit their speech.

One court has stated the following:

---

[4]*Id.* at 512-13.

[5]There are at least three major Supreme Court decisions dealing with student free speech activities. The students in *Tinker* involved an eight-year-old second grader, an eleven-year-old fifth grader, a thirteen-year-old eighth grader, and a fifteen and a sixteen-year-old in the eleventh grade. The students in *Board of Education v. Mergens*, 110 S. Ct. 2356 (1990), involved a public secondary school. Public secondary schools, depending on state law, include middle schools and/or junior high schools and high schools. The students in *Widmar v. Vincent*, 454 U.S. 263 (1981), involved college students. Though the latter two cases pertained to student clubs within a public secondary school or college, these cases were based on student free speech rights.

[6]*Tinker*, 393 U.S. at 506.

[7]*Epperson v. Arkansas*, 393 U.S. 97, 104 (1968).

[8]*Tinker*, 393. U.S. at 516.

[9]*But see DeNooyer v. Livonia Public Schools*, 799 F. Supp. 744, 752 (E.D. Mich. 1992), *aff'd sub nom, DeNooyer v. Merinelli*, 1 F.3d 1240 (6th Cir. 1993).

[P]ublic schools are dedicated, in part, to accommodate students during prescribed hours for personal intercommunication. Unless the students' speech is curriculum-related, the speech cannot be limited during those hours on the school campus without a strong showing of interference with school activities or with the rights of other students. As the Court stated, 'Dedication to specific uses [including student interpersonal communication] does not imply that the constitutional rights of persons entitled to be there are to be gauged as if the premises were purely private property.'[10]

According to the Supreme Court ruling in *Tinker*, the "principle use to which schools are dedicated is to accommodate students during prescribed hours for the purpose of certain types of activities. Among those activities is personal intercommunication among the students."[11] Though "the holding in *Tinker* did not depend upon a finding that the school was a public forum,"[12] *Tinker* clearly acknowledged that schools by virtue of their very existence are dedicated to personal intercommunication among the students. Thus, in a sense, schools are by their very nature a designated or limited public forum and can be none other than a limited or designated public forum by virtue of the fact that they are dedicated "to accommodate students during prescribed hours."[13] Recently one federal district court recognized this important aspect of *Tinker* by declaring,

In the light of *Tinker*, I conclude that government intent to create public secondary schools as limited public forums, during school hours, for the first amendment personal speech of the students who attend those schools, is intrinsic in the dedication of those schools. Only when the schools cease operating is that intent negated.[14]

In other words, it is improper to analyze student-initiated speech under a public forum framework, and to state, in turn, that schools can limit the public forum and thus prohibit student speech. First, students are commanded to be on public school campuses by law. Once there, the government cannot restrict their speech unless their speech disrupts the ordinary operation of the school or interferes with the rights of other students. Schools may not prohibit student speech simply because another student objects to the content of the message by the speaker. "If school officials were permitted to prohibit expression to which other students objected, absent any further justification, the officials would have a license to prohibit virtually every type of expression."[15] Additionally, the phrase "interferes with

---

[10]*Slotterback v. Interboro School District*, 766 F. Supp. 280, 293 (E.D. Pa. 1991) (quoting *Tinker*, 393 U.S. at 512 n.6).
[11]*Tinker*, 393 U.S. at 739.
[12]*Rivera v. East Otero School District*, 721 F. Supp. 1189, 1193 (D. Colo. 1989).
[13]*Tinker*, 393 U.S. at 739.
[14]*Slotterback*, 766 F. Supp. at 293.
[15]*Clark v. Dallas Independent School District*, 806 F. Supp. 116, 120 (N.D. Tex. 1992) (citing *Rivera*, 721 F. Supp. at 1189; and *Slotterback*, 766 F. Supp. at 280).

the rights of other students" found in *Tinker* means student speech that is sexually explicit, libelous or defamatory toward another student.[16] Second, even if a public forum analysis were used within a public school context, the Supreme Court and other federal cases suggest that by their very nature, schools are dedicated to student interpersonal communication. Only when schools cease being schools is that public dedication extinguished. Just as schools could not prohibit students from verbally speaking to one another between class, on the playing field, in the cafeteria, or during noninstructional times before or after class sessions, schools cannot prohibit other forms of student expression. "In the absence of a specific showing of constitutionally valid reasons to regulate their speech, students are entitled to freedom of expression of their views."[17] Indeed, the "vigilant protection of constitutional freedoms is nowhere more vital than in a community of American schools."[18]

In the context of student-initiated prayer, one court stated "students can do what the State acting on its own cannot do."[19]

Regardless of the arguments presented by opponents of student-initiated speech, the Supreme Court in "*Tinker* made clear that school property may not be declared off limits for expressive activity by students. . . ."[20]

LITERATURE DISTRIBUTION

The Supreme Court has long recognized "that the right to distribute flyers and literature lies at the heart of the liberties guaranteed by the speech and press clauses by the First Amendment."[21] "It is axiomatic that written expression is pure speech."[22] The well-settled constitutional cases confirm "that the guarantee of freedom of speech that is enshrined in the First Amendment encompasses the right to distribute peacefully."[23] "From the time of the founding of our nation, the distribution of written material has been an essential weapon in the defense of liberty."[24]

The right of free speech includes the right to distribute literature.[25] In fact, the distribution of *printed* material is considered pure speech.[26] Consequently, peaceful distribution of literature is protected speech.[27]

---

[16]*Hazelwood School District v. Kuhlmeier*, 484 U.S. 260, 274 (1988); *Bethel School District v. Fraser*, 478 U.S. 675 (1986).

[17]*Clark*, 806 F. Supp. at 119 (quoting *Tinker*, 393 U.S. at 511).

[18]*Shelton v. Tucker*, 364 U.S. 479, 487 (1967).

[19]*Jones v. Clear Creek Independent School District*, 977 F.2d 963 (5th Cir. 1992), *cert. denied*, 113 S. Ct. 2950 (1993).

[20]*Grayned v. City of Rockford*, 408 U.S. 104, 118 (1972).

[21]*ISKCON v. Lee*, 112 S. Ct. 2711, 2720 (1992).

[22]*Slotterback*, 766 F. Supp. at 288.

[23]*Id.*

[24]*Paulsen v. County of Nassau*, 925 F.2d 65, 66 (2d Cir. 1991).

[25]*Martin v. City of Struthers*, 319 U.S. 141 (1943).

[26]*Texas v. Johnson*, 491 U.S. 397, 406 (1989) ("The Government generally has a freer hand in restricting expressive conduct than it has in restricting the written or spoken word.")

[27]*United States v. Grace*, 461 U.S. 169, 176 (1983) ("Leafletting is protected speech."); *Lovell v. City*

Literature distribution includes anything in printed format such as brochures, pamphlets, newspapers, cards, stamps, books, and pictures that are not considered obscene.

Religious speech enjoys the same protection as political speech.[28] Indeed, the right to persuade, advocate, or proselytize a religious viewpoint is protected by the First Amendment. The Supreme Court in *Thomas v. Collins*, stated that "free trade in ideas means free trade and the opportunity to persuade, not merely to describe facts."[29] The burden on the government (public school) to justify an exclusion of free speech requires the government to show that the denial of speech is necessary to serve a compelling state interest and that complete denial is the least restrictive alternative to achieve that end.[30] Mere disagreement with the content of the speech is not sufficient reason to deny student speech.[31]

The Supreme Court has held that a school principal may restrict the content of a school-sponsored newspaper which was published as part of the course work for a journalism class because the newspaper was not a public forum and because it was part of the educational curriculum and a regular classroom activity.[32] However, the Court distinguished the newspaper case from literature distribution by stating:

> The question whether the First Amendment requires a school to tolerate particular student speech—the question that we addressed in *Tinker*—is different from the question whether the First Amendment requires a school affirmatively to promote particular student speech. The former question addresses educators' ability to silence a student's personal expression that happens to occur on the school premises. The latter question concerns educators' authority over school-sponsored publications, theatrical productions, and other expressive activities that students, parents, and members of the public might reasonably perceive to bear the imprimatur of the school. These activities [that is, writing an article in a school-sponsored newspaper] may fairly be characterized as part of the

---

of *Griffin*, 303 U.S. 444, 451-52 (1938) ("Liberty of circulating is as essential to [freedom of speech] as liberty of publishing; indeed, without circulation, the publication would be of little value.").

[28]*Widmar v. Vincent*, 454 U.S. 263, 269 (1981) (citing *Heffron v. ISKCON* 452 U.S. 640 (1981)). See also *Niemotko v. Maryland*, 340 U.S. 268 (1951); *Saia v. New York*, 334 U.S. 558 (1948).

[29]323 U.S. 516, 537 (1945).

[30]*Carey v. Brown*, 447 U.S. 455, 461, 464-65 (1980); *Widmar*, 454 U.S. at 270.

[31]*Clark*, 806 F. Supp. at 120.

[32]*Hazelwood School District v. Kuhlmeier*, 484 U.S. 260 (1988). In *Desilets v. Clearview Regional Board of Education*, 266 N.J. Super. 531, 630 A.2d 333 (N.J. Sup. Ct. 1993), a New Jersey state appeals court ruled that a school violated the First Amendment Free Speech Clause when it censored from a school-sponsored newspaper a student's movie reviews of the R-rated films *Mississippi Burning* and *Rainman*. The court reasoned that the censorship was based on the content of the movie reviews and was not associated with pedagogical concern such as grammar, writing, research, bias or prejudice, or vulgar or profane language. Since the censorship was purely based on the content of the movie being R-rated, the school violated the student's free speech right. The court ruled that any school newspaper censorship case must be read in light of the Supreme Court's decision in *Tinker*, 393 U.S. at 503. The court also ruled that if the school was concerned about the appearance that it endorsed R-rated movie reviews, the school could add a disclaimer to the newspaper.

school curriculum, whether or not they occur in a traditional classroom setting, so long as they are supervised by faculty members and designed to impart particular knowledge or skills to student participants and audiences.[33]

The same distinction makes literature distribution different from *Bethel School District v. Fraser*,[34] in which the Court ruled that a student was appropriately disciplined by the school authorities for the offensive tone of a nominating speech at a school assembly.[35]

The difference between the Supreme Court decision in *Hazelwood* (school-sponsored newspaper), *Fraser* (an offensive nominating speech at a school assembly), and *Tinker* (student-initiated speech) is important. The Court in *Hazelwood* ruled that a school could censor student speech when that speech occurred in a school-sponsored newspaper. There were two reasons the Court allowed the school to censor this speech. First, the student speech occurred in a school-sponsored newspaper. This school newspaper was clearly a school-sponsored publication in which other faculty members participated in the production thereof, and the school newspaper contained the school logo, thus giving the appearance that the school sponsored the content of the newspaper. The second reason was that the article dealt with fellow students who had become pregnant. The article did not name the students, but so specifically described the circumstances that everyone within the school would know to whom the article was referring. As such, this article could have been defamatory toward the students and thus interfered with the right of particular students under the *Tinker* analysis. Similarly, the student nominating speech in *Fraser* was also somewhat defamatory or libelous. In this particular case the student gave a nominating speech and used sexual innuendoes, describing as it were, a sexual act between himself and the student body.

The Supreme Court, however, indicated that there is a clear difference between "whether the First Amendment requires a school to tolerate a particular student's speech [as was addressed in *Tinker*] from the question of whether the First Amendment requires a school affirmatively to *promote* particular student speech [the question addressed in *Hazelwood*]."[36] The reason the school could censor the content of the student newspaper was in part because the production of that newspaper was "supervised by faculty members and designed to impart particular knowledge or skills to student participants and audiences."[37] However, student interpersonal communi-

---

[33]*Hazelwood*, 484 U.S. at 270-71.

[34]478 U.S. 675 (1986).

[35]Another federal court of appeals ruled that "civility" is a legitimate pedagogical concern of a school and therefore school officials could declare a high school student ineligible to run for student office as a sanction for an offensive campaign speech delivered at a school assembly in which the student ridiculed an assistant principal. *Poling v. Murphy*, 872 F.2d 757 (6th Cir. 1989), *cert. denied*, 493 U.S. 1021 (1990).

[36]*Hazelwood*, 484 U.S. at 270-71 (emphasis added).

[37]*Id.* at 271. A federal court of appeals ruled that a school board could properly reject Planned

cation, either verbally or through printed format, has no supervision of faculty and is not designed to impart knowledge or skills to other participants or audiences. As such, the school has no reason to censor this form of student speech unless the student speech interrupts the ordinary operation of the school or interferes with the rights of other students such as libelous or defamatory expressions. Students may therefore distribute literature during noninstructional time—before, after, and between classes. As *Tinker* stated, when a student is "in the cafeteria, or on the playing field, or on the campus during the authorized hours, he may express his opinions."[38] The only compelling reason to prohibit literature distribution is when such activities substantially interfere with the work of the school or impinge upon the rights of other students.[39]

The distribution of religious literature is a powerful evangelization tool. Students should not be intimidated from using this form of expression. Students may distribute religious literature before or after school while students are arriving on the campus. Bus stops and hallways are prime areas for the distribution of literature. They may also distribute literature or verbally express themselves between classes. Other times appropriate for student expression include lunchtime, in the cafeteria, or on the playing field. Any period where there is noninstructional time, students have the right to express themselves. Students should not attempt to distribute literature during class time. However, outside of class time, a flat "ban on the distribution of student-initiated religious literature cannot be constitutionally justified."[40]

Sometimes the bigotry and ignorance of some school officials is astonishing. One eighth grader brought the religious newspaper *Issues and Answers* to school, planning to distribute this literature to her fellow students during noninstructional time. She asked the assistant principal for permission to distribute the literature. After reviewing the contents of the literature and noting that it was religious and had Bible verses, the assistant principal responded that students were not permitted to bring Bibles, religious literature, or literature that quoted the Bible on public school campuses. Therefore, the request for distribution was flatly denied. Liberty Counsel represented this student and brought a suit against the school

---

Parenthood's advertisement for publication in high school newspapers and other school publications because in such a school-sponsored publication, the school had the right to maintain a position of neutrality on controversial issues. *Planned Parenthood of Southern Nevada, Inc. v. Clark County School District*, 941 F.2d 817 (9th Cir. 1991).

[38]*Tinker*, 393 U.S. at 512-13.

[39]*Id.* at 509, 511. *Accord Baughman v. Freienmuth*, 478 F.2d 1345 (4th Cir. 1973); *Quarterman v. Byrd*, 453 F.2d 54 (4th Cir. 1971); *Rivera*, 721 F. Supp. at 1189.

[40]*Widmar*, 454 U.S. at 269-70. It should be noted that distribution of literature by outside groups is treated differently than distribution of literature by students. Though some courts have ruled in favor for Gideons, most courts have ruled that Gideons may not come on public school campuses for the purpose of distributing Bibles. *Cf. Meltzer v. Board of Public Instruction of Orange County*, 548 F.2d 559 (5th Cir. 1977) and 577 F.2d 311 (5th Cir. 1978) (en banc) (Gideons may distribute Bibles on public school campuses) *with Berger v. Rensselaer Central School Corporation*, 992 F.2d 1160 (7th Cir. 1993) (Gideons may not distribute Bibles on public school campuses.)

board for denial of the student's free speech rights. The day after filing suit, one school board member was quoted by the media as saying that religion had no place on public school campuses and that students had no right to bring religious literature to school. This statement by the school board member was later retracted when the school board agreed with Liberty Counsel's position and further agreed that the student had a First Amendment right to distribute her literature before and after class, in between classes, in the cafeteria, or on the playing field.

Some schools have attempted to regulate student literature distribution by requiring that any literature be reviewed by school officials prior to distribution. However, the requirement of giving advance notice of a student's intent to speak inherently inhibits free speech.[41] The Supreme Court has stated that prior notification is "quite incompatible with the requirements of the First Amendment."[42] Indeed, the "simple knowledge that one must inform the government of his desire to speak and must fill out appropriate forms and comply with applicable regulations discourages citizens from speaking freely."[43] Certainly the "delay inherent in advance notice requirements inhibits free speech by outlawing spontaneous expression."[44] The Supreme Court has further noted that when "an event occurs, it is often necessary to have one's voice heard promptly, if it is to be considered at all."[45]

Most of these school policies requiring advance notice prior to distribution are insufficient because they lack specific guidelines. These policies often leave so much discretion to the school officials so as to allow the school officials to censor the speech without using objective criteria. These pre-distribution review requirements are presumptively invalid because, essentially, they require a license from the government prior to speaking.[46] One case concluded that a one day advanced notification requirement was unconstitutional.[47] In striking down an advanced notification requirement, a federal court noted that "a policy which subjects all nonschool sponsored communications to pre-distribution review for content censorship violates the First Amendment. . . . [N]o . . . content control is justified for communication among students which is not part of the educational program."[48] The "majority of courts of appeals considering policies similar to the one

---

[41]*NAACP v. City of Richmond,* 743 F.2d 1346 (9th Cir. 1984).
[42]*Thomas v. Collins,* 323 U.S. 516, 540 (1945).
[43]*City of Richmond,* 743 F.2d at 1455 (citing *Rosen v. Port of Portland,* 641 F.2d 1243 (9th Cir. 1981)).
[44]*City of Richmond,* 743 F.2d at 1355.
[45]*Shuttlesworth v. City of Birmingham,* 394 U.S. 147, 163 (1969).
[46]"It is well established that in the area of freedom of expression an overbroad regulation may be subject to review and invalidation, even though its application in the case under construction may be constitutionally unobjectable." *Forsyth County v. Nationalist Movement,* 112 S. Ct. 2395, 2400 (1992). *See also Secretary of State of Maryland v. Joseph Munson Company,* 467 U.S. 947 (1984); *Shuttlesworth v. Birmingham,* 394 U.S. 147 (1969); *Freedman v. Maryland,* 380 U.S. 51 (1965); *Talley v. California,* 362 U.S. 60 (1960); *Abramson v. Gonzalez,* 949 F.2d 1567 (11th Cir. 1992); *Sentinel Communications Company v. Watts,* 936 F.2d 1189 (11th Cir. 1991).
[47]*Rosen v. Port of Portland,* 641 F.2d 1243 (9th Cir. 1981) (dealing with an international airport).
[48]*Burch v. Barker,* 861 F.2d 1149 (9th Cir. 1988).

at issue here [a pre-distribution review policy] found them violative of the First Amendment because they were overly broad and inadequately focused on avoidance of disruption and interference with school discipline."[49]

Reviewing a pre-distribution review literature distribution policy within the context of the public school, a federal court found such a policy unconstitutional because it gave school officials "unfettered discretion."[50] The court went on to state that such a policy gave

> the government the power to suppress speech in advance, while imposing no time limits or other procedural obligations on school officials that would insure that speech is suppressed to the minimum extent possible, or that the speech is supported for good and expressed reasons, rather than at the whim of the school officials. This policy gives the school authorities the power to extinguish the right of students to speak through inaction and delay.[51]

One school district argued that all literature brought on campus by students must be approved by the school superintendent prior to distribution. In a case brought on behalf of a fifth-grade student whose literature was confiscated by a school principal, Liberty Counsel argued that the policy placed an impermissible restraint on free speech. The school argued that it must pre-review the literature for religious content. The court stated the following:

> It is beyond dispute that the school policy imposes a prior restraint on speech. It is also beyond dispute that the restraint is based on content, for only after reviewing content does the school decide whether particular materials may be distributed.[52]

Recognizing that students on public school campuses, including fifth-grade students, are protected by the constitutional right to free speech, the court declared:

> In order for the State in the person of school officials to justify prohibition of a particular expression of opinion, it must be able to show that its action was caused by something more than a mere desire to avoid the discomfort and unpleasantness that always accompany an unpopular viewpoint. . . .

> Following *Tinker*, a school seeking to impose a content-based prior restriction on student speech must show that the restricted speech would materially and substantially interfere with school operations or with the

---

[49]*Id.* at 1157.
[50]*Rivera*, 721 F. Supp. at 1198.
[51]*Id.*
[52]*Johnston-Loehner v. O'Brien*, 859 F. Supp. 575, 579 (M.D. Fla. 1994).

rights of other students. Mere fear of possible interference is not sufficient to sustain a content-based prior restraint on student speech.[53]

The court ruled that the policy requiring literature to be reviewed for approval prior to its distribution was unconstitutional.

The courts have disdained pre-distribution review policies because they essentially allow the government to suppress speech in advance. Those policies which do not contain time limits in which the government official has to grant or deny the request essentially allow the government to suppress speech either through inaction or delay of the granting or denial of the request. One federal court of appeals stated that "*Tinker* in no way suggests that students may be required to announce their intentions of engaging in certain conduct beforehand so school authorities may decide whether to prohibit the conduct."[54] These pre-distribution review policies are essentially a licensing law, and the Supreme Court has made "clear that a person faced with such an unconstitutional licensing law may ignore it and engage with impunity in the exercise of the right of free expression for which the law purports to require a license."[55] Clearly, a policy which requires students to present their literature for pre-distribution literature review is flatly unconstitutional.

A final way schools have attempted to restrict student distribution of literature is to require the literature to be placed at a designated location. Some schools will argue that it is not a violation of student free speech if the students can exercise their free speech on the public sidewalks surrounding the school or place their literature in a designated rack within the school. However, the Supreme Court has stated that "one is not to have the exercise of his liberty of expression in appropriate places abridged on the plea that it may be exercised in some other place."[56] Actually, requiring students to place literature at a designated location creates a First Amendment Establishment Clause conflict rather than alleviating such a problem. This is so because the designated location, like a school newspaper, carries with it a seal of sponsorship, endorsement, or approval by the school facility. It has already clearly been pointed out that student speech does not violate the Establishment Clause or raise any church-state issues. One school argued that it must prohibit student distribution of literature because to allow it would violate the Establishment Clause or the so-called separation of church and state. Therefore, the school instead allowed the distribution of literature, but only if it were placed at a specific designated location. A court reviewing this situation ruled that the designated location restriction created an Establishment Clause problem which the school attempted to avoid.[57]

---

[53]*Id.* at 580.

[54]*Fujishima v. Board of Education,* 460 F.2d 1355, 1358 (7th Cir. 1972).

[55]*Shuttlesworth,* 394 U.S. at 151.

[56]*Schneider v. New Jersey,* 308 U.S. 147 (1939).

[57]*Johnston-Leohner v. O'Brien,* 859 F. Supp. 575 (M.D. Fla. 1994); *Hedges v. Wauconda Community Unit School District No. 118,* 807 F. Supp. 444 (N.D. Ill. 1992). The Establishment Clause is not implicated by student-initiated literature distribution during noninstructional time.

First, to place student literature at a designated location creates the appearance of school sponsorship or endorsement. Second, it is unreasonable to require students to speak only at a designated location. Just as it would be ludicrous to require students to go to a designated location in order to pass out a love note or directions, or to verbally express themselves to one another, it is ludicrous and unreasonable to require students to place their literature at a designated location. Remember, verbal speech is equivalent to written speech, and the two should be treated equally. The only difference between the two would be a concern involving litter. However, schools should prohibit the one who litters and not try to use littering or some other invalid reason to restrict speech in general.

Some schools have attempted to restrict student-initiated speech on the basis that it violates the Establishment Clause of the First Amendment, or the so-called "separation of church and state." For example, Liberty Counsel brought suit on behalf of Amber Johnston-Loehner against one school district which claimed it had to prohibit a fifth grade student's distribution of literature to her fellow students because, the school argued, to allow this distribution would violate the Establishment Clause. In this case, a principal confiscated and destroyed religious tracts which the fifth grade student wanted to distribute to her fellow students during noninstructional time. The school argued that if it allowed this student to distribute material to her fellow classmates, the other students would perceive that the school was endorsing the message within these tracts, and since the school was prohibited from endorsing or promoting religion, the distribution of these tracts would violate the Establishment Clause or the so-called "separation of church and state." Thus, in order to avoid a constitutional problem on behalf of the school, the school's position was that it must prohibit all religious expression by students.

The federal court ruled that the school board's "asserted interest in avoiding a violation of the Establishment Clause is invalid because permitting student distribution of religious materials does not violate the Establishment Clause."[58]

The school district's reasoning was, of course, flawed. Students as well as school officials have the affirmative protection of the First Amendment Free Speech and Free Exercise Clauses. However, only teachers and school officials have the restriction of the Establishment Clause and are restricted in their promotion of religion. The Establishment Clause applies only to governmental entities and does not apply to individuals who are not associated with the government. Therefore, students do not have the restriction imposed by the Establishment Clause. Students cannot establish a religion, only governmental entities and their agents can establish a religion.

When the school sought to restrict student literature distribution by requiring that the literature be "distributed" only in a placement rack provided by the school, the school created, rather than avoided, an Establishment Clause violation.

[58]*Johnston-Loehner v. O'Brien*, 859 F. Supp. 575 (M.D. Fla. 1994).

Consequently, students have all the affirmative protection of the Free Speech and Free Exercise Clauses of the First Amendment and do not have any restriction or prohibition of the First Amendment Establishment Clause. While schools and their agents are prohibited from actively promoting and proselytizing a particular religious tenet, students have absolutely no prohibition in this regard. The Supreme Court has already recognized that "there is a crucial difference between *government* speech endorsing religion, which the Establishment Clause forbids, and *private* speech endorsing religion, which the Free Speech and Free Exercise Clauses protect."[59]

Voluntary, student-initiated, student-led distribution of religious literature on public school property has never been prohibited by the courts on the basis that it violates the separation of church and state. "It is only when individuals seek to observe their religion in ways that unduly involve the government that their expressive rights may be circumscribed."[60] There has never been any case in which student initiated activity has constituted a violation of the Establishment Clause or the separation of church and state.

A Texas court has rejected the Establishment Clause argument on the basis that the Establishment Clause "is not a restriction on the rights of individuals acting in their private lives."[61] Another court has also rejected this argument by stating the following:

> The Establishment Clause is a limitation on the power of governments; it is not a restriction on the rights of individuals acting in their private lives. The threshold question in any Establishment Clause case is whether there is sufficient governmental action to invoke the prohibition. In *Bethel* and *Hazelwood*, the Supreme Court recognized a distinction between school-affiliated speech and the private speech of students. It is clear that the mere fact that student speech occurs on school property does not make it government supported. It is undisputed in this case that the students are not government actors, are not acting in concert with the government, and do not seek school cooperation or assistance with their speech. Accordingly, the Establishment Clause simply is inapplicable.[62]

CLOTHES

Expressive activity through the wearing of clothes that have writing or articles of clothing such as crosses or religious jewelry which do not substantially interfere with the work of the school or impinge upon the rights of other students also retains First Amendment protection. The *Tinker* case involved students wearing black arm bands to school as a symbolic protest

---

[59]*Mergens*, 110 S. Ct. at 2360.
[60]*Berger v. Rensselaer Central School Corporation*, 992 F.2d 1160, 1168 (7th Cir. 1993).
[61]*Clark*, 806 F. Supp. at 121. *Accord Mergens*, 110 S. Ct. 2356 (1990); *Rivera*, 721 F. Supp. at 1195.
[62]*Rivera*, 721 F. Supp. at 1195. *See also Clark*, 806 F. Supp. at 121; *Thompson v. Waynesboro Area School District*, 673 F. Supp. 1379 (N.D. Pa. 1987).

to the Vietnam War. The Supreme Court held that such expression was protected by the First Amendment.[63]

The analysis used for clothing should be the same analysis used for literature distribution. Courts have already established that students have free speech rights on public school campuses and literature is considered free speech. Printed words on clothing such as t-shirts is another form of free speech. Just like the students in *Tinker* who wore the black armbands protesting involvement in the Vietnam War, students have the right to wear printed wording on clothing expressing themselves. This expression should be limited only if it interferes with the ordinary operation of the school or with the rights of other students. In the case of interfering with the rights of other students, the issue is whether the wording is defamatory or libelous to another student, not whether it is offensive.[64] Simply because another student disagrees with the content of the message does not permit the school to restrict the wearing of the shirt.

One student contacted Liberty Counsel after listening to a national radio broadcasts on this topic. The student apparently had worn a t-shirt to school with a pro-life message on it and the principal had required her to change clothes and not wear the shirt again. The shirt had the message "God created woman with a womb, not a tomb." The student was instructed that she should proceed with respect for those in authority over her, but this also involved her religious conviction and her right to speak under the First Amendment. Therefore, we advised her that she had the right to wear the shirt to school again. When she showed up at school wearing the shirt again, the principal questioned her, stating, "Why are you wearing that t-shirt again?" The student responded, "Because my attorney said I have a constitutional right to do so." That was the end of the discussion. After contacting the superintendent, the principal agreed that the student had a right to wear the shirt.

In one case, junior high school students designed t-shirts on the back of which were the words: "The best of the night's adventures are reserved for people with nothing planned."[65] School officials told the students to remove the t-shirts because the officials believed the message promoted an alcohol advertisement. However, the students contended that the message was meant to convey a message of being spontaneous and having fun. The federal court found that students' speech was "presumptively protected by the First Amendment."[66] The court further noted that the t-shirts worn during regular school hours did not bear the imprimatur or sponsorship of the school and therefore neither the *Hazelwood* case (the school newspaper

---

[63]*Tinker*, 393 U.S. at 506, 511.
[64]*Clark*, 806 F. Supp. at 120.
[65]*McIntire v. Bethel Independent School District*, 804 F. Supp. 1415, 1421 (W.D. Ok. 1992).
[66]*Id.* at 1424. *See also Roth v. United States*, 354 U.S. 476, 484 (1957) ("All ideas having even the slightest redeeming social importance—unorthodox ideas, controversial ideas, even ideas hateful to the prevailing climate of opinion, have the full protection of the guarantees [of the First Amendment].")

case) nor the *Fraser* case (the nominating speech case) applied. Finally, the court ruled that a forum analysis was not appropriate and that the proper test was to apply *Tinker*.[67] The court therefore concluded that the students had a First Amendment right to wear the t-shirts, and they could not be prohibited unless there was evidence of "substantial disruption or material interference with school activities."[68]

One shirt that is particularly intriguing was created by a pro-life group in Orlando, Florida. On the front of the shirt are the words "CHOOSE LIFE." The word "CHOOSE" is written across the top of the shirt. Underneath, in big letters approximately eight inches tall, is the word "LIFE." On the back of the shirt is the following:

> 4,352 babies Killed in abortions each day in U.S.A. • 18 days after conception the child's heart starts beating • In the year 2,000, over $1/2$ of our population will be 50 and older • 1 out of every 3 pregnancies end in abortion • 99% of all abortions performed are for social reasons • Less than 1% of all abortions are for rape, incest & medical reasons • Only half the people that go into abortion clinics come out alive • Mother's womb: the most dangerous place on earth • Abortions are performed legally through all 9 months of pregnancy •All of the unborn child's organs are formed and functioning at 2 months • Child is dependent on mother's body; not part of it • Genetic code is set from moment of conception • Brainwaves are detected at 40 days • Nervous system functioning before 12 weeks • Birth is merely changing place of residence, dining habits, and airwaves • Abortion: the worst form of child abuse • Just because it's legal, doesn't make it right.

Below this inscription are the words: "This is dedicated to all those whose lives were brutally ended by abortion. We mourn their deaths, but know their souls are with God."

This message is written in black interspersed with red highlighted words to break up the paragraph. As a student sits in class, the student behind the student with the t-shirt obviously sees the writing. During class, discussion about the writing is probably not appropriate, but after class or in between class, discussion of the message is appropriate. This shirt provides an outstanding opportunity for students to discuss pro-life issues.

HAIR

Though hair is an issue that will not often arise as a religious liberty matter, the length of hair is clearly important to certain religious beliefs. School dress codes requiring males to have short hair may conflict with the beliefs of some Native American students. A federal court has ruled that it is

---

[67]*McIntire*, 804 F. Supp. at 1427.
[68]*Id.* at 1420.

unconstitutional for a school to require Native American male students to have short hair contrary to their religious belief that short hair is only to be worn to show mourning when a close family member dies. Since wearing long hair for males of certain religious beliefs may actually be a First Amendment expressive activity, some dress codes may be ruled unconstitutional.[69] When considering the constitutionality of dress codes, the student who is negatively impacted by such a code must have a sincerely held religious belief that is negatively impacted.

CLASS DISCUSSION AND REPORTS

The issue often arises as to whether students may ask questions or even challenge their teachers during class when the subject matter being taught is disagreeable to the student. Another interesting question arises as to whether students may give religious verbal or written reports.

Again, student speech, whether verbal or written, is protected by the First Amendment. A student cannot stand up in a math class and begin speaking about religion if the speech has no relation to the topic being studied. However, if the subject matter is evolution, the student can certainly ask questions regarding creation science or abrupt appearance, and can even express disagreements with the teacher. The student may express views on any subject being taught so long as it is consistent with the subject matter being discussed at that time. Moreover, if students are asked to give verbal or written reports, students may give these reports on religious matters, so long as it falls within the parameters of the context of study. For example, in a literature class, if students are required to read a book and give a written or oral report, a student may read a religious book and give a report on this book. If a teacher prohibited the student from giving the report simply because the content of the report was religious, this would be a violation of the student's free speech and free exercise rights.[70]

One person called Liberty Counsel and advised that the students were required to give a written report on the fall season. The student wrote in the report that God created the fall season. When the student presented this paper to the teacher and the teacher realized that it contained information in it regarding God, the teacher ripped up the paper and threw it away, stat-

---

[69]*Alabama and Coushatta Tribes of Texas v. Trustees of the Big Sandy Independent School District,* 817 F. Supp. 1319 (E.D. Tex. 1993).

[70]*But see DeNooyer v. Livonia Public Schools,* 799 F. Supp. 744 (E.D. Mich. 1992), *aff'd sub nom, DeNooyer v. Merinelli,* 1 F.3d 1240 (6th Cir. 1993) (A school may prohibit a second grade student from showing during show and tell time a videotape of herself singing a proselytizing religious song and advocating accepting Jesus Christ as Savior because the school teacher believed that showing the videotape was inappropriate in that it was inconsistent with the purpose of the class, which was designed to develop self-esteem through oral presentations in the classroom.); *Duran v. Nitsche,* 780 F. Supp. 1048 (E.D. Pa. 1991) (A fifth grade teacher may prohibit a student from giving an oral presentation to her class about her belief in God because, even though the teacher allowed oral presentations, the classroom was not open for all forms of discussion.).

ing that it violated the separation of church and state. This is clearly a big-oted action and violative of the First Amendment.

In addition, students may object to participating in certain kinds of class activities if the activity violates a sincerely held religious belief. If a class project, assignment, or activity violates a student's sincerely held religious beliefs, the student may opt out and request alternative accommodations.

ACCESS TO BOOKS AND FILMS

The Supreme Court has declared that a student's "right to receive ideas is a necessary predicate to the recipient's meaningful exercise of his or her own right of speech."[71] While a school may not be forced to place a book in the library, once a book is placed there, the discretion to remove the book is circumscribed by the First Amendment. The book may not be removed simply because the school disagrees with the content. However, the book could be removed if it lacked "educational suitability" or if it contained pervasive vulgarity.[72] Similarly, the Bible cannot be removed from a library on the basis of its religious content.[73] Finally, although a school has wide latitude in the selection and retention of curriculum, content-neutral criteria may be necessary to remove a film from part of the curriculum.[74]

One student called Liberty Counsel because her library did not have any pro-life literature. She obtained certain books and donated them to her school library, and the library accepted the books and placed them on the library shelves. Once accepted, the library has certain restrictions on removing the books. These books cannot be removed simply because the content of the speech is disagreeable or offensive. The so-called political correctness movement wants to remove certain speech that offends various classes of society. This is an absolute violation of the First Amendment and should be resisted. One individual contacted Liberty Counsel and stated that the school principal told her that a Bible could not be in the school library because it violated the so-called separation of church and state. This is absolutely untrue. Schools may and should have religious literature in their libraries. Schools that remove religious material simply because the content is religious violate the First Amendment because such decisions are based on the content of the literature.

RELEASE TIME

Release time programs may allow public school students a certain time each week to leave school to attend religious instruction.[75] The instruction must

---

[71]*Board of Education, Island Trees Union Free School District No. 26 v. Pico,* 457 U.S. 853, 867 (1982).
[72]*Id.* at 871.
[73]*But see Roberts v. Madigan,* 702 F. Supp. 1505 (D. Colo. 1989).
[74]*Pratt v. Independent School District,* 670 F.2d 771 (8th Cir. 1982).
[75]*Zorach v. Clauson,* 343 U.S. 306 (1952).

be given by non-school personnel off campus.[76] Portable instruction sites must not be on school premises and no academic credit should be given for such instruction.[77] Finally, the printing cost of attendance cards should be borne by the religious institution providing the instruction,[78] and elective credit should not be given.[79]

THE PLEDGE OF ALLEGIANCE

The Pledge of Allegiance has been attacked in two forms. The first attack has been from a free exercise standpoint, and the second has been from an Establishment Clause position. The first type of challenge has been upheld while the second has been rejected.

Jehovah's Witnesses have a sincerely held religious belief against saluting flags which they consider to be idols. The United States Supreme Court ruled that a Jehovah's Witness should be excused from the requirement of saluting the flag.[80] Indeed, anyone who opposes saluting the flag should be excused from the requirement without regard to whether their refusal is based on religious or nonreligious grounds. To compel a student to salute the flag would not only be a violation of the Jehovah's Witnesses' free exercise rights, but it could be a violation of other individuals' free speech rights by virtue of the state compelling a specific type of speech.

The United States Supreme Court case deciding the flag salute issue with regard to Jehovah's Witnesses occurred in 1943. However, in 1954, the Pledge of Allegiance was amended to add the phrase "under God." In 1992, an atheist brought suit against an Illinois school board claiming that the flag salute was an unconstitutional establishment of religion by the state because it required individuals, at the direction of the state, to confess belief in God. The Illinois federal appeals court found that the pledge was "a secular rather than sectarian vow" and therefore did not violate the First Amendment Establishment Clause.[81] The court, therefore, ruled that the pledge was constitutional, merely recognizing "the historical fact that our Nation was believed to have been founded 'under God'."[82] The court went on to say that "reciting the pledge may be no more of a religious exercise than the reading allowed of Lincoln's Gettysburg Address, which contains an allusion to the same historical fact."[83]

In summary, students in public schools should have the option to refuse

---

[76]*Lanner v. Wimmer*, 662 F.2d 1349 (10th Cir. 1981).
[77]*Doe v. Shenandoah County School Board*, 737 F. Supp. 913 (W.D. Va. 1990).
[78]*Lanner*, 662 F.2d at 1349.
[79]*Id. See Minnesota Federation of Teachers v. Nelson*, 740 F. Supp. 694 (D. Minn. 1990).
[80]*West Virginia State Board of Education v. Barnette*, 319 U.S. 624 (1943).
[81]*Sherman v. Community Consolidated School District*, 980 F.2d 437 (7th Cir. 1992), *cert. denied*, 113 S. Ct. 2439 (1993).
[82]*Id.* at 447.
[83]*Id.*

to say the Pledge of Allegiance. Without this option, there may be a constitutional violation.

EQUAL ACCESS ON PUBLIC SCHOOLS CAMPUSES

The Equal Access Act of 1984 (herein referred to as the "Act")[84] has been affirmatively upheld by the Supreme Court in *Board of Education v. Mergens*.[85] If the public secondary school receives federal funds and allows one or more noncurriculum-related student groups to meet on campus, then the school cannot prohibit other noncurriculum-related student groups from meeting on campus unless such clubs "materially and substantially interfere with the orderly conduct of educational activities within the school."[86] A noncurriculum-related student group is interpreted broadly to mean "any student group that does not *directly* relate to the body of courses offered by the school."[87] The Court indicated that "a student group directly relates to a school's curriculum if the subject matter of the group is actually taught, or will soon be taught, in a regularly offered course; if the subject matter of the group concerns the body of courses as a whole; if the participation in the group is required for a particular course; or if participation in the group results in academic credit."[88] Examples of noncurriculum-related groups are chess clubs, stamp collecting clubs, or community service clubs. Equal access means exactly what it says—equal access to every facility of the school which is used by at least one or more other noncurriculum related student groups, which would include use of classroom facilities, copy machines, intercom systems, bulletin boards, school newspaper, yearbook pictures, and annual club fairs.[89]

The application of the Act is simple—all groups must be treated equally without discrimination. Religious and political groups must be treated equally with other social or activity groups. According to the United States Supreme Court in *Mergens*, Congress passed the Act in order "to prevent discrimination against religious and other types of speech."[90]

In the *Mergens* case the Westside High School already allowed a Christian club to meet informally in the school facilities after school hours. However, the Christian club was denied official recognition which allowed other student clubs to be a part of the student activities program and allowed access to the school newspaper, bulletin boards, the public address system, and the annual club fair. According to *Mergens*, since the Westside High School officially recognized other noncurriculum related student

---

[84]20 U.S.C. §§ 4071-74. This Act is reproduced in Appendix C.
[85]110 S. Ct. 2356 (1990).
[86]*Id.* at 2364, 2367.
[87]*Id.* at 2366.
[88]*Id.*
[89]As for use of bulletin boards and yearbooks, the school can designate space to "noncurriculum-related student clubs" thus avoiding the appearance of school endorsement.
[90]*Mergens*, 110 S. Ct. at 2371.

groups, allowed those groups access to the school newspaper, bulletin boards, public address system and the annual club fair, but did not allow the same privileges to the Christian club, the school violated the Act. Thus, if any club is given the opportunity of access to use school facilities, then a school must allow the same access to other groups. As one group is treated, all groups must be treated.

Application of Equal Access

The Act provides a safe harbor in which a school may operate. The Act should be viewed as a floor and not a ceiling. In other words, it presents the bare minimum that a school may provide to student groups, but a school may grant even more rights to student groups than the Act requires.

The Act applies to any (1) public secondary school (2) which receives federal funds and (3) which has a limited open forum. Identifying a public school providing secondary education which receives federal funds is easy. A limited open forum occurs "whenever such school grants an offering to or opportunity for one or more noncurriculum related student groups to meet on school premises during noninstructional time."[91]

The Supreme Court in *Mergens* defined a noncurriculum-related student group "broadly to mean any student group that does not *directly* relate to the body of courses offered by the school."[92] The Court further stated that

> a student group directly relates to a school's curriculum if the subject matter of the group is actually taught, or will soon be taught, in a regularly offered course; if the subject matter of the group concerns the body of courses as a whole; if participation in the group is required for a particular course; or if participation in the group results in academic credit.[93]

A student government group would generally relate directly to the curriculum to the extent that it addresses concerns or solicits opinions and formulates proposals pertaining to the body of courses offered by the school. If participation in the school band or orchestra were required for the band or orchestra classes, or resulted in academic credit, then those groups would directly relate to the curriculum.

On the other hand, some examples of noncurriculum-related student groups include, but are by no means limited to, the chess club, a stamp collecting club, a community service club, camera club, diving club, music groups, Key Club, debate groups, business groups, political groups, and religious groups.[94]

---

[91]20 U.S.C. § 4071(b).
[92]*Mergens*, 110 S. Ct. at 2366.
[93]*Id.*
[94]*See Mergens*, 110 S. Ct. at 2366; *Bender v. Williamsport Area School District*, 741 F.2d 538, 539 n.18 (3rd Cir. 1984), *vacated on other grounds*, 475 U.S. 534 (1986); *Student Coalition for Peace v. Lower Merion School District*, 633 F. Supp. 1040, 1042 (E.D. Pa. 1986); 130 Cong. Rec. H 7732 (daily ed. July 25, 1984) and 130 Cong. Rec. S 8365 (daily ed. July 27, 1984).

Organizing a School Club

Under the Act a student club must be initiated by the students. Once initi-ated, the student group, no matter the size, must be given equal treatment as all other existing clubs. If the school requires a constitution or a state-ment of purpose from the other clubs, then a constitution or a statement of purpose may also be required of the new club.[95] The school may require a faculty member or any other school employee to be a sponsor of the group if a sponsor is required of the already existing groups. The school faculty member or employee may attend the student meetings. The basic principle is that the student group must be initiated and predominantly led by stu-dents, although the students may on occasion bring in outside speakers.

Equal Access and Disruptive Clubs

A concern that was brought up during the legislative hearings on the Act was that equal access would allow groups in public schools which are racist, hate groups, or disruptive.[96] However, the Act has been in effect since 1984; yet, an influx of disruptive hate groups disturbing schools has not occurred.

The Act specifically indicates that it "shall not be construed to limit the authority of the school, its agents or employees, to maintain order and dis-cipline on school premises, to protect the well-being of students and faculty, and to assure that attendance of students at meetings is voluntary."[97] If a group substantially interferes with the normal operation of the school or is disruptive, the school under the Act is free to prohibit such a group from meeting on campus. The school must be able to show that the group is, in fact, disruptive. A simple fear that a group may be disruptive in the future is probably not enough to support denial of equal access, but the actual dis-ruption or a threatened disruption by a group may be enough to restrict equal access. Satanic, occultic, racist, and hate groups may at some time cause disruption, but time has shown that schools have not seen an influx of these groups. Simply because some students or faculty disagree with the content of a group's speech is not enough to prohibit that group from equal access. However, if such a group is disruptive to the ordinary operation of the school, then the administrators retain the authority under the Act to maintain an orderly operating school. A school cannot deny access to a group simply because the content of the group's speech is distasteful or offensive. Moreover, a school cannot deny access to a group merely because an affiliate or parent organization at some other location has been shown to be disruptive.[98] The United States Supreme Court has stated

---

[95]Liberty Counsel has produced a model constitution which can be used as an example. This constitution is reproduced in Appendix D.
[96]See *U.S. Code Congressional and Administrative News*, P.L. 95-561 Vol. 5 pp. 4971-5226 (1978).
[97]20 U.S.C. § 4071(f).
[98]*Healy v. James*, 408 U.S. 169 (1972).

Among the rights protected by the First Amendment is the right of individuals to associate to further their personal beliefs. While the freedom of association is not explicitly set out in the Amendment, it has long been held to be implicit in the freedoms of speech, assembly, and petition.[99]

The Supreme Court has also observed the following,

> It should be obvious that the exclusion of any person or group—all-Negro, all-Oriental, or all-white—from public facilities infringes upon the freedom of the individual to associate as he chooses. . . . The associational rights which our system honors permit all white, all black, all brown, and all yellow groups to be formed. They also permit all Catholic, all Jewish, or all agnostic clubs to be established. Government may not tell a man or woman who his or her associates must be. . . . The freedom to associate applies to the beliefs we share, and to those we consider reprehensible. It tends to produce the diversity of opinion that oils the machinery of democratic government and insures peaceful, orderly change.[100]

On one university campus, a school tried to prohibit the formation of a student group because its national affiliate or parent organization was known to have violent or disruptive behavior. However, there was no evidence that the local student group had created any violent or disruptive behavior. The school denied access to the student group simply because of the affiliation with its national parent. The United States Supreme Court ruled that denying access to this student group based upon the activities of other individuals was a violation of the First Amendment.[101] Consequently, though school administrators have the right to maintain an orderly process on campus, mere distaste for the content of the student group's speech or an undifferentiated fear of disruption is not enough to prohibit access. Moreover, it is not enough to prohibit access simply because some other parent or affiliate organization similar to the one seeking access is known to be violent or disruptive. Certainly schools can prohibit violent or disruptive groups, but the school must have specific information to support the violent or disruptive behavior of the particular group requesting access.

Equal Access and the Constitution

On June 4, 1990, the Supreme Court of the United States upheld the constitutionality of the Act.[102] Specifically, the *Mergens* case ruled that the Act was not prohibited by the First Amendment Establishment Clause. Although the Supreme Court in 1986 hinted that the Act was constitutional

---

[99]*Id.* at 181.
[100]*Gilmore v. City of Montgomery*, 417 U.S. 556, 575 (1974) (quoting *Moose Lodge No. 107 v. Irvis*, 407 U.S. 163, 179-80 (1972) (Douglas, J., dissenting)).
[101]*Healy*, 408 U.S. at 169.
[102]*Mergens*, 110 S. Ct. at 2356.

in the case of *Bender v. Williamsport Area School District*,[103] the *Mergens* case left no doubt as to the constitutionality of the Act.[104]

Although the United States Supreme Court in 1990 clearly upheld the constitutionality of the Act, some schools still have not heard the message. In one situation, Liberty Counsel was contacted by a concerned parent because the school discriminated against religious clubs. Religious clubs were allowed to meet, but only after school hours, while the secular clubs were allowed to meet during school hours. Fortunately the situation was resolved by sending one of Liberty Counsel's brochures to the school officials. After reading the brochure, the school officials agreed that they had wrongly discriminated against the clubs and decided to allow them to meet during the school hours as they allowed the secular clubs. In one month, the Youth Alive club grew from six to sixty students and the Fellowship of Christian Athletes club doubled in size. The rate of growth of these clubs was so enormous that school officials requested assistance from other teachers to be sponsors of these clubs.

In another case, Liberty Counsel was contacted because the school would not allow the religious clubs to be pictured in the school annual. Though the other secular clubs had their pictures in the school annual, the school stated it would not allow the religious clubs to be pictured in the annual because to do so would violate the so-called separation of church and state. After several weeks of negotiation and a trip to the school board, the school agreed that it had violated the Act and decided to treat the clubs equally. Consequently, the school allowed the religious clubs to have their picture in the annual just like they allowed the secular clubs.

Students should take advantage of student-initiated Bible clubs. Much can be accomplished through these clubs. For example, students may announce through these clubs such activities as the annual "See You at the Pole." If the other secular clubs are allowed to use the intercom system or bulletin boards, then the religious clubs can use these same facilities to make announcements. Periodically students may work through these clubs to bring outside events onto campus, assuming, of course, that the school allows other outside events to come on campus.

Guidelines for Starting a Club

The following are suggested steps for starting a club. These steps are not required by the Act but are presented here to show practical guidelines.

(1) A club must be initiated by a student. One student should talk to friends to see if there is an interest in starting a club. The students should share ideas about the club. What will the club do? What will

---

[103]*Bender*, 475 U.S. at 534.
[104]*Mergens*, 110 S. Ct. at 2356.

the name of the club be? What is the purpose? How often will the club meet?

(2) After the idea of the club has been formulated, one or two students should ask a school employee to be its sponsor. Meet with the sponsor to share your ideas. Not all schools require a sponsor, so talk to members of other clubs to see if they have a sponsor.

(3) Prepare a constitution which states the club's name and purpose. A constitution can be anything from one paragraph to several pages. If you need assistance, Liberty Counsel's model constitution is reproduced in Appendix D.

(4) One or two student leaders of the club should meet with the principal or one of the vice principals in charge of clubs. Present your request to form a club and your constitution at this meeting.

(5) The school should then consider your request and give you guidance for beginning your meetings.

SUMMARY

In summary, students on public school campuses do not shed their constitutional rights at the schoolhouse gate. Before, after, and between classes as well as during the lunch period and on the playing field, students have the First Amendment right to free speech. This speech can be exercised during noninstructional time so long as it is not disruptive to the ordinary operation of the school. Students can communicate with each other verbally, through literature, or through clothing with inscribed messages.

During class discussions, students have a constitutional right to ask questions and discuss religious issues so long as the question or discussion is related to the curriculum being studied. Students have the First Amendment right to express themselves through projects or reports. To allow other students to present secular reports while prohibiting religious reports is to show hostility toward religion, which the Constitution forbids.

The First Amendment rights of students also permit them to have access to various books and films, and place certain limitations upon schools for removing books or films from libraries if the school's decision to remove the book or film is based upon the content of the speech. Students also have free exercise of religion rights which would permit a school to provide for release time allowing students to leave campus for off-site religious instruction.

Since students have First Amendment free speech and free exercise of religion rights, schools cannot compel a student to say a pledge of allegiance to a flag if the student has a sincerely held religious belief prohibiting the student from saying a pledge or simply objects to the pledge for nonreligious reasons.

Finally, students have free speech rights to be able to gather together in student clubs under the Equal Access Act. Even if the Equal Access Act was not in existence, the First Amendment still grants First Amendment free speech rights for students to form noncurriculum-related student clubs. If a school allows any noncurriculum-related club, it must allow all noncurriculum-related student clubs, even if the content of their speech is religious. All clubs must be treated equally.

Students are clearly protected by the Constituton while on public school campuses and may exercise their religious rights by sharing their faith with other students.

4

Graduation Prayers in
Public Schools

The United States Supreme Court decision in *Lee v. Weisman*[1] has caused some confusion as to whether prayers are permissible at public school graduation ceremonies. While prayers have been restricted at public school graduations, they have not been completely prohibited. It is important to know what the Court did and did not say.

WHAT IS PROHIBITED?

To understand what is presently prohibited by the United States Supreme Court decision in *Lee v. Weisman*, it is important to know some of the history regarding that case. The Supreme Court focused on the following three factors: (1) the school principal decided that an invocation and benediction would be given at the ceremony and placed prayer on the agenda; (2) the principal chose the religious participant; and (3) the principal provided the clergyman with a copy of *Guidelines for Civic Occasions*, produced by the National Council of Christians and Jews, outlining suggestions for delivering nonsectarian prayers. Justice Kennedy found that these three factors actually placed the school in the position of guiding and directing the prayer during a public ceremony, and based upon his opinion, this participation and guidance of the prayer was a violation of the First Amendment Establishment Clause.

What the Supreme Court prohibited can be summed up as follows. School officials cannot direct that prayer be part of a public school graduation ceremony, cannot specifically select a religious participant to say a prayer during a public graduation ceremony, and cannot give guidelines on how to say a prayer during a public graduation ceremony, even if these guidelines are meant to be used in a nonsectarian manner. In practical terms, a public school cannot invite a clergyman to say a prayer at a grad-

---

[1]112 S. Ct. 2649 (1992).

uation ceremony and direct him on how to say the prayer. As an additional note, this decision probably does not affect graduation prayers at post-secondary schools.

Clearly the Supreme Court did not say that all prayers at graduation were flatly prohibited. In fact, the Court stated that its ruling was limited to the facts of that particular case.[2] Therefore, any change in the factual situation presented in *Lee* could change the outcome. Justice Scalia wrote in his dissenting opinion that merely adding a disclaimer to the graduation program would make the same set of facts constitutional.[3] Justice Scalia stated the following:

> All that is seemingly needed is an announcement, or perhaps a written insertion at the beginning of the graduation program, to the effect that, while all are asked to rise for the invocation and benediction, none is compelled to join in them, nor will be assumed, by rising, to have done so. That obvious fact recited, the graduates and their parents may proceed to thank God, as Americans have always done, for the blessings He has generously bestowed on them and on their country.[4]

WHAT IS PERMITTED?

Though a school cannot invite clergy to say a prayer at a public school graduation ceremony, prayers are still permissible at such ceremonies. A school retains a number of options for the continuation of prayer.

Option One

If a school avoided placing prayer on the agenda and avoided a specific selection of a clergyman to recite a prayer, it would avoid two of the major concerns of the Supreme Court. Consequently, school officials could use secular criteria for selecting the participants. A secular criteria would simply be one that does not specifically look for someone who is a religious participant to say a specific religious message. If a school chose a speaker because of some contribution the speaker made to society and not because the speaker happened to be a clergyman, then the school would avoid one of the concerns of the Supreme Court. In short, school officials could choose a speaker or participant because of some recognized contribution to society. A clergyman could be a participant as long as the selection was made using secular criteria and not solely because the participant is religious.

An individual selected using secular criteria could then participate in the public graduation ceremony and could voluntarily offer a prayer. In this way, the school does not specifically select a religious person for the purpose of offering prayer. For the school to forbid this participant from say-

[2]*Id.* at 2655.
[3]*Id.* at 2685 (Scalia, J., dissenting).
[4]*Id.*

ing a prayer may be a violation of that person's First Amendment right to freedom of expression. Furthermore, if a school prohibited such a person from saying a prayer, either before or after the fact, could violate the First Amendment Establishment Clause because the school would be showing hostility toward religion. In summary, a school could select a participant on a secular basis, and that participant could voluntarily pray.

Option Two

Similar to option one, another option is for a valedictorian, salutatorian, president of the senior class, or any other student participant chosen based upon academic criteria or other secular standards to be a part of the graduation ceremony to pray voluntarily. In this circumstance, the school would not specifically be placing prayer on the agenda and would not be selecting the student for the specific purpose of praying. The school may not even know that the participant would pray until the participant actually stood up and did pray. Again, under this particular option, for the school to prohibit this student participant from praying could be construed as a violation of the First Amendment Free Speech and Establishment Clauses in that the school would be restricting speech and showing hostility toward religion.

In one case, Liberty Counsel was contacted by a high school senior class president who was chosen to be the keynote speaker at graduation. The class president wanted to thank God in his speech. When he spoke to the principal, the principal warned that the student must not mention anything regarding religion. After discussing this situation with Liberty Counsel, we advised that, of course, he must have respect for his authorities, but this issue dealt with the expression of his religious conviction and the First Amendment. We advised that he had the right to speak about his relationship with Jesus Christ. He was rightfully there on the platform by virtue of his position as a class officer, and while there, he had the right to speak freely, so long as he did not speak libelous or defamatory remarks toward other students. When he did speak during the graduation ceremony, he acknowledged and thanked God for his accomplishments. At the end of the speech, he got a standing ovation. Afterwards, he received numerous cards from students and parents congratulating him for having the courage to speak about God. The response was so overwhelming that the principal who originally warned against speaking about God also wrote the student a thank you card.

In one school, the valedictorian sneezed after giving the valedictory address. All of the students in unison responded, "God bless you." Of course, this is a humorous way of acknowledging God during a ceremony, and students do not need to resort to these type of tactics. When student speakers enter the podium during a graduation ceremony, they do not shed their constitutional rights to freedom of expression, just like they do not shed these rights when they enter the schoolhouse gate.[5]

---

[5]*Tinker v. Des Moines Independent School District*, 393 U.S. 503, 506 (1969).

Option Three

Similar to option two, prayer could still be conducted at a graduation ceremony if the student body was permitted to elect a student chaplain or speaker. This chaplain or speaker could be elected by the student body in the same way that the student body elects class officers. Some class sections already elect student chaplains along with the election of other class officers. As part of the graduation ceremony, the student chaplain could address the student body along with the other officers of the class, and the address could include a prayer. In this manner, the school would not be directly endorsing the school officers since they would be elected by the student body. The school chaplain could certainly be placed on the agenda, and the school should avoid any efforts to guide or direct the prayer or address given by the school chaplain. While not required, the chaplain could announce, or the bulletin could state, that while all are asked to rise for the invocation and benediction, none are compelled to do so. If this option is chosen, the bulletin should state that the school does not control, review, promote, or endorse the content of student messages.

Option Four

The Court in *Lee* was concerned that school officials specifically placed prayer on the agenda, selected a clergyman, and gave the clergyman guidelines for saying nonsectarian prayers. If these factors were avoided, prayers would be permissible. One way that these factors could be avoided is for school officials to allow a parent and/or student committee to create the agenda for graduation ceremonies. This parent-student committee could then come up with its own agenda, which could include prayer. This parent-student committee could specifically choose a religious participant to say a prayer and could, in fact, discuss the prayer with the participant. By permitting a parent-student committee to create the agenda and select the participants, the school would avoid any appearance of sponsorship. The school could note that the graduation ceremony or baccalaureate service was not actually sponsored by the school, but rather was sponsored by the parents and students. The parents and students could request to use the school facilities in order to conduct the graduation ceremonies.

A federal court of appeals ruled in *Jones v. Clear Creek Independent School District* that "a majority of students can do what the State acting on its own cannot do to incorporate prayer in public high school graduation ceremonies."[6] It is important to note that the *Jones* case was decided in November of 1992, *after* the Supreme Court's decision in *Lee*. In fact, the *Jones* case discusses the *Lee* decision and states that its situation is clearly distinguishable from that presented in *Lee*. In *Jones*, the school district passed a resolution permitting the high school graduating seniors to vote

---

[6]*Jones v. Clear Creek Independent School District*, 977 F.2d 963, 972 (5th Cir. 1992), *cert. denied*, 113 S. Ct. 2950 (1993).

whether or not to have a fellow student lead the graduating class in prayer. Quoting the Supreme Court's decision in *Board of Education v. Mergens*, the *Jones* court stated that "there is a crucial difference between *government* speech endorsing religion, which the Establishment Clause forbids, and *private* speech endorsing religion, which the Free Speech and Free Exercise Clauses protect."[7] In other words, what the government cannot do through its school officials, individual students can do acting on their own.

The Supreme Court has clearly stated that students on public school campuses do not "shed their constitutional rights to freedom of speech or expression at the schoolhouse gate."[8] The Court recognized that students have free speech rights "in the cafeteria, on the playing field, or on campus during authorized hours."[9] Therefore, a student clearly has the First Amendment right to lead fellow students in a prayer during a graduation ceremony. First, in allowing a student to pray during a graduation ceremony, there would be no church-state problem as encountered in *Lee* because the prayer would be conducted by a private individual rather than school officials. Second, to prohibit the student from saying a prayer would actually result in a violation of the student's free speech rights. Prohibiting prayer in this context could subject the school to lawsuits.

A federal court ruled that student-initiated prayer during graduation ceremonies was constitutional. An Idaho court found that "the practice of allowing students to determine whether or not to include prayer in their graduation ceremonies [did] not violate the Establishment Clause."[10] If this option is chosen, the bulletin should state that the school does not control, review, promote, or endorse the content of student messages.

Option Five

Similar to options three and four, a school could choose to allow student-initiated, student-led messages. This option does not mention prayer but instead focuses on student messages. The students are then permitted to choose whatever topic they wish to address. This method is actually preferable to one focusing on student-initiated prayers. The difference between this option and option four is that option four states that students may choose to include *prayer* in the graduation, whereas this option states that students may choose to present a *message* during graduation.

One school district developed the following guidelines:

1. The use of a brief opening and/or closing message, not to exceed two minutes, at high school graduation exercises shall rest within the discretion of the graduating senior class.

2. The opening and/or closing message shall be given by a student vol-

---

[7]*See Mergens*, 110 S. Ct. at 2360. Though the school district in *Jones* required the student prayers to be nonsectarian, schools should avoid this requirement because it injects the school into religion by mandating that school officials monitor the prayer.

[8]*Tinker*, 393 U.S. at 506.

[9]*Id.* at 512-513.

[10]*Harris v. Joint School District No. 241*, 821 F. Supp. 638 (D. Idaho 1993).

unteer, in the graduating senior class, chosen by the graduating senior class as a whole.

3. If the graduating senior class chooses to use an opening and/or closing message, the content of that message shall be prepared by the student volunteer and shall not be monitored or otherwise reviewed by school officials, its officers, or employees.[11]

During the first year in which the above policy was operative within the school district, ten of the seventeen high schools opted for messages that constituted various forms of religious prayer. The remaining seven schools had either no message at all or their message was entirely secular in nature.[12] A policy allowing student messages truly focuses on the initiation of the student to choose the contents of the message. Moreover, the policy restricts all forms of review or censorship of the message by school officials. Students may say whatever they wish with impunity. In the case in which this policy arose, the American Civil Liberties Union sued the school board requesting that the policy be declared unconstitutional. Liberty Counsel intervened on behalf of students ranging from seventh through twelfth grade to defend the school. A federal court ruled that the policy was constitutional and that students have First Amendment rights to free speech during the graduation ceremony. As in options three and four, it is advisable for the bulletin to note that the school does not control, review, promote, or endorse the content of student messages.

Option Six

Under the above options one through five, prayer could still be conducted during public school graduation ceremonies. The First Amendment permits prayer as noted above but does not require prayer. In other words, prayer could still be conducted under the circumstances presented above, but the First Amendment would not require the speaker or participant to pray, the student to pray, or the school officials to allow a parent-student committee. Under options one through five, there may be some years when prayer would be conducted and other years when it would not be conducted. In order to insure that prayer would be conducted on a consistent basis during public school graduations, community leaders and churches could privately sponsor graduation ceremonies. Currently many schools are not large enough to conduct public graduation ceremonies. Such schools often use outside facilities, and many use church auditoriums. Churches throughout the community could organize public graduation ceremonies or baccalaureate services. The time, place, and manner could be organized by the churches or other community leaders, and student groups could publicize the information through their on campus clubs. Public school students along with teachers and staff could be invited to participate in the cere-

---

[11]*Adler v. Duval County School Board*, 851 F. Supp. 446, 449 (M.D. Fla. 1994).
[12]*Id.* at 449-450.

mony, so long as the ceremony was held off campus, designed and choreographed by nonschool officials.

School officials could participate in ceremonies conducted at churches as long as they were not necessarily organizing it as part of a sponsorship of the local school. At such a service, there would be no prohibition against inviting a religious speaker to address the students.

If a public school allows use of its facilities by outside secular organizations, then the public school must allow use of the same facilities by religious organizations including use for religious purposes. Such a purpose can be the performance of a graduation or baccalaureate ceremony. In one case, a United Methodist Church sued a school board because it wished to rent the facilities for a graduation ceremony. The school refused, and an Alabama federal court ruled that disallowing use of the facilities by the Methodist church was a violation of the First Amendment Free Speech Clause because the school allowed use of its facilities by other outside secular organizations.[13] Indeed, the United States Supreme Court stated that "if a State refused to let religious groups use facilities open to others, then it would demonstrate not neutrality, but hostility toward religion."[14] In another case, a group of parents and graduating senior students requested use of a high school gymnasium to conduct a baccalaureate ceremony. The baccalaureate ceremony was privately-sponsored and open to the public. Participation by the students was completely voluntary. However, the school board decided not to rent the gymnasium because its use would be for a religious purpose. The school board had on other occasions allowed use of its facilities to outside secular organizations. A federal court in Wyoming ruled that refusal to rent the gymnasium to the parents and students to conduct the religious baccalaureate service was an unconstitutional violation of the First Amendment.[15]

SUMMARY

Prayers at public school graduations have been limited by the United States Supreme Court. The tradition that can be dated back as far as July of 1868, when the first public school graduation is officially documented, will no longer continue as it has for so many years. However, prayer is still permissible at public school graduation ceremonies.

The Supreme Court has ruled that a school cannot place prayer on the

---

[13] *Verbena United Methodist Church v. Chilton County Board of Education,* 765 F. Supp. 704 (M.D. Ala. 1991).

[14] *Mergens,* 110 S. Ct. at 2371. *See also Grace Bible Fellowship, Inc. v. Maine School Admin. District #5,* 941 F.2d 45 (1st Cir. 1991); *Gregoire v. Centennial School District,* 907 F.2d 1366 (3rd Cir. 1990), *cert. denied,* 111 S. Ct. 253 (1993); *Concerned Woman for America v. Lafayette County,* 883 F.2d 32 (5th Cir. 1990).

[15] *Shumway v. Albany County School District #1,* 826 F. Supp. 1320 (D. Wyo. 1993); In *Pratt v. Arizona Board of Regents,* 520 P.2d 514 (Ariz. 1974), the Arizona Supreme Court ruled that the rental of the Sun Devils Stadium on a university campus to an evangelist for a religious service did not violate the First Amendment Establishment Clause.

agenda of a public graduation ceremony, cannot select a religious participant for the purpose of praying, and cannot give guidelines to a religious
participant as to how that participant should pray. However, prayer is still
permissible if a school selects a participant using secular criteria and the participant voluntarily prays. Prayer is also permissible if a student participant
who was selected to be a part of the graduation ceremony based upon some
outstanding achievement voluntarily prays. Prayer could also be conducted
by a student chaplain or speaker elected by the student body in the same
way class officers are elected. Additionally, prayer is permissible if the
school officials permit a parent and/or student committee to create the
agenda and to select the participants. In this instance, the school should
avoid any sponsorship of the ceremony and may even want to place in the
bulletin that the ceremony is being sponsored by the parents and students.
Finally, prayer at a public school graduation ceremony is permissible if
organized and conducted by nonschool officials, without school sponsorship, and on or off school premises.[16]

---

[16]After the *Lee v. Weisman* decision in the summer of 1992, some schools attempted to prohibit
student-initiated prayer at graduation ceremonies. In one case, a community college student was
elected by her class peers to say a prayer at their graduation service. However, the nursing director
prohibited the student from saying the prayer and instead insisted that she must say a secular poem.
The student refused to say a secular poem and, therefore, was not part of the graduation ceremony
although her name was printed in the bulletin. Liberty Counsel negotiated with the community
college, and the president of the college eventually realized that the student had been deprived of
her First Amendment right to speak. The president then wrote the following acknowledgment and
apology:

> Please accept this letter as my personal apology and that of the staff of . . . Community
> College for any embarrassment that you suffered as a result of the decision of the nursing
> staff of the college to not allow you to offer the invocation which you wrote at the request
> of your fellow students for the Pinning Ceremony. . . .
>   I hope that you will also accept my representation that they thought that they were doing
> what they were required to do under the law as they understood it at the time. They did not
> have the benefit of either the legal memoranda that your attorneys of the Liberty Counsel
> have since furnished to the college or the recent Supreme Court decision that essentially con-
> firmed the Liberty Counsel position.
>   It may be possible that unfortunate incidents work out for the best in the long run. I
> have always been a strong supporter of the provisions of the First Amendment, especially
> as it relates to the educational process. Because of this situation having come to my atten-
> tion, I have asked our college attorney to draft a policy for the college that should prevent
> any future occurrence of this nature.

In the spring of 1993, many schools allowed student-initiated graduation prayer. Approximately
four schools nationwide were sued by students objecting to student-initiated graduation prayer.
These cases include *Harris v. Joint School District No. 241*, 821 F. Supp. 638 (D. Idaho 1993),
Adler v. Duval County School Board, 851 F. Supp. 446 (M.D. Fla. 1994), and *ACLU v. Black
Horse Pike Regional Board of Education*, Case No. 93-CV2651(JEI) (D.N.J. 1993). In the *Adler*
case, the ACLU represented three Jewish students in an attempt to prohibit student-initiated prayer.
Liberty Counsel intervened on behalf of eleven other students, grades seven through eleven. These
students became co-defendants with the school board. This is one of the first cases of its kind in
the country where students have been allowed to intervene in a case to defend their right to free
speech. The federal court ruled that students have the constitutional right to pray. To censor their
speech because of religious content would violate their right to free speech.

5

Students' Rights in Research, Experimental Programs, and Testing

A former educator and United States Senator, Samuel I. Hayakawa, warned the United States Senate in 1978 that schools had become vehicles for a "heresy that rejects the idea of education as the acquisition of knowledge and skill," and stated that schools regarded their "fundamental task in education as therapy."[1] Congress responded by amending the General Education Provisions Act to include a section entitled *Protection of Pupil Rights Amendment*, commonly called the *Hatch Amendment*. This amendment is reproduced in Appendix E.

Notwithstanding the passage of the so-called Hatch Amendment, educators never implemented this federal law until 1984 when the Department of Education promulgated rules after extensive hearings. These hearings revealed that schools were using federal funds to implement experimental testing programs making personal inquiries into students' individual personal, sexual, family, and religious lives.

This federal law requires that all instructional material, including teacher's manuals, films, tapes, or other supplementary instructional material that are used in connection with any research or experimentation program or project be made available for inspection by the parents or guardians of the children involved in such program or project. The term "children" means any person under the age of 21 or not above the elementary or secondary education level as defined by state law. The term "research or experimentation program or project" refers to any program or project designed to explore or develop new or unproved teaching methods or techniques.

The amendment further states that without the prior consent of the student, or in the case of an unemancipated minor, without the prior written con-

---

[1]Phyllis Schlafly, ed., *Child Abuse in the Classroom* (Wheaton, Illinois: Crossway Books) 1985, 13.

sent of the parent, no student shall be required to submit to a psychiatric examination, testing, or treatment, or psychological examination, testing, or treatment in which the primary purpose is to reveal information concerning: (1) political affiliation; (2) mental and psychological problems potentially embarrassing to the student or his family; (3) sexual behavior and attitudes; (4) illegal, anti-social, self-incriminating and demeaning behavior; (5) critical appraisals of other individuals with whom respondents have close family relationships; (6) legally recognized privileged and analogous relationships, such as those of lawyers, physicians, and ministers; or (7) income (other than that required by law to determine eligibility for participation in a program or for receiving financial assistance under such program).

The term "psychiatric or psychological examination or test" or "psychiatric or psychological treatment" means any method of obtaining information, including a group activity, that is not directly related to academic instruction and that is designed to elicit information about attitudes, habits, traits, opinions, beliefs or feelings or any activity involving the planned, systematic use of methods or techniques that are not directly related to academic instruction and that is designed to affect behavioral, emotional, or attitudinal characteristics of an individual or group.

Reading the testimony taken by the Department of Education in 1984 is enlightening and concerning. One parent testifying in the state of Washington stated that the guidance counseling program asked the following questions of the students:

● Do you believe in a God who answers prayer?
● Do you believe that tithing—giving one-tenth of one's earnings to the church—is one's duty to God?
● Do you pray about your problems?
● Do you read the Bible or other religious writings regularly?
● Do you love your parents?
● Do you believe God created man in His own image?
● If you ask God for forgiveness, are your sins forgiven?[2]

A parent from Oregon stated that her son was required to participate in a Magic Circle where the students would hold hands and divulge personal information about their thoughts, feelings, values, and beliefs. The student was also given questionnaires asking whether he drank alcohol, used drugs, lied to his parents, or believed in God.[3] One question asked "Are you going to practice religion just like your parents?" Another question queried "What is your parents' income?" Surprisingly, one question discussed in third grade asked, "How many of you ever wanted to beat up your parents?"[4]

---

[2]*Id.* at 29-30.
[3]*Id.* at 55-56.
[4]*Id.* at 57.

In another school, one course entitled Risk Taking required students to arrange themselves in small groups and roll dice to determine which category of questions they would discuss. Some of the questions they were to discuss in the personal and social category required the students to consider swimming in the nude at a private beach with friends, not telling your parents the truth about where you are going and what you will be doing, and having sexual intercourse with your boyfriend or girlfriend. The grade level for these questions was seventh through ninth grade.[5]

Another parent testified during these hearings that a *Values Clarification Handbook* used by the teacher indicated that the purpose of the program was to have students "begin to realize that on most issues there are many shades of gray, and they are more likely to move away from either/or black-and-white thinking which often occurs when controversial issues are discussed in the classroom."[6]

The Department of Education was also presented with testimony from a Michigan parent regarding teachers of senior high students doing the following:

> First ask the students to relax, feel comfortable and close their eyes. Then ask them to fantasize and design a form of birth control that they would enjoy using. If possible, they should include in their design how the contraceptive would work to prevent pregnancy, but this is not necessary.[7]

In another case, students were to be divided up in three groups representing eight- and nine-year-olds, twelve- and thirteen-year-olds, and young adults. They were to discuss issues such as abortion, teenage pregnancies, contraceptives, and seeing a person of the opposite sex naked.[8] A vocabulary brainstorming program was to be conducted by dividing the class up into groups of five or six to list as many synonyms in three to five minutes using such words as "penis, vagina, intercourse, [or] breast."[9]

After being subjected to this kind of social behavior testing, one student testified as follows:

> I was severely depressed. I didn't know what I believed about myself. I didn't know who I was or anything. Even things I was positive about earlier, I just didn't know. I had to learn to know myself all over again. I had to learn what I believed all over again, using all the sources that the school taught me were outdated, such as my mom and dad, my pastor, and my Bible. I had to learn to make decisions again, the hardest part of all, and one that now, four years later, I am still having problems with.[10]

---

[5]*Id.* at 72-73.
[6]*Id.* at 95.
[7]*Id.* at 146.
[8]*Id.* at 147-48.
[9]*Id.* at 148.
[10]*Id.* at 124.

These kinds of psychological and behavior modification programs are not new to the public school system. The Hatch Amendment is meant to return some student and parental control over these types of intrusions into private lives. Students and parents should become familiar with the Hatch Amendment and utilize it when necessary.

School administrators often pretend that the Hatch Amendment does not exist. Students and parents should insist on schools abiding by the Hatch Amendment. In addition to this federal law, many states have laws requiring that public schools reveal all records, which includes teaching materials, to parents upon request. If schools refuse this request, oftentimes state laws provide for the award of attorney's fees if a parent has to retain an attorney to obtain such documents.

Similar to the Hatch Amendment's requirement of prior consent, parents or students may insist on parental consent or opt-out provisions when confronted with objectionable situations not covered by the Hatch Amendment. For example, a New York court ruled that New York City schools were prohibited from dispensing condoms to unemancipated minor students without the prior consent of their parents or guardians, or without an opt-out provision.[11] Despite the importance of education on HIV infection and AIDS, the court noted the following:

> The primary purpose of the Board of Education is not to serve as a health provider. Its reason for being is education. No judicial or legislative authority directs or permits teachers and other public school educators to dispense condoms to minor, unemancipated students without the knowledge or consent of their parents. Nor do we believe that they have any inherent authority to do so.[12]

The court concluded that by excluding parental involvement, the condom availability program "impermissibly trespasses" on parental rights.[13]

Consequently, the Hatch Amendment and parental rights may be utilized to restrict a school's intrusion into experimental or other parent-student relationships.

---

[11]*Alfonso v. Fernandez*, 606 N.Y.S.2d 259 (N.Y. App. Div. 1993).
[12]*Id.*
[13]*Id.*

6

Teachers' Rights on Public School Campuses

CLASSROOM AS THE BATTLEGROUND

Teachers in today's public schools often find themselves in difficult positions. Most teachers sincerely want the best for their students. They unfortunately find themselves in a very litigious environment. For the most part, disciplinary actions in schools have all but disappeared under the threat of lawsuits. Child abuse allegations against public school teachers have increased. Trying to protect their school, administrators often side with parents rather than teachers in student-teacher disputes. The classroom is becoming more violent and disruptive. One study found that over 130,000 students bring guns to school every day. In the areas of religion, many school administrators have become so cautious that they have erroneously erased all traces of religion. Many have run roughshod over teachers. Others have attempted to squelch all discussion of religion.

The public school has become a battleground for religion. John Dunphy, a secular humanist, wrote in *The Humanist* magazine:

I am convinced that the battleground for humankind's future must be waged and won in the public school classroom by teachers who correctly perceive their role as the proselytizers of a new faith: a religion of humanity that recognizes and respects the spark of what theologians call divinity in every human being. These teachers must embody the same selfless dedication as the most rabid fundamentalist preacher, for they will be ministers of another sort, utilizing a classroom instead of a pulpit to convey humanist values in whatever subjects they teach regardless of the educational level—preschool daycare or large state university. The classroom must and will become an arena of conflict between the old and the new—the rotting corpse of Christianity together with all its adjacent evils and misery and the new faith of humanism, resplendent in its promise of a world in which the never realized Christian idea of "love thy neighbor" will be finally achieved.[1]

John Dewey, the so-called father of modern education, hoped to replace sectarian religion with "a religious faith that shall not be confined to sect, class, or race."[2] Some have referred to the religion envisioned by John Dewey as a religion of secular humanism. Indeed, the Supreme Court has recognized secular humanism as a religion.[3] As a result of the secularization of public education, many teachers have the mistaken view that religion is forbidden on public campuses.

Notwithstanding the confusion over religion, teachers still have constitutionally protected rights and should seek to exercise these rights. Teachers play a critical role in educating our future generation. Indeed, schools were founded upon the basis of religion to instill religious principles. With the exception of the University of Pennsylvania, every collegiate institution prior to the Revolutionary War was established by some branch of the Christian church.

Aristotle understood the importance of teaching when he stated "all who have meditated on the art of governing mankind are convinced that the fate of empires depends on the education of youth." Martin Luther once stated that he was "afraid that schools will prove to be great gates of hell unless they diligently labor in explaining the Holy Scriptures, engraving them in the hearts of youth. I advise no one to place his child where the Scriptures do not reign paramount. Every institution in which men are not increasingly occupied with the word of God must become corrupt." However, Martin Luther was not operating under the present day interpretations of the United States Supreme Court. Yet, teachers do maintain a unique position inculcating values for the next generation. Under the present constitutional makeup, teachers still have great latitude in reviewing religious topics. The United States Supreme Court has observed the following:

> It can hardly be argued that either students or teachers shed their constitutional rights to freedom of speech or expression at the schoolhouse gate.[4]

TEACHER AS INDIVIDUAL AND STATE AGENT

Though the First Amendment of the Constitution initially applied only to restrict the authority of the federal government and did not apply to the states, the United States Supreme Court in 1940 began to apply the First

---

[1]*The Humanist,* January/February 1982, p. 26.
[2]*A Common Faith* (New Haven, Conn.: Yale University Press, 1934), pp. 86, 87.
[3]*Torcaso v. Watkins,* 367 U.S. 488 (1961).
[4]*Tinker v. Des Moines Independent School District,* 393 U.S. 503, 506 (1969).

Amendment to the states through the Fourteenth Amendment.[5] The First Amendment is now interpreted to protect the free exercise of religion of individuals and to prohibit the establishment of religion by a state entity.

Teachers stand in unique positions because they are both individuals and agents of the state. Consequently, the First Amendment serves to protect their freedom of speech and free exercise of religion, and to prohibit a teacher from establishing a religion. In other words, since teachers are employees of the state, they are, in a sense, an extension of the state. As such, the First Amendment Establishment Clause, prohibiting the government from establishing a religion, applies to place restrictions on teachers' activities in matters of religion. On the other hand, teachers do not lose their constitutional free speech and freedom of religion rights simply because they are employees of the state. The First Amendment allows teachers to freely speak and to freely exercise their religious beliefs. Students, on the other hand, are not actors of the state and do not have the restrictions of the Establishment Clause. Students have the affirmative protection of the Free Speech and Free Exercise Clauses. Therefore, students can do what teachers cannot do in certain circumstances.

The First Amendment has been interpreted to mean that a state may not affirmatively promote or proselytize a particular religious viewpoint, but neither can the state be hostile toward religion. Thus, while teachers may not encourage their students to have a saving faith in Jesus Christ, teachers may objectively overview the teachings of Jesus as long as the overview is consistent with the subject matter being taught.

ASSERTING YOUR RIGHTS

The teacher is protected by the Constitution as are other individuals and should assert those rights when deemed appropriate. A teacher can assert not only constitutional rights but also the status of tenure, which should at least guarantee notice and reason for a hearing in the event of a complaint.[6]

FREEDOM OF SPEECH

Teachers have the constitutional right to free speech on a public school campus.[7] Neither students nor teachers "shed their constitutional rights to freedom of speech or expression at the schoolhouse gate."[8] A teacher can discuss religious topics with other teachers in the school lounge or between

---

[5]*Cantwell v. Connecticut,* 310 U.S. 296 (1940) (Free Exercise Clause); *Everson v. Board of Education,* 330 U.S. 1 (1947) (Establishment Clause); *Illinois ex rel. McCollum v. Board of Education,* 333 U.S. 203 (1948) (same).
[6]On occasion the Apostle Paul utilized his status as a Roman citizen to his benefit. Acts 22:25. Indeed, Paul used his status as a Roman citizen to have his case heard in Rome before Caesar where he stated "I am standing before Caesar's tribunal, where I ought to be tried." Acts 25:10.
[7]*Tinker,* 393 U.S. at 506.
[8]*Id.*

classes. If a school allows its facilities to be used by teachers for meetings unrelated to the curriculum, it probably cannot prohibit teachers from meeting with other teachers during noninstructional time solely on the basis of religion.[9]

Clearly, during nonschool hours and while off school property, teachers are individual citizens and not actors of the state. As such, they enjoy the affirmative protection of the Free Speech and Free Exercise clauses. In this context, they are not actors of the state and therefore do not have the restrictions imposed by the First Amendment Establishment Clause.

While on school campus but before or after school hours, teachers may have certain restrictions imposed by the First Amendment Establishment Clause. In this context, some courts have looked at the age of students and their impressionability. The younger the student, the more careful the teacher must be in matters of religion. The courts have reasoned that younger students are not able to easily separate the acts of the teacher from the acts of the school. The courts have considered older students as having more capabilities of making a distinction between the teacher as an individual and the actions of the school. Unfortunately, no clear line has been decided as to when this age differential changes. No matter the age, however, teachers may not proselytize students in a captive setting. Thus, for example, if several teachers were to congregate before school in a classroom to pray, the teachers would not want to invite students and would not want to publicize the meeting to the students. To do so may give the impression that the school is affirmatively promoting religion. However, a teacher does not have to be so paranoid as to avoid a student's religious inquiry.

ACADEMIC FREEDOM

Academic freedom means "the principle that individual instructors are at liberty to teach what they deem to be appropriate in the exercise of their professional judgment."[10] According to the Supreme Court, academic freedom "is a special concern of the First Amendment."[11] However, academic freedom is not absolute. A teacher cannot use the classroom to indoctrinate the students in religious faith, but a teacher should be free to disseminate information in an objective manner so long as the information is reasonably related to the subject matter being taught in the curriculum.[12] Therefore, academic freedom or the right to free speech should permit an objective discussion of religion as it relates to the curriculum. In fact, no subject can be thoroughly taught without some discussion of religion.

---

[9]*Cf. Widmar v. Vincent*, 454 U.S. 263 (1981); *May v. Evansville-Vanderbaugh School Corporation*, 787 F.2d 1105 (7th Cir. 1986); *Police Department of Chicago v. Mosley*, 408 U.S. 92 (1972).
[10]*Edwards v. Aguillard*, 482 U.S. 578, 586 n.6 (1987).
[11]*Keyishian v. Board of Regents*, 385 U.S. 589, 603 (1967).
[12]Free speech or academic freedom is not unlimited. *Cf. Krizek v. Cicero-Stickney Township High School District*, 713 F. Supp. 1131 (N.D. Ill. 1989) (school did not renew the contract of a nontenured teacher who showed an R-rated film during class).

The teacher would probably be prohibited from talking about a biblical reason for sexual abstinence before marriage in a math class, but a teacher in a health class should be able to discuss sexual abstinence and various objective religious views on sexual abstinence. Biblical literature could be discussed in literature class, but probably not in a math class. If the content of speech is consistent with the course being studied, the teacher is probably free to objectively overview religious contributions and viewpoints dealing with the issue.

Certainly schools have "important, delicate and highly discretionary functions" to perform.[13] These functions, however, must be performed "within the limits of the Bill of Rights."[14] "The vigilant protection of constitutional freedoms is nowhere more vital than in a community of American schools."[15] Since the "classroom is peculiarly the market place of ideas,"[16] teachers should have the opportunity to lead robust discussions and to present information, including religious information, in an objective manner.

One teacher who is a personal friend of mine teaches space technology in a public high school and has been voted teacher of the year. He has used innovative approaches to the classroom, including having his class directly link to the space shuttle and verbally communicate with the astronauts on board. This class deals with anything relative to space technology, including the technology used in laser guided bombs during the Persian Gulf War, astronomy, satellite hookups, and other forms of technology.

During the Persian Gulf War, this teacher focused on the technology used by the military forces. During the discussion, he brought up the issue of war in the Middle East, which naturally led to the various confrontations among the warring religious sects. It is virtually impossible to address the Persian Gulf War without looking at the religious and cultural issues involved.

This teacher also focuses on astronomy, and as such, must address the Big Bang theory and the origin of the universe. Not long ago the Big Bang theory was discredited among scientists. This theory is replete throughout many science books, and even after the repudiation of the Big Bang theory, many science books continue to rely upon this outdated and unfounded principle. A good teacher brings up this information, critiques it, and then the natural question arises as to what other theories have been put forth regarding the origin of the universe. Within this context, the teacher is able to overview theories of abrupt appearance. As Wendell Bird has shown in his two volume work entitled *The Origin of the Species Revisited*,[17] abrupt

[13]*West Virginia State Board of Education v. Barnette*, 319 U.S. 624, 637 (1943).
[14]*Id.* at 637.
[15]*Shelton v. Tucker*, 364 U.S. 479, 487 (1967).
[16]*Keyishian*, 385 U.S. at 603 (1967).
[17]Wendell R. Bird, *The Origin of the Species Revisted*, 2 Vol. (New York: Philosophical Library) 1989.

appearance can be viewed as science. The theory of abrupt appearance is a classic example of an issue that can be objectively overviewed in class. [18] Abrupt appearance does not need to use the Bible as the textbook. However, when overviewing theories of the origin of the universe, the astute teacher can present evidence proffered for evolution and for abrupt appearance. In the final analysis, neither can be scientifically proven, and both must be accepted by faith. However, when discussing the scientific data, in order to adequately overview the entire subject, cultural and religious views may be discussed in an objective manner. Many religions have created theologies regarding creation in addition to the Judeo-Christian religion. Egyptian theology on this matter can be found in *The Memphite Theology of Creation*.[19] Likewise, the Akkadians, as well as those in the Far East, had creation epics.

Similarly, when studying geographical topography such as the Grand Canyon, the theory of deluge must be overviewed. The Sumerians, the Akkadians, and the Babylonians all had similar flood stories.[20] To ignore this rich religious and cultural history is to neglect the topic and to cheat the students of a broad education.

No topic can be adequately studied without objectively overviewing religious contributions. When studying sociology, demographic studies may be brought in showing the geographical distribution of the various religious faiths. Glenmary Research Center in Atlanta, Georgia,[21] publishes demographic maps of the United States showing the distribution of religious faiths within the states. This is certainly relevant to sociology and is a permissible form of teaching. Religious contributions and musical compositions may be studied in music class. Religious art may be studied in art class. History or political science cannot be studied properly without considering

---

[18]The United States Supreme Court struck down the State of Arkansas' anti-evolution statute which prohibited the teaching of evolution within public schools because the court found that the primary purpose of this statute was religious and had no objective secular basis. *Epperson v. Arkansas*, 393 U.S. 97 (1968). The Supreme Court ruled in *Edwards v. Aguillard*, 482 U.S. 578 (1987), that a state could not mandate the teaching of creationism by requiring that creation theories be taught whenever evolutionary theories are taught. The principle in this case was that the state statute had primarily a religious and not a secular aspect which indeed required the teaching of creationism. It is an entirely different matter when a teacher objectively overviews origins of the universe theories without religious advocacy. A federal appeals court has ruled that a principal may prohibit a teacher from teaching nonevolutionary theories of creation in the classroom without violating the teacher's First Amendment rights. *Webster v. New Lenox School District*, 917 F.2d 1004 (7th Cir. 1990). In the *Webster* case, the issue was not so much whether teaching on evolutionary creation violates the First Amendment Establishment Clause, but whether a principal had the right to control the curriculum within the school contrary to the individual desires of teachers within that school. The court noted the essence of the case was that "an individual teacher has no right to ignore the directives of duly appointed education authorities." *Id.* at 1008. The court further noted that the teacher had "not been prohibited from teaching any nonevolutionary theories or from teaching anything regarding the historical relationship between church and state" but that the teacher was merely prohibited from "religious advocacy." *Id.* at 1006.

[19]James B. Pritchard, ed., *The Ancient Near East*, Vol. 1. (New Jersey: Princeton University Press) 1958, p. 1.

[20]*Id.* at 28, 31; N. Bailkey, ed., *Readings In Ancient History From Gilgamesh To Diocletian* (Lexington, Massachusetts: Tulane University) 1976, p. 12.

[21]Glenmary Research Center, 750 Piedmont Avenue, NE, Atlanta, Georgia, 30308.

the Roman Catholic, Protestant, evangelical, or charismatic impacts. Literature cannot be fully studied without considering religious influences. For example, today's book format arose out of Christian evangelization. Prior to the formation of books, Old Testament scriptures were contained on bulky scrolls. The New Testament Christians cut these scrolls in pieces and sewed the edges together to form what is known as a codex, which is now known as a book. Printing presses were developed primarily to reproduce the Bible. In short, no subject matter can be taught adequately without considering and overviewing the impact of religion. Teachers have a constitutional right to do so and should not shirk their responsibility.

TEACHING ABOUT RELIGION

In *School District of Abington Township v. Schempp*,[22] the Supreme Court stated that study of the Bible or religion when presented objectively as part of a secular program of education is consistent with the First Amendment. The Bible could be studied as literature in a literature course. Some books on the Bible as literature include *The Bible as Literature*[23] and Leland Ryken's *The Literature of the Bible*.[24] Religious literature could be used in any course in which the message is relevant to the subject matter, but the teacher should be careful not to proselytize.

The Bible is an excellent source for literature. For example, the entire Book of Lamentations is written in acrostic form.[25] Hebrew literature also contains parallelisms,[26] and approximately one-third of the Old Testament

---

[22]374 U.S. 203 (1963).
[23](New York: Webster/McGraw-Hill).
[24](Grand Rapids, Mich.: The Zondervan Corp.).
[25]An acrostic is a mnemonic device utilizing the twenty-two letters of the Hebrew alphabet. Chapter one of Lamentations contains twenty-two verses, each verse successively begins with the corresponding letter of the alphabet. Verse one begins with the aleph, the first letter of the alphabet, and verse twenty-two ends with a tau, the last letter of the Hebrew alphabet. Chapter two continues this sequence and also contains twenty-two verses. Chapter three, the very middle chapter, has a slightly different version. This chapter contains sixty-six verses, the alphabet multiplied by three. These verses follow the alphabet in sequence but are grouped in three's. Verses one, two, and three begin with the first letter of the alphabet while verses four, five, and six begin with the second letter of the Hebrew alphabet and so on. Chapter four again contains twenty-two verses, each starting with the successive letter of the alphabet. Chapter five, though containing twenty-two verses, departs from the acrostic pattern. The most famous acrostic of all is Psalm 119. This psalm contains twenty-two sections, each section containing eight verses. The first eight verses begin with the first letter of the Hebrew alphabet while the second series of eight verses begin with the second letter of the Hebrew alphabet and so on.
[26]By and large there is no rhyme in terms of sound as we know it in English, but the rhyme or rhythm is based on thought parallelisms. For example, synonymous parallelism is found in Isaiah 1:3 where the same thought is expressed in successive stichs: "The ox knows its owner, and the ass its master's crib." The "ox" is equivalent to the "ass" and the "owner" is equivalent to the "master." Another example is found in Amos 5:24. Antithetic parallelism means that the second stich is in contrast to the first, as found in Psalm 1:6, "For the Lord knows the way of the righteous, but the way of the wicked will perish." In Matthew 7:18, Jesus stated "A sound tree cannot bear evil fruit, nor can a bad tree bear good fruit." The most famous one of all is in Matthew 10:19 where Jesus declared "He who finds his life will lose it, and he who loses his life for my sake will find it." Formal or synthetic parallelism contains neither repetition nor contrasted assertions but is where the first stich is carried further in thought through the second stich. Psalm 14:2 is an example, "The Lord looks

and parts of the New Testament are written in poetry.[27] Clearly the Bible as literature is a fascinating book. The *Chronicles of Narnia* is also a work that can be studied from a literary point of view. When studying religious works as literature, the teacher should be objective. Indeed, to ignore religious literature, including the Bible, ignores a vast amount of educational material that ultimately is the detriment of the student.

SYMBOLS, MUSIC, ART, DRAMA, AND LITERATURE

The same principles outlined in Chapter Seven regarding nativity scenes are applicable to symbols, music, art, drama, or literature, whether in public school or in association with other public entities.

Probably the best illustration of the permissibility for the use of symbols, music, art, drama, and literature within the public school system is the school board policy of Sioux Falls School District in Sioux Falls, South Dakota. The school policy begins by stating that tolerance and understanding should be promoted and that "students and staff members should be excused from participating in practices which are contrary to their religious beliefs" unless there are clear issues of overriding concern that would prevent excusal.[28]

The policy goes on to state the following:

1. The several holidays throughout the year which have a religious and a secular basis may be observed in the public schools.
2. The historical and contemporary values and the origin of religious hol-

---

down from heaven, upon the children of men." Climatic parallelism is found in Psalm 28:1 where the second stich echoes or repeats the first part of the stich and adds to it an element of thought such as the following: "Ascribe to the Lord, oh heavenly beings, ascribe to the Lord glory and strength." These examples are what is known as Internal Parallelism. Examples of External Parallelism are found between dystichs, such as that found in Isaiah 1:27-28:

> Zion shall be redeemed by Justice,
> And those in her who repent, by righteousness.
> But rebels and sinners shall be destroyed together,
> And those who forsake the Lord shall be consumed.

[27]Hebrew poetry had meter with the most frequent pattern being 3:3, that is a dystich with three stressed syllables in each stich. An example is found in Job 14:1-2. The shorter 2:2 meter is used to convey intense emotion and urgency as found in Isaiah 1:16-17. The 3:2 pattern is known as the Qinah or the Lament or dirge meter. This is the prevailing meter used in the book of Lamentations. An example is also found in Amos 5:2. Other but less frequently used patterns are 4:4, 2:2:2, and 3:3:3. In the original Hebrew, alliteration is found in Psalm 122:6-7, where the effect of the passage is gained by juxtaposition of words or syllables which begin with the same consonant. Assonance is found in Psalm 90:17, where the same vowel sound is often deliberately repeated. An interesting concept is found in Judges 5:2 known as onomatopoeia, where the writer uses words which actually sound like the described activity. This is the Song of Deborah describing the galloping of horses and the actual speaking of the Hebrew sounds like the galloping of horses' hooves. Paranomasia, or a play on words, is aptly found in Isaiah 5:7. There, Isaiah says that God looked for "justice" (mishpat), but instead he found only "bloodshed" (mispah); he looked for "righteousness" (sedhaqah) but instead found only a "cry" (seaqah).

[28]*Florey v. Sioux Falls School District 49-5,* 619 F.2d 1311, 1319 (8th Cir.), *cert. denied* 449 U.S. 987 (1980).

idays may be explained in an unbiased and objective manner without sectarian indoctrination.

3. Music, art, literature, and drama having religious themes or basis are permitted as part of the curriculum for school-sponsored activities and programs if presented in a prudent and objective manner and as a traditional part of the cultural and religious heritage of the particular holiday.

4. The use of religious symbols such as a cross, menorah, crescent, Star of David, crèche, symbols of Native American religions or other symbols that are part of a religious holiday [are] permitted as a teaching aid or resource provided such symbols are displayed as an example of the cultural and religious heritage of the holiday and are temporary in nature. Among these holidays are included Christmas, Easter, Passover, Hanukkah, St. Valentine's Day, St. Patrick's Day, Thanksgiving and Halloween.

5. The school district's calendar should be prepared so as to minimize conflicts with religious holidays of all faiths.[29]

The same school board policy also correctly addresses religious literature in the curriculum as follows:

Religious institutions and orientations are central to human experience, past and present. An education excluding such a significant aspect would be incomplete. It is essential that the teaching about and not of religion be conducted in a factual, objective and respectful manner.[30]

The policy then goes on to outline the following:

1. The District supports the inclusion of religious literature, music, drama, and the arts in the curriculum and in school activities provided it is intrinsic to the learning experience in the various fields of study and is presented objectively.

2. The emphasis on religious themes in the arts, literature and history should be only as extensive as necessary for a balanced and comprehensive study of these areas. Such studies should never foster any particular religious tenets or demean any religious beliefs.

3. Student-initiated expressions to questions or assignments which reflect their beliefs or non-beliefs about a religious theme shall be accommodated. For example, students are free to express religious belief or non-belief in compositions, art forms, music, speech and debate.[31]

The above cited school board policy of the Sioux Falls School District is presented here because it concisely and correctly outlines the parame-

---

[29]*Id.* at 1319-20.
[30]*Id.* at 1320.
[31]*Id.*

ters for the celebration of religious holidays, the display of symbols, the performance of music or drama, and the study of religious literature within the public school system and in association with public entities. The constitutionality of this school board policy was upheld by the Eighth Circuit Court of Appeals. As for the issue of music, the United States Supreme Court has acknowledged that "[m]usic without sacred music, architecture minus the Cathedral, or painting without the Scriptural themes would be eccentric and incomplete, even from a secular view."[32] As it pertains to religious literature within the public school system, the United States Supreme Court declared that the "study of the Bible or of religion, when presented objectively as a part of a secular program of education," is consistent with the First Amendment.[33] Indeed, the Supreme Court has reiterated that the Bible may constitutionally be used as an appropriate study of history, civilization, ethics, comparative religion, or the like.[34] In other words, a public school teacher may teach about religion in an objective manner, but should avoid promoting belief in a particular religion and should likewise avoid degrading or showing hostility toward any religion.

In summary, religious symbols, music, art, drama, and literature may clearly be taught and presented in the public school system and in association with other public entities so long as the presentation is done in a prudent and objective manner consistent with the topic or the holiday occasion. Contrary to some popular opinion, religious Christmas carols are still permitted in the public school, religious art, drama, and literature are still permitted as part of the curriculum, and religious symbols are still permissible. The key is to present the information, display, or performance objectively and in combination with other secular aspects surrounding the holiday or subject matter. To exclude religion from the public school system or from other public entities is to show nothing less than hostility toward religion, and clearly, the First Amendment demands accommodation and absolutely forbids hostility.

RELIGIOUS HOLIDAYS

The Supreme Court has upheld display of religious symbols on public property if the context of the religious symbols have other nonreligious symbols associated which would also emphasize the secular nature of the

---

[32]*McCollum*, 333 U.S. at 206 (Jackson, J., concurring).

[33]*Abington Township*, 374 U.S. at 225.

[34]*Stone v. Graham*, 449 U.S. 39, 42 (1980). The Supreme Court in *Stone* struck down the display of the Ten Commandments on a classroom bulletin board because, standing alone in the absence of a secular context, it was not integrated into the school curriculum, where the Bible may constitutionally be used as an appropriate study of history, civilization, ethics, comparative religion, or the like. Presumably, if the Ten Commandments were displayed on the bulletin board in association with other secular symbols of law-based society, the Supreme Court may well have ruled the display to be constitutional.

holiday.[35] The classic example is a nativity scene in the context of a Christmas tree, a menorah, and Santa Claus. All these symbols should be in close proximity to each other.

The Eighth Circuit Court of Appeals ruled in 1980 that a school Christmas program may include religious carols so long as they are presented "in a prudent and objective manner and as a traditional part of the cultural and religious heritage of the particular holiday."[36] The Supreme Court has long ago acknowledged that "[m]usic without sacred music, architecture minus the cathedral, or painting without the Scriptural themes would be eccentric and incomplete, even from a secular view."[37] Teachers should not shun celebrations of religious holidays. This includes permitting students to give reports, whether oral or written, on religious holiday topics. This also includes the display of a nativity scene within the classroom setting. A nativity scene is certainly permissible in a classroom setting if, within the same setting as the nativity scene, secular symbols of Christmas are also displayed. For example, a teacher could display a nativity scene so long as within that same context are displayed secular symbols such as a Christmas tree and Santa Claus. Jewish celebrations of Hanukkah may also be displayed. The background of Hanukkah can be found by reading the Apocryphal book of Maccabes, which describes the Jews taking back and cleansing the temple from the Syrians on Kislev 25, or the ninth month of the Jewish calendar.[38]

Unfortunately, teachers and administrators have mistakenly concluded that students are no longer permitted to sing religious Christmas carols during the Christmas season. However, Christmas carols, including Christian carols such as "Silent Night, Holy Night," are permissible within a public school setting so long as other secular songs of Christmas, such as "Rudolph the Red Nosed Reindeer" are sung as well.[39]

CLOTHING

According to *Tinker v. Des Moines Independent School District*, a teacher should be permitted to wear religious symbols. Like the students in *Tinker*, a federal appeals court permitted teachers to wear black arm bands as a symbolic protest to the Vietnam war.[40]

In contrast to a student's ability of free expression through articles of clothing, a teacher has a few limitations. If the content of the message is not religious, a teacher probably has greater latitude to wear clothing with inscribed words. However, the First Amendment Establishment Clause

---

[35]*Lynch v. Donnelly*, 465 U.S. 668 (1984); *County of Allegheny v. American Civil Liberties Union*, 492 U.S. 573 (1989).
[36]*Florey*, 619 F.2d at 1311 (8th Cir. 1980).
[37]*McCollum*, 333 U.S. at 206 (Jackson, J., concurring).
[38]1 Maccabes 4.
[39]For more information, see the model school board policy in Appendix B.
[40]*James v. Board of Education*, 461 F.2d 566 (2d Cir. 1972), *cert. denied*, 409 U.S. 1042 (1972), *reh'g denied*, 410 U.S. 947 (1973).

places certain restrictions on a teacher with respect to promoting religion. Nevertheless, a teacher should be able to wear religious articles of clothing or jewelry. Articles of clothing with religious writing moves a little bit more into a gray area. The more objective the writing without promoting a religious view, the more likely the teacher is able to wear that article of clothing. This is a somewhat untested area. If any questions arise on a specific case, competent counsel should be contacted for advice.

OUTSIDE SPEAKERS

Teachers should be able to bring in outside speakers to present views on a particular topic. The teacher can even utilize a debate format to present both sides of an issue. This avoids the problem of the school endorsing the speaker and allows for experts in various areas to present religious information to students. The teacher should avoid a regular pattern of inviting outside speakers to present only one viewpoint. Also, the school should not pay for or sponsor the outside speaker.[41]

STUDENT BIBLE CLUBS

According to the Equal Access Act, schools may require that student-initiated Bible Clubs have a teacher sponsor. Schools may only require a sponsor of religious clubs if the same requirements are made of secular clubs. According to the Equal Access Act, the provision of a school sponsor, whether an employee, agent, or otherwise, does not mean that the school is actually endorsing the club.[42] Moreover, the employee or agent of the school should be present at such religious meetings "only in a nonparticipatory capacity."[43] This "nonparticipatory" attendance means that the teacher should not actively lead or direct the group. The club must be student-initiated and student-led. The activity must primarily be the activity of the students, not of the school. Teachers or other school employees certainly may be in attendance but should not take active leadership roles in these clubs. Certainly the sponsors can give advice and counsel, but the clubs should remain student-initiated and student-led. However, teachers may invite the students to their homes, and in the off-campus setting, teachers may take active participation roles.

Some teachers have requested the opportunity to pray with students during the annual "See You at the Pole" event. Constitutionally this is probably risky. Like Bible Clubs, "See You at the Pole" should be primarily student-initiated and student-led. If teachers desired, they could meet separately in a room out of the view of the public to offer prayers for the school. However, under current Supreme Court interpretations, it would

---

[41] *Wilson v. Chancellor*, 418 F. Supp. 1358 (D. Or. 1976).
[42] 20 U.S.C. § 4072(2).
[43] 20 U.S.C. § 4071(c)(3).

probably not be advisable to meet with the students or to meet openly to pray on the campus during school hours in the presence of the student body.

SUMMARY

Teachers on public school campuses are protected by the First Amendment Free Speech and Free Exercise Clauses. Teachers are also limited by the First Amendment Establishment Clause. Teachers retain the constitutional right to bring information to the classroom that is related to the curriculum being taught. The more relevant the information to the curriculum, the stronger the constitutional protection. Teachers may objectively instruct about religion but should be careful not to proselytize. Almost every subject taught in public school has in some way been impacted by religion, and to ignore religion is to render a disservice to the curriculum being taught and to the students.

7

Religious Symbols on Public Property

The relationship between religion and the United States Constitution is often misunderstood. Some have assumed that the Constitution requires total separation of the state and religion. However, according to the United States Supreme Court, "[t]otal separation is not possible in the absolute sense. Some relationship between government and religious organizations is inevitable."[1]

Though some have argued that there must be a "wall of separation between church and state," the Supreme Court has stated that this so-called "wall" metaphor is not an "accurate description" of the relationship between church and state.[2] Accordingly, the Supreme Court has stated that it "has never been thought either possible or desirable to enforce a regime of total separation. . . ."[3] The Constitution does not "require complete separation of church and state; it affirmatively mandates accommodation, not merely tolerance, of all religions, and forbids hostility toward any."[4] Anything less than mandating affirmative accommodation of religion would require "callous indifference," which the Constitution never intended.[5]

Total separation of church and state would actually result in hostility toward religion and would bring this country into "war with our national tradition as embodied in the First Amendment's guarantee of the free exercise of religion."[6]

A correct interpretation of the First Amendment must be in accord "with what history reveals was the contemporaneous understanding of its

---

[1]*Lemon v. Kurtzman*, 403 U.S. 602, 614 (1971).
[2]*Lynch v. Donnelly*, 465 U.S. 668, 673 (1984).
[3]*Committee for Public Education & Religious Liberty v. Nyquist*, 413 U.S. 756, 760 (1973).
[4]*Lynch*, 465 U.S. at 673. See, e.g., *Zorach v. Clauson*, 343 U.S. 306, 314 (1952); *Illinois ex rel. McCullom v. Board of Education*, 333 U.S. 203, 211 (1948).
[5]*Zorach*, 343 U.S. at 314; *Lynch*, 465 U.S. at 673.
[6]*McCullom*, 333 U.S. at 211-212.

guarantees."[7] The Supreme Court recognizes "that religion has been closely identified with our history and our government."[8] The history of this country "is inseparable from the history of religion."[9] History clearly indicates that "[w]e are a religious people whose institutions presuppose a Supreme Being."[10]

Clearly, the First Amendment requires that the state affirmatively accommodate religion and prevents the state from showing hostility toward any religion. Examples of accommodation of religion throughout history include legislation providing paid chaplains for the House and Senate, adopted by the First Congress in 1789 when the First Amendment was framed;[11] national days of thanksgiving;[12] Executive Orders proclaiming Christmas and Thanksgiving as national holidays,[13] the national motto "In God We Trust;"[14] the term "one nation under God" as part of the Pledge of Allegiance;[15] art galleries supported by public revenues displaying religious paintings of the 15th and 16th centuries, including the National Gallery in Washington maintained by government support exhibiting masterpieces with religious messages such as the Last Supper and paintings depicting the Birth of Christ, the Crucifixion, and the Resurrection, along with many other explicit Christian themes,[16] and the inscription of Moses with the Ten Commandments etched in stone in the Supreme Court of the United States of America.[17] These are just a few of many examples. Clearly, "our history is pervaded by expressions of religious beliefs."[18] Consequently, government would do well to "respect the religious nature of our people."[19]

The Judeo-Christian history of this country is evident when considering religious symbols on public property. These symbols include crosses perched atop water towers, crosses within city seals, the Ten Commandments on public buildings, scripture verses etched in stone, nativity scenes, and many, many other symbols. One cannot walk through our nation's capitol without realizing the Judeo-Christian impact on this country. Indeed, in the United States Supreme Court, inscribed directly above the Chief Justice, is Moses with the Ten Commandments. The centrality of the Ten Commandments within the United States Supreme Court is meant to symbolize that all other laws throughout history are based upon and

---

[7]*Lynch*, 465 U.S. at 673.
[8]*School District of Abington Township v. Schempp*, 374 U.S. 203, 212 (1963).
[9]*Engel v. Vitale*, 370 U.S. 421, 434 (1962).
[10]*Zorach*, 343 U.S. at 313.
[11]*Lynch*, 465 U.S. at 674.
[12]*Id.* at 675.
[13]*Id.* at 676.
[14]36 U.S.C. § 186. The national motto was also mandated for currency. 31 U.S.C. § 5112(d)(1).
[15]*Lynch*, 465 U.S. at 676.
[16]*Id.* at 677. The National Gallery regularly exhibits more than 200 similar religious paintings. *Id.* at 677 n.4.
[17]*Id.* at 677.
[18]*Id.*
[19]*Zorach*, 343 U.S. at 314; *Lynch*, 465 U.S. at 678.

derived from the Ten Commandments. Each day the court is in session, the justices sit below the Ten Commandments purportedly to apply its principles.

Religious symbols within the public sector have come under attack. The battle over nativity scenes greatly contributed to pushing my career from ministry to law. Every year as I read about one nativity scene falling after another, I became frustrated, and as I entered the study of law, I began to realize that nativity scenes are still constitutional when formatted in the proper context.

NATIVITY SCENES

Some have the mistaken idea that nativity scenes on public property or maintained by public entities are unconstitutional. This is clearly not the law as stated by the United States Supreme Court. In the famous case of *Lynch v. Donnelly*,[20] the United States Supreme Court ruled that the city of Pawtucket, Rhode Island, could continue to display its nativity scene, which it had done for the previous forty years.

When considering the constitutionality of the nativity scene, the Court addressed the following three questions: (a) whether the display had a secular purpose, (b) whether the display had the primary effect of advancing religion, and (c) whether the display fostered excessive governmental entanglement.

Whether There is a Secular Purpose

In addressing this first question, the Court stated that the focus must be on the entire Christmas display, not simply on the nativity scene (crèche) as separated from the context of the Christmas display. Also, it is important to note that there must only be *a* secular purpose. There certainly may be a religious purpose in parts of the display, but when looking at the display in its entirety, if a secular aspect does exist, then there would be a secular purpose. Thus, a nativity scene by itself may only have a religious purpose, but when placed in the context of the Christmas holiday season, and in the context of other secular symbols of Christmas such as Santa Claus and a Christmas tree, the entire display may be said to have at least *a* secular purpose. In fact, the Supreme Court stated that the display was sponsored by the city "to celebrate the Holiday and to depict the origins of that Holiday. These are legitimate secular purposes."[21]

Whether the Primary Effect is to Advance Religion

In looking at this question, the issue is whether the *primary* effect is to advance religion by the entire context of the display. Though the nativity scene by itself

---

[20]465 U.S. 668 (1984).
[21]*Lynch*, 465 U.S. at 681.

may be said to advance religion, when viewed in the entire context of the surrounding secular symbols, it cannot be said that the *primary* purpose is to advance religion. In making this decision, the *Lynch* Court cited other examples of governmental aid to religion which did not have the primary effect of advancing religion, namely expenditures of large sums of public money for textbooks supplied throughout the country to students attending church-sponsored schools,[22] expenditure of public funds for transportation of students to church-sponsored schools,[23] federal grants for college buildings of church-sponsored institutions of higher education combining secular and religious education,[24] noncategorical grants to church-sponsored colleges and universities,[25] tax-exemptions for church properties,[26] Sunday Closing Laws,[27] release time programs for religious training during public school hours,[28] and legislative prayers.[29] Since the Supreme Court has in the past found all of these activities to be consistent with the Constitution, the mere display of a nativity scene within a Christmas display provides no greater aid to religion and clearly would not violate the Constitution. In fact, the Court noted that not every law which confers an indirect, remote, or incidental benefit upon religion is, for that reason alone, constitutionally invalid.[30]

The Supreme Court in *Lynch* specifically noted that the "display of the crèche is no more an advancement or endorsement of religion than the Congressional and Executive recognition of the origins of the Holiday as 'Christ's Mass,' or the exhibition of literally hundreds of religious paintings in governmentally-sponsored museums."[31]

Whether There is Excessive Governmental Entanglement

In displaying a nativity scene during the Christmas season, the *Lynch* Court found that there was no excessive governmental entanglement because there was no excessive administrative entanglement between the state and church authorities concerning the content or design of the exhibit, and any money that was expended toward the display of the nativity scene was minimal. In fact, the display required far less ongoing, day-to-day interaction between church and state than religious paintings in public galleries.[32]

As the above shows, the context of the nativity scene is all important. In one case, the United States Supreme Court ruled that a nativity scene was unconstitutional while a Jewish menorah was constitutional.[33] In the

---

[22]*Board of Education v. Allen*, 392 U.S. 236, 244, (1968).
[23]*Everson v. Board of Education*, 330 U.S. 1, 17 (1947).
[24]*Tilton v. Richardson*, 403 U.S. 672 (1971).
[25]*Roemer v. Maryland Board of Public Works*, 426 U.S. 736 (1976).
[26]*Walz v. Tax Commissioner*, 397 U.S. 664 (1970).
[27]*McGowan v. Maryland*, 366 U.S. 420 (1961).
[28]*Zorach*, 343 U.S. at 306.
[29]*Marsh v. Chambers*, 463 U.S. 783 (1983).
[30]*Lynch*, 465 U.S. at 683 (citing *Nyquist*, 413 U.S. at 771).
[31]*Lynch*, 465 U.S. at 683.
[32]*Id.* at 684.
[33]*County of Allegheny v. American Civil Liberties Union*, 492 U.S. 573 (1989).

County of Allegheny case, the Supreme Court considered two recurring holiday displays located on public property in downtown Pittsburgh. The first was a crèche depicting the Christian nativity scene which was placed on the Grand Staircase of the Allegheny County courthouse. This was the main and apparently the most beautiful and most public part of the courthouse. The crèche was donated by the Holy Name Society, a Roman Catholic group, and bore a sign to that effect. The second holiday display was an eighteen-foot Hanukkah menorah, or candelabrum, which was placed just outside the city-county building next to the city's forty-five foot decorated Christmas tree. The menorah was owned by Chabad, a Jewish group, but was stored and erected by the city each year.

Splitting hairs in this case, the Supreme Court ruled that the nativity scene violated the First Amendment Establishment Clause, but the menorah did not. The reasoning was that the nativity scene was at the prime entrance to the courthouse and was not surrounded by any secular symbols of Christmas. However, the menorah was not at the prime entrance and was in fact surrounded by secular symbols of Christmas such as the Christmas tree. Presumably, the nativity scene would have been constitutional had the menorah and the Christmas tree been at the same entrance or had the nativity scene been at the other location with a menorah and the Christmas tree. However, because the nativity scene did not have any corresponding secular symbols of Christmas in its presence, the Court ruled that this was unconstitutional and had the primary effect of endorsing religion.

The main teaching to be gleaned from the *County of Allegheny* case is that for a nativity scene to be constitutional it must be within close proximity to some other secular symbol of Christmas such as a Christmas tree or Santa Claus and the reindeer. Though this seems to be splitting hairs, and is clearly not the original intent of the First Amendment, under this analysis a nativity scene can still be displayed on any public property. Unfortunately, some city officials have become frustrated and jettisoned the whole idea of nativity scenes. Such drastic measures are not required by the Supreme Court's interpretation of the Constitution.

In a slightly different but related matter, a federal appeals court in Illinois ruled that privately displayed nativity pictures in a public park were constitutional. In 1956, the Ottawa Retail Merchants Association, a private organization, commissioned the painting of sixteen canvases depicting scenes from the life of Christ in an effort to "put Christ back in Christmas."[34] These paintings were displayed in Washington Park located in the center of the city of Ottawa, Illinois, during the Christmas season from 1957 to 1969. These paintings were again displayed from 1980 through 1988. Except for the years 1964 through 1967, when the city arranged for the erection of the paintings, the display had been exhibited by private parties. However, these paintings were not displayed during the

---

[34]*Doe v. Small*, 964 F.2d 611, 612 (7th Cir. 1992) (en banc).

1970s but were stored in an old grandstand structure and apparently forgotten. A newspaper article in 1980 discussed the paintings, upon which a local chapter of the Junior Chamber of Commerce (Jaycees), a national service-oriented organization, contacted the city and volunteered to take charge of the paintings.

When these private paintings were displayed in the city park, they occupied less than one-half of the west side of Washington Park. These paintings were accompanied by a sign that stated: "THIS DISPLAY HAS BEEN ERECTED AND MAINTAINED SOLELY BY THE OTTAWA JAYCEES, A PRIVATE ORGANIZATION, WITHOUT THE USE OF PUBLIC FUNDS."[35] In considering this situation, the court of appeals found that the park was a traditional public forum and as such obviously open to the public. This public park had been open to the public and space had always been allocated on a first-come, first-served basis. Since this was a public park, and the displays were owned and maintained privately with a disclaimer indicating private ownership, the federal court ruled that it was constitutionally permissible to display these paintings and to remove these paintings would actually be a violation of the First Amendment Free Speech Clause.

Similar to the Seventh Circuit Court of Appeals, the Sixth, Ninth and Eleventh Circuit Courts of Appeals have ruled that the private display of a Jewish menorah in a public park during Hanukkah is constitutionally permissible activity under the First Amendment Free Speech Clause.[36] The city of Grand Rapids had since 1964 granted Chabad House of Western Michigan a permit to display a twenty foot high steel menorah during the eight days of the Jewish holiday of Hanukkah. The menorah was purchased entirely with private funds and was owned by Chabad House, a private

---

[35]*Id.* at 612.
[36]*Kreisner v. City of San Diego*, 1 F.3d 775 (9th Cir. 1993) (the private sponsorship in a public park of a display of life-size statuaries depicting biblical scenes from the life of Christ having a disclaimer sign indicating that the display was privately sponsored is constitutional and is protected free expression); *Americans United for Separation of Church and State v. City of Grand Rapids*, 980 F.2d 1538 (6th Cir. 1992) (en banc). In another case, the City of Cincinnati enacted an ordinance which stated "The proposed use including presence of any display, exhibit, or structure, will not occur in Fountain Square between the hours of 10:00 p.m. and 6:00 a.m." However, this limitation on the use of the public square exempted "agencies, political subdivisions and instrumentalities of governments of the United States, the State of Ohio, the County of Hamilton, the City of Cincinnati, and the Board of Education of the City of Cincinnati." The Congregation Lubavitch wished to display its eighteen-foot high menorah during Hanukkah. It had displayed this menorah in the past. The assembly and disassembly of this structure took approximately six hours. The new city ordinance requiring that no use of Fountain Square could occur between 10:00 p.m. and 6:00 a.m. would have required the dismantling of this menorah everyday. Congregation Lubavitch sued the city of Cincinnati, claiming that the ordinance was not content-neutral because, as applied to them, it violated their First Amendment right to free speech. Unlike other outside organizations, Congregation Lubavitch would not be able to adequately use Fountain Square with this limitation. A federal court of appeals agreed stating that the ordinance was not content-neutral and therefore violated the Constitution. *Congregation Lubavitch v. City of Cincinnati*, 997 F.2d 1160 (6th Cir. 1993). *See also Chabad-Lubavitch of Georgia v. Miller*, 5 F.3d 1383 (11th Cir. 1993) (en banc) (ruling that a state could not deny permission to a private Jewish organization to display in a designated or limited public forum its fifteen foot tall menorah in the State Capitol Rotunda because not being accompanied by other secular symbols and without a disclaimer of private sponsorship the display would violate the First Amendment Establishment Clause).

organization. The city of Grand Rapids had no role in the planning, erecting, removal, maintenance, or storage of the menorah. All the display costs were privately funded, except for a small cost for providing electricity.

The display was located in Calder Plaza in the center of downtown Grand Rapids and was the principal public plaza in the area. The city required that the menorah be accompanied by two signs measuring two feet by three feet, which were illuminated at night. The signs read as follows:

HAPPY CHANUKAH TO ALL
This Menorah display has been erected by Chabad House,
a private organization. Its presence does not constitute
an endorsement by the City of Grand Rapids of
the organization or the display.[37]

The city of Grand Rapids had made the plaza available to the public for all forms of speech and assembly and clearly this was a traditional public forum. Since this was a traditional public forum, and since other members of the public had access to the public forum for expressive activities, the appeals court ruled that the Jewish organization had a right to display the menorah, and that to prohibit display of the menorah would be content-based censorship and violative of the First Amendment Free Speech Clause.

In summary, governmental entities may display nativity scenes so long as the governmental entity surrounds the nativity scene by other secular symbols of Christmas such as Santa Claus or a Christmas tree. Other alternative approaches that have been found constitutional include the private display of religious symbols or pictures in traditional public or designated public forums. In this setting, the government has no activity, and if the government were to prohibit the religious displays while permitting other secular displays, this would clearly violate the First Amendment Free Speech Clause. Added constitutional protection to private displays could include disclaimers showing private sponsorship.

OTHER SYMBOLS

There has been a great deal of litigation regarding the display of crosses on public property. Many crosses have been removed from water towers and from city seals.

In the city of St. Cloud, Florida, the city owned and maintained a water tower on top of which was a lighted cross. This cross was not surrounded by any other object and was plainly visible throughout the entire city. A federal court ruled that this display of a Latin cross on top of a city water tower was unconstitutional.[38] Similarly, a federal court ruled that a Latin cross in a county seal was unconstitutional.[39]

---

[37]*City of Grand Rapids*, 980 F.2d at 1540.
[38]*Mendelsohn v. City of St. Cloud*, 719 F. Supp. 1065 (M.D. Fla. 1989).
[39]*Friedman v. Board of County Commissioners of Beralillo County*, 781 F.2d 777 (10th Cir. 1985).

In the state of California, the city of La Mesa and the city of San Diego were sued for the display of crosses. The Mt. Helix cross was erected as a memorial to a private citizen and was originally on privately-owned land on one of the highest hills in San Diego County. It was visible from a substantial distance. In 1929, the owner of this private land conveyed the property to San Diego County and the conveyance obligated the county to maintain the cross. A cross was also placed atop Mt. Soledad by private citizens on a piece of land owned by the city of San Diego. This land was dedicated as a public park in 1916.

Relying upon the California Constitution rather than the federal Constitution, the federal court ruled that both of these crosses were unconstitutional under the state's constitution. The factors considered were the religious significance of the display, the size and visibility of the display, the inclusion of other religious symbols, and the historical background of the display, as well as the proximity of the display to government buildings or religious facilities. Interestingly, after the filing of the federal lawsuit, the city of San Diego voted to authorize the sale of a fifteen square foot portion of land underneath the Mt. Soledad cross to the Mt. Soledad Memorial Association. San Diego County similarly voted to give the San Diego Historical Society the Mt. Helix cross and a thirty foot diameter partial of land beneath the cross. The effect of these transfers to private citizens meant that the crosses would no longer be on publicly-owned land, and as such, there would be no constitutional violation because constitutional limitations do not apply to individuals but only to governmental entities.

Two Illinois towns, the cities of Zion and Rolling Hills, both displayed Latin crosses in their city seals. The Illinois federal court of appeals ruled that the display of these Latin crosses in the city seals violated the First Amendment Establishment Clause.[40] However, in response to this court's ruling, the city of Zion removed the Latin cross and replaced the cross with the national motto, "In God We Trust." The city seal, therefore, carried the words of the national motto. The Society of Separationists which sued the city to remove the Latin cross again sued the city to remove the national motto. However, this time the federal court ruled that the national motto, "In God We Trust," was constitutional.[41] Indeed, there are more than sixty federal cases that suggest that the national motto is constitutional.[42]

---

[40]*Harris v. City of Zion*, 927 F.2d 1401 (7th Cir. 1991).
[41]*Harris v. City of Zion*, No. 87-C-7204, slip op. (N.D. Ill. 1992).
[42]*County of Allegheny v. American Civil Liberties Union*, 492 U.S. 573 (1989); *Regan v. Time, Inc.*, 468 U.S. 641 (1984); *Lynch v. Donnelly*, 465 U.S. 668 (1984); *Marsh v. Chambers*, 463 U.S. 783 (1983); *Stone v. Graham*, 449 U.S. 39 (1980); *Wooley v. Maynard*, 430 U.S. 705 (1977); *School District of Abington Township v. Schempp*, 374 U.S. 203 (1963); *Engel v. Vitale*, 370 U.S. 421 (1962); *Sherman v. Community Consolidated School District*, 980 F.2d 437 (7th Cir. 1992), cert. denied, 113 S. Ct. 2439 (1993); *Americans United for Separation of Church and State v. City of Grand Rapids*, 980 F.2d 1538, (6th Cir. 1992)(en banc); *Murray v. City of Austin*, 947 F.2d 147 (5th Cir. 1991), cert. denied, 112 S. Ct. 3028 (1992); *North Carolina Civil Liberties Union Legal Foundation v. Constangy*, 947 F.2d 1145 (4th Cir. 1991), cert. denied, 112 S. Ct. 3027 (1992); *Society of Separationists, Inc. v. Herman*, 939 F.2d 1207 (5th Cir. 1991), on rehearing, 959 F.2d

The issue of whether Latin crosses will remain on public property has not yet been finally decided. A federal appeals court in Texas ruled that the display of a Latin cross within a city seal was constitutional. In Austin, Texas, the home of atheist Madalyn Murray O'Hair, her son Jon Murray brought suit against the city of Austin claiming that the Latin cross within the city seal was unconstitutional. However, the federal court ruled that the display of the Latin cross within the context of that particular city seal did not violate the First Amendment Establishment Clause.[43]

The United States Supreme Court has ruled that the Ten Commandments standing alone may not be placed on a classroom bulletin board,[44] but the Ten Commandments may still be displayed on public property so long as within the same context is displayed other depictions of secular law-

---

1283 (5th Cir) (en banc), *cert. denied,* 113 S. Ct. 191 (1992); *Jones v. Clear Creek Independent School District,* 930 F.2d 416 (5th Cir. 1991), *on rehearing,* 977 F.2d 963 (5th Cir. 1992), *cert. denied,* 113 S. Ct. 2950 (1993); *Harris v. City of Zion,* 927 F.2d 1401 (7th Cir. 1991); *Doe v. Village of Crestwood,* 917 F.2d 1476 (7th Cir. 1990); *Mather v. Village of Mundelein,* 864 F.2d 1291 (7th Cir. 1989); *Jager v. Douglas County School District,* 862 F.2d 824 (11th Cir. 1989) *cert. denied,* 490 U.S. 1090 (1989); *American Jewish Congress v. City of Chicago,* 827 F.2d 120 (7th Cir. 1987); *Stein v. Plainwell Community Schools,* 822 F.2d 1406 (6th Cir. 1987); *American Civil Liberties Union v. City of Birmingham,* 791 F.2d 1561 (6th Cir. 1986); *American Civil Liberties Union of Illinois v. City of St. Charles,* 794 F.2d 265 (7th Cir. 1986); *United States v. Covelli,* 738 F.2d 847 (7th Cir. 1984), *cert. denied,* 469 U.S. 867 (1984); *Chambers v. Marsh,* 675 F.2d 228 (8th Cir. 1982); *Hall v. Bradshaw,* 630 F.2d 1018 (4th Cir. 1980), *cert. denied,* 450 U.S. 965 (1981); *Florey v. Sioux Falls School District 49-5,* 619 F.2d 1311 (8th Cir. 1980), *cert. denied,* 449 U.S. 987 (1980); *O'Hair v. Murray,* 588 F.2d 1144 (5th Cir. 1979), *cert. denied, O'Hair v. Blumenthal,* 442 U.S. 930 (1979); *United States v. Nabrit,* 554 F.2d 247 (5th Cir. 1977); *Tollett v. United States,* 485 F.2d 1087 (8th Cir. 1973); *Aronow v. United States,* 432 F.2d 242 (9th Cir. 1970); *Stevens v. Summerfield,* 257 F.2d 205 (D.C. Cir. 1958); *Doe v. Louisiana Supreme Court,* 1992 WL 373566 (E.D. La. 1992); *Carpenter v. City and County of San Francisco,* 803 F. Supp. 337 (N.D. Cal. 1992); *Sherman v. Community Consolidated School District 21 of Wheeling Township,* 758 F. Supp. 1244 (N.D. Ill. 1991); *North Carolina Civil Liberties Union v. Constangy,* 751 F. Supp. 552 (W.D.N.C. 1990); *Memorandum Opinion and Standing Rule for Courtroom of William M. Acker, Jr.,* 1990 WL 126265 (N.D. Ala. 1990); *Allen v. Consolidated City of Jacksonville,* 719 F. Supp. 1532 (M.D. Fla. 1989), *aff'd,* 880 F.2d 420 (11th Cir. 1989); *Sherman v. Community Consolidated School District,* 714 F. Supp. 932 (N.D. Ill. 1989); *Horn & Hardart Co. v. Pillsbury Co.,* 703 F. Supp. 1062 (S.D.N.Y. 1989), *Judgement aff'd,* 888 F.2d 8 (2nd Cir. 1989); *Smith v. Lindstrom,* 699 F. Supp. 549 (W.D. Va. 1988); *Jewish War Veterans of United States v. United States,* 695 F. Supp. 3 (D.D.C. 1988); *Berlin by Berlin v. Okaloosa County School District,* 1988 WL 85937 (N.D. Fla. 1988); *Shomon v. Pott,* 1988 W: 4960 (N.D. Ill. 1988); *benMiriam v. Office of Personnel Management,* 647 F. Supp. 84 (M.D.N.C. 1986); *American Jewish Congress v. City of Chicago,* 1986 WL 20750 (N.D. Ill. 1986); *Libin v. Town of Greenwich,* 625 F. Supp. 393 (D. Conn. 1985); *Greater Houston Chapter of American Civil Liberties Union v. Eckels,* 589 F. Supp. 222 (S.D. Tex. 1984); *Time, Inc. v. Regan,* 539 F. Supp. 1371 (S.D.N.Y. 1982), *aff'd in part, rev'd in part,* 468 U.S. 641 (1984); *Citizens Concerned for Separation of Church and State v. City and County of Denver,* 526 F. Supp. 1310 (D. Colo. 1981), *cert. denied,* 452 U.S. 963 (1981); *Voswinkel v. City of Charlotte,* 495 F. Supp. 588 (W.D.N.C. 1980); *McRae v. Califano,* 491 F. Supp. 630 (E.D.N.Y. 1980), *rev'd, Harris v. McRae,* 448 U.S. 297 (1980); *Citizens Concerned for Separation of Church and State v. City and County of Denver,* 481 F. Supp. 522 (D. Colo. 1979); *Gavin v. Peoples Natural Gas Co.,* 464 F. Supp. 622 (W.D. Pa. 1979), *vacated,* 613 F.2d 482 (3rd Cir. 1980); *O'Hair v. Blumenthal,* 462 F. Supp. 19 (W.D. Tex. 1978); *United States v. Handler,* 383 F. Supp. 1267 (D. Md. 1974); *Reed v. Van Hoven,* 237 F. Supp. 48 (W.D. Mich. 1965); *Crown Kosher Super Market of Mass., Inc. v. Gallagher,* 176 F. Supp. 466 (D. Mass. 1959), *rev'd,* 366 U.S. 617 (1961); *Stevens v. Summerfield,* 151 F. Supp. 343 (D.D.C. 1957); *Petition of Plywacki,* 107 F. Supp. 593 (D. Hawaii 1952), *rev'd, Plywacki v. United States,* 205 F.2d 423 (9th Cir. 1953).

43*Murray v. City of Austin,* 947 F.2d 147 (5th Cir. 1991), *cert. denied,* 112 S. Ct. 3028 (1992).

44*Stone v. Graham,* 449 U.S. 39 (1980).

givers. Commenting on the religious and secular mix, one Supreme Court Justice stated the following:

> [A] carving of Moses holding the Ten Commandments, if that is the only adornment on a courtroom wall, conveys an equivocal message, perhaps of respect for Judaism, for religion in general, or for law. The addition of carvings depicting Confucious and Mohammed may honor religion, or particular religions, to an extent that the First Amendment does not tolerate any more than it does "the permanent erection of a large Latin cross on the roof of city hall." Placement of secular figures such as Caesar Augustus, William Blackstone, Napoleon Bonaparte, and John Marshall alongside these three religious figures, however, signals respect not for great proselytizers but for great lawgivers. It would be absurd to exclude such a fitting message from a courtroom, as it would to exclude religious paintings by Italian Renaissance masters from a public museum.[45]

Thus, like a nativity scene, the display of the Ten Commandments would be permissible under current law if placed in the context of other secular laws or lawgivers.

In summary, the courts are presently split on whether Latin crosses on public property are constitutional. As noted under the section dealing with nativity scenes and in this section dealing with crosses, there are other unique ways to display religious symbols within a public setting. One way might be for governmental officials to convey parts of public land to private entities. However, another way is to display privately-owned symbols within a public forum such as a park. Other methods can be used by placing secular symbols in the context of the religious symbols.

---

[45]*County of Allegheny*, 492 U.S. at 652 (Stevens, J., concurring in part and dissenting in part) (citations and footnote omitted).

8

Use of Public Facilities

The use of public facilities is an important aspect of religious liberty. Use of such facilities is significant as a means for public meeting places. Unfortunately, oftentimes those charged with scheduling use of these facilities have the mistaken idea that religious persons should be prohibited from conducting any meetings because to do so would violate the so-called separation of church and state. Sometimes this misunderstanding occurs from ignorance, and sometimes it occurs from blatant hostility or bigotry toward religion.

TRADITIONAL PUBLIC FORUMS

Parks, Streets, and Sidewalks

For free speech in general and religious speech in particular, public parks, streets, and sidewalks have been critical areas in the discussion of public debate. The United States Supreme Court has consistently ruled that public parks, streets, and sidewalks "have immemorially been held in trust for use of the public . . . and are properly considered traditional public fora [forums]."[1] The Court has also noted that the "purpose of the public forum doctrine is to give effect to the broad command of the First Amendment to protect speech from governmental interference."[2]

Unlike a limited or designated public forum, a traditional public forum such as a park, street, or sidewalk is always open to the public and cannot be permanently closed to public use.[3] A speaker can be prohibited from using a traditional public forum only if the government has a compelling

---

[1]*Frisby v. Schultz,* 487 U.S. 474, 481 (1988). *See also Perry Education Ass'n. v. Perry Local Educators' Ass'n.,* 460 U.S. 37 (1983).

[2]*ISKCON v. Lee,* 112 S. Ct. 2711, 2717 (1992).

[3]In an interesting case, a federal court of appeals ruled that the Naturist Society, which advocated "clothing optional" lifestyles and educated the public through writings, lectures, and public demonstrations could use a Florida park near a public beach to distribute literature, circulate petitions, and display a sign because the park was a public forum. *Naturist Society, Inc. v. Fillyaw,* 958 F.2d 1515 (11th Cir. 1992).

interest and has used the least restrictive means in order to achieve that compelling interest. Reasonable content neutral[4] restrictions may be placed upon the use of a public forum such as time, place, and manner restrictions. For example, so long as the restriction has nothing to do with the content of the message, the government may allow use of a street for a parade only at certain hours so as not to interfere with rush hour traffic. However, the government cannot flatly prohibit parades.

One case which was brought to Liberty Counsel's attention dealt with a public park in Texas. The park allowed use of its facilities by the general public. However, churches were required to sign a waiver that they would not offer prayer in the public park or perform baptisms there. This was clearly unconstitutional, and once brought to our attention at Liberty Counsel, it was quickly changed. Public parks can be used by religious groups for evangelization, drama, skits, speaking, congregating, or distributing religious literature. Streets may also be used by religious speakers for parades.

Public sidewalks are traditional public forums that may be used by religious speakers. While the use of sound magnification devices may be restricted to certain levels,[5] and blocking ingress or egress is not permissible, peaceful picketing on a public sidewalk is clearly protected First Amendment activity. Simply because the government disagrees with the content of the protesters' message does not allow the government to restrict speech in a traditional public forum. Indeed, the government "may not prohibit the expression of an idea simply because society finds the idea itself offensive or disagreeable."[6] The Supreme Court has also noted that its prior cases have "consistently stressed that we are often captives outside the sanctuary of the home and subject to objectionable speech."[7] Restricting speech within a public forum based upon the content of the speech is repugnant to the Constitution. Stressing its disdain for content-based restrictions on speech, the United States Supreme Court has stated:

> But, above all else, the First Amendment means that the government has no power to restrict expression because of its message, its ideas, its subject matter or its content. . . . The essence of this forbidden censorship is content control. Any restriction on expressive activity because of its content would completely undercut the "profound national commitment to

---

[4]Content-neutral regulations are those that are "justified without reference to the content of the regulated speech." *Virginia State Board of Pharmacy v. Virginia Citizens Consumer Council*, 425 U.S. 748, 771 (1976).

[5]*Saia v. New York*, 334 U.S. 558 (1948); *Kovacs v. Cooper*, 336 U.S. 77 (1949) (anti-noise ordinances must meet the strict tests of vagueness and overbreadth); *U.S. Labor Party v. Pomerlau*, 557 F.2d 410 (4th Cir. 1977).

[6]*Simon & Schuster v. New York Crime Victims Board*, 112 S. Ct. 501, 509 (1991). *See also Cohen v. California*, 403 U.S. 15 (1971) (overturning a criminal conviction based on a breach of the peace charge for wearing a t-shirt in a public forum with the words "F— the Draft").

[7]*Cohen*, 403 U.S. at 21.

the principles that debate on public issues should be uninhibited, robust and wide open."[8]

Sidewalks within residential neighborhoods are also considered traditional public forums. Picketing within a residential neighborhood is a constitutionally protected First Amendment right. The United States Supreme Court has ruled that a person can picket within a residential neighborhood so long as the picketing is not targeted toward a specific residence.[9] In other words, so long as the picketer moves about within the residential neighborhood on the public sidewalk and does not localize the picketing activities in front of one specific residence, the picketing is permissible speech activity. Picketers should, therefore, continually move on the public sidewalk within the residential neighborhood and not constantly stand in front of the same residential address.

LIMITED OR DESIGNATED PUBLIC FORUMS

Facilities such as public schools, libraries, public housing, or any other public facility other than parks, streets, or sidewalks, are considered limited or designated public forums. As mentioned earlier, parks, streets, and sidewalks are considered traditional public forums. As such, parks, streets, and sidewalks are always open to the public. On the other hand, limited or designated public forums such as schools, libraries, housing facilities, or other public facilities are to be governed according to the limited or designated public forum analysis. To be a limited or designated public forum, the public facility must intentionally open use of that facility to the general public. This is an important key to the use of these public facilities. Thus, if a public school allows use of its facilities after school hours as a meeting place for a Rotary club or a Tupperware party, then that public school is probably deemed to have opened its facilities for use by the general public. The same holds true for a library, which frequently opens its facilities to use by the public for meeting places. Public housing facilities frequently open use of the facilities either to the residents for meeting places, and as such it would be open to residents on a general basis, or to nonresidents for outside meetings, and in such cases it would be open on a general basis to outside organizations.

In order to determine whether a public facility is a limited or designated public forum, one must consider who and what type of organizations use the facility. Once it is clear that outside persons or groups use the facilities,

---

[8]*Police Department of Chicago v. Mosley*, 408 U.S. 92, 95-96 (1972) (quoting *New York Times Co. v. Sullivan*, 376 U.S. 254, 270 (1963)).

[9]*Frisby v. Schultz*, 487 U.S. 474 (1988). *See also Madsen v. Women's Health Center, Inc.*, 114 S. Ct. 2516 (1994); *Carey v. Brown*, 447 U.S. 455 (1980); *Vittitow v. City of Upper Arlington*, 830 F. Supp. 1077 (S.D. Ohio 1993) (picketing near the home of a physician who performs abortions is permissible so long as the protestors move about the neighborhood and do not solely target one residence).

then it is also clear that the public facility must not discriminate against outside organizations even if the organizations are religious in nature. Once open for use by the general public, the same analysis as is found in parks, streets, or sidewalks should be used. The government is not required to keep the facility open to the public and can therefore close the forum so long as it closes it to all outside use. While it is open to use for the public, a speaker can be excluded only when such exclusion is necessary to serve a compelling state interest and the exclusion is narrowly drawn to achieve that interest. Of course, use of these facilities can be restricted in terms of time, place, and manner so long as the restriction has nothing to do with the content of the message and ample alternative channels of communications are available. In other words, a public school could require that use of its facilities by outside organizations occur after 4:00 P.M., or use of its facilities only includes the cafeteria, the gym, or the public school classrooms. This type of restriction is permissible so long as that same restriction is applicable to all organizations and is not done based on the content of a particular organization's message.

Public Schools

The landmark decision governing use of public schools by outside organizations is the United States Supreme Court's opinion in *Lamb's Chapel v. Center Moriches Union Free School District*.[10] In *Lamb's Chapel*, New York law authorized local school boards to adopt reasonable regulations permitting the after-hours use of school property for ten specified purposes. Religious purposes were not one of the ten specified. In fact, the school district, while allowing use of its facilities to secular organizations, specifically prohibited use to any group for religious purposes. An evangelical church and its pastor requested to use the school facilities in order to show a six-part film series containing lectures by Dr. James Dobson. The content of this film included traditional Christian family values. Because the content was religious, the school district denied the request.

Since the school offered use of its facilities to outside secular organizations, the United States Supreme Court agreed that the school had become a limited or designated public forum. The school argued that it was offering use of its facilities to religious groups in a nondiscriminatory manner, namely that it did not allow any religious group to use its facilities. Indeed, the principle that had already previously emerged from Supreme Court opinions was that "the First Amendment forbids the government to regulate speech in ways that favor some viewpoints or ideas at the expense of others."[11]

The school also argued that to allow use of its facilities by religious organizations would violate the First Amendment Establishment Clause because it

---

[10]113 S. Ct. 2141 (1993).
[11]*City Council of Los Angeles v. Taxpayers for Vincent*, 466 U.S. 789, 804 (1984).

would give the appearance that the school was endorsing religion. However, the United States Supreme Court rejected this argument stating that because the school offered use of its facilities to other secular organizations, "there would have been no realistic danger that the community would think that the District was endorsing religion or any particular creed, and any benefit to religion or to the Church would have been no more than incidental."[12] In short, the school violated the First Amendment when it offered use of its facilities to secular organizations but denied use of the same facilities to a religious organization.

The principle is clear that if a school opens its facilities to the "community for meetings and discussions during nonschool hours, then it becomes a public forum for the community" which cannot exclude religious groups.[13] Clearly a high school cannot legally prohibit a religious group from using its auditorium when the auditorium is made available to nonreligious groups.[14] Moreover, if a school is a limited or designated public forum for outside use purposes, religious organizations such as churches may request use of the school facility to conduct, for example, a public school graduation ceremony.[15] On one occasion, a federal court ruled that the Arizona Board of Regents did not violate the First Amendment Establishment Clause when it rented the Sun Devil Stadium to an evangelist in order to conduct an evangelistic service.[16]

The Supreme Court of Delaware found that the University of Delaware's absolute ban on use of its common facilities by students for religious activities was unconstitutional.[17] The court stated that

the University cannot support its absolute ban of all religious worship on the theory that, without such a ban, University policy allowing all student groups, including religious groups, free access to dormitory common areas would necessarily violate the Establishment Clause. The Establishment cases decided by the United States Supreme Court indicate that neutrality is the safe harbor in which to avoid First Amendment violations: 'neutral accommodation' of religion is permitted, while 'promotion' and 'advancement' of religion are not. University policy without the worship ban could be neutral towards religion and could have the primary effect of advancing education by allowing students to meet together in the commons room of their dormitory to exchange ideas and share mutual interests. If any religious group or religion is accommodated or benefited thereby, such accommodation or benefit is purely incidental, and would not, in our judgment, violate the Establishment Clause.[18]

---

[12]*Lamb's Chapel v. Center Moriches Union Free School District*, 113 S. Ct. 2141, 2148 (1993).
[13]*Country Hills Christian Church v. Unified School District*, 560 F. Supp. 1207 (D. Kan. 1983).
[14]*Gregoire v. Centennial School District*, 674 F. Supp. 172 (E.D. Pa. 1987); *See also Gregoire v. Centennial School District*, 907 F.2d 1366 (3rd Cir. 1990) *cert. denied*, 498 U.S. 899 (1990).
[15]*Verbena United Methodist Church v. Chilton County Board of Education*, 765 F. Supp. 704 (M.D. Ala. 1991). *See also Shumway v. Albany County School District #1*, 826 F. Supp. 1320 (D. Wyo. 1993).
[16]*Pratt v. Arizona Board of Regents*, 110 Ariz. 466, 520 P.2d 514, (Ariz. 1974).
[17]*Keegan v. University of Delaware*, 349 A.2d 18 (Del. Supr. 1975), *cert. denied*, 424 U.S. 934 (1976).
[18]*Id.* at 16 (citations omitted).

Some schools have charged rental fees for use of their facilities by religious organizations. Additionally, some schools have allowed churches to use their facilities as places of worship only if the church has a building permit or is actively seeking another site with the intention of moving from the public school. In *Fairfax Covenant Church v. Fairfax County School Board,*[19] the school board allowed a church to use its facilities as a place of worship. In addition to allowing the church to use its facilities for Sunday worship, an array of other community groups were also allowed to rent the facilities during weeknights and weekends. However, the regulation governing use of the school facilities stated that "church/religious groups may be authorized usage after five years of use at increasing rental values until the full commercial rates become effective in the ninth year of use." Thus, for the first five rental years, churches were permitted to rent school facilities at the same rate as all other groups. However, after five years only churches were required to pay the increasingly higher rate. Moreover, the school policy required churches to provide "satisfactory evidence of progress towards the construction or acquisition of a church site."[20] No other rental group was required to make such a showing.

The school board argued that it must treat religious groups differently from secular groups, especially when religious groups use the facilities on a long term basis, because to do otherwise would violate the First Amendment Establishment Clause. The court reasoned that since the school facilities were open to other community groups, the school had created a limited or designated public forum. The court noted that "religious speech cannot be barred from a limited public forum simply because it is religious speech."[21] Indeed, a limited or designated public forum "does not confer any imprimatur of state approval on religious sects or practices."[22] The court stated that "by creating a forum generally open for use by various groups, the Fairfax County School Board does not thereby endorse or promote any of the particular ideas aired there."[23] The court further noted that "First Covenant Church cannot be treated differently from other groups that use the forum simply because of the content of its speech."[24] The court warned that to single out a religious organization as opposed to a secular organization would not only violate the Free Speech Clause but would also violate the Free Exercise Clause of the First Amendment.[25] Certainly "the government may not impose special disabilities on the basis of religious views or religious status."[26] Courts must "strictly scrutinize governmental classifications based on religion."[27] Finally, the court rejected the school's

---

[19]*Fairfax Covenant Church v. Fairfax County School Board,* 811 F. Supp. 1137 (E.D. Va. 1993).
[20]*Id.* at 1138.
[21]*Id.* at 1139.
[22]*Widmar v. Vincent,* 454 U.S. 263, 274 (1981).
[23]*Fairfax Covenant Church,* 811 F. Supp. at 1139.
[24]*Id.*
[25]*Id.* (relying on *Employment Division v. Smith,* 494 U.S. 872 (1990)).
[26]*Smith,* 494 U.S. at 877.
[27]*Id.* at 886, n.3.

argument that it must exclude the religious organization in order to not violate the First Amendment Establishment Clause. Since the school offered use of its facilities to other secular groups, offering such use to a religious group does not in any way violate the First Amendment Establishment Clause or raise any church/state problems. The court further rejected the idea that it was providing a monetary benefit to the school. The court noted that "the Supreme Court has also ruled that it does not violate the Establishment Clause for religious groups to partake of governmental financial benefits that are available for everyone."[28] The result of the *Fairfax Covenant Church* case was that the policy requiring increased rent and evidence of progress toward the construction or acquisition of a church site was ruled unconstitutional. Since the school had overcharged the church $235,000.00, the court ordered that the money be refunded.

Public Libraries

Public libraries are to be governed by the same analysis used for public schools. Both are public facilities, and whenever a public library opens its facilities for use by the general public, it has created a designated or limited public forum. When this occurs, religious organizations must be treated equal to the treatment provided to the other secular groups. Unfortunately, many libraries retain unconstitutional policies that specifically prohibit use of facilities by political or religious organizations. These policies violate the First Amendment.

The religious organization, Concerned Women for America, came face to face with one of these discriminatory policies in Mississippi. The library had created a limited or designated public forum. A library policy allowed outside persons to use its facilities for meetings of a "civic, cultural or educational character." However, the library policy specifically excluded use of its facilities by religious groups. The federal court rightfully found that this was a violation of the First Amendment.[29]

Public Housing Facilities

Almost every city or county contains some form of public housing facilities. Often these facilities have general meeting rooms. These general meeting

---

[28]*Fairfax Covenant Church*, 811 F. Supp. at 1141 (citing *Mueller v. Allen*, 463 U.S. 388 (1983)) (upholding the Minnesota tax deduction for student expenses at all schools including parochial schools); *Witters v. Washington Department of Services for the Blind*, 474 U.S. 481 (1986) (rejecting a claim by the State of Washington that it was required to ban a blind person from a state program funding the college educations of blind people because he wanted to go to a Bible college); *Bowen v. Kendrick*, 487 U.S. 589 (1988) (upholding a federal program to teach sexual chastity to teenagers that funded many secular as well as religious groups to promote that goal); *Walz v. Tax Commission*, 397 U.S. 664 (1970). Another case which could be cited, but which was not because it was not decided until after *Fairfax Covenant Church*, is the United States Supreme Court decision in *Zobrest v. Catalina Foothills School District*, 113 S. Ct. 2462 (1993) (providing government funds for the services of an interpreter to a student attending a religious school does not violate the Establishment Clause).

[29]*Concerned Women for America v. Lafayette County and*, 883 F.2d 32, 34 (5th Cir. 1989).

rooms are used by the residents, and frequently these meeting places are made available to the general public.

Sometimes religious tenants or outside religious groups have been discriminated against when attempting to use these type of public facilities. The analysis in a public housing facility is basically the same as for schools and libraries. The only difference is whether the person requesting the meeting is a tenant or a nontenant. For example, a public housing facility can allow use of its facilities by tenants only and thereby exclude all nontenants. That would be permissible under the First Amendment because it seems reasonable to accommodate the tenants over and above the nontenants. It would probably be unreasonable to allow use of the facilities by nontenants while excluding the tenants.

If use of the facilities is allowed for tenants, then there must be no discrimination based upon the content of the tenant's speech. Tenants who use such a facility for religious Bible studies or religious purposes should be allowed the same use of the facility as tenants who use it for secular purposes. Likewise, if use of the facilities is offered to nontenants, a nontenant speaker should be treated equally even if the content of the speech is religious.

A tenant living in a public housing facility in Atlanta wanted to use the facility to conduct a Bible study. Though the housing authority allowed use of its facilities by tenants for secular purposes, it tried to discriminate against this tenant. Part of the reasoning was that the use of the facilities by tenants should benefit all tenants rather than just a few. After several requests, a representative of the housing authority agreed to allow use of the facilities for a Bible study on Friday evenings. However, since many of the tenants were elderly, the Friday evening time was not convenient in that most were in their homes at that time. Over the objection of the tenant, the housing authority would not change its position. Consequently, the tenant conducted the Bible study anyway during the day at another time. The housing authority called the police and had the tenant arrested for conducting a Bible study. The federal court of appeals ruled that the housing authority violated the First Amendment by limiting the time for the Bible study to a Friday night when it did not equally apply this time limitation to other secular usages.[30] If the housing authority allows use of its facilities by tenants or nontenants for secular purposes, it must offer its facilities on an equal basis to tenants or nontenants who seek to conduct religious meetings.

Shopping Malls

The issue of shopping malls has proved to be difficult for the United States Supreme Court. If the shopping mall is owned by a governmental entity, then the first consideration is whether the government has opened up use of the shopping mall to outside persons for expressive activity. If so, those

---

[30]*Crowder v. Housing Authority of the City of Atlanta*, 990 F.2d 586 (11th Cir. 1993).

desiring access to the government-owned facility cannot be turned away simply because the content of their speech is religious.

However, most shopping malls are privately-owned. As such, there is no government action in the purest sense and, therefore, no application of the First Amendment. Notwithstanding, the issue has not been clear from its inception.

The United States Supreme Court developed a doctrine known as the "public function doctrine" which is distinguished from the public forum doctrine. One authority describes it as follows:

> It is now clear that constitutional limitations on state activities restrict the manner in which governmental functions are conducted. If private persons are engaged in the exercise of governmental functions their activities are subject to similar constitutional restrictions. The state cannot free itself from the limitations of the Constitution in the operations of its governmental functions merely by delegating certain functions to otherwise private individuals. If private actors assume the role of the state by engaging in these governmental functions then they subject themselves to the same limitations on their freedom of action as would be imposed upon the state itself.[31]

The fact that a private person engages in activity that could be performed by a governmental entity does not transform the activity into a public function. Only "those activities or functions which are traditionally associated with sovereign governments, and which are operated almost exclusively by governmental entities . . . will be deemed public functions."[32]

In 1946, the United States Supreme Court considered a case involving a "company town" which was a privately-owned area including residential and commercial districts. The Golf Shipbuilding Corporation owned and governed the area but had no direct connections with governmental authorities. Jehovah's Witnesses wished to distribute religious literature in the area but were prohibited from doing so. The Supreme Court stated that this was a violation of the First Amendment.[33] The Court reasoned that the state allowed private ownership of land and property to such a degree as to allow the private corporation to replace all the functions and activities which would normally belong to a city. Since the area served as an equivalent of a community shopping district in a city, the First Amendment applied.

The Court considered a similar issue in 1968. The Logan Valley Plaza was a privately-owned shopping center where striking laborers attempted to picket a store during a labor dispute. The Supreme Court ruled that the shopping center was the functional equivalent of a company town and

---

[31]Nowak, Rotunda, and Young, *Constitutional Law*, 3rd Ed. (St. Paul, Minn.: West Publishing Co.) 1986 p. 426.
[32]*Id.*
[33]*Marsh v. Alabama*, 326 U.S. 501 (1946).

therefore the picketers were protected by the First Amendment.[34] The Supreme Court in *Loyd Corporation* altered its opinion in 1972 when confronted with a group of anti-war demonstrators who desired to enter a private shopping mall to distribute literature. The Supreme Court attempted to distinguish this case from the two previous cases on the basis that in *Logan Valley Plaza* the labor picketing was directly related to the shopping mall, but here the anti-war literature distribution was not related to the shopping center's purpose, and consequently, the private mall could prohibit the literature distribution.[35]

Finally, in 1976, the Supreme Court ruled in *Hudgens* that the First Amendment does not apply to privately-owned shopping centers. Unfortunately, the Court could not agree on how they reached that decision. A majority agreed that the result in denying the application of the First Amendment to a private shopping mall was permissible in this particular case.[36] Justice Stevens did not take part in the decision. Two Justices wrote opinions concurring in the result but specifically mentioned that the prior Supreme Court decision in *Logan Valley Plaza* was not overruled while two other Justices dissented relying upon the prior decision in *Logan Valley Plaza*.

One other case is relevant to this inquiry. In 1990, the United States Supreme Court in *Pruneyard Shopping Center* considered a case involving a state statute which specifically granted access for free speech purposes to privately-owned property. The private property owners challenged the constitutionality of the statute. The court ruled that the statute was constitutional and then went further to indicate that the First Amendment protects this type of activity.[37] The Supreme Court noted that its 1976 ruling in *Hudgens* did not preclude a state from granting First Amendment free speech protection in privately-owned shopping centers.

As is clear from the analysis above, this issue is far from settled. Clearly, if a shopping center is a governmentally-owned institution, the First Amendment is applicable, and presumably literature could be distributed at such malls. Verbal discussion should clearly be permitted at such malls. If the shopping center is privately-owned, the United States Supreme Court's position is somewhat murky. If the shopping mall is performing a public function, presumably the First Amendment would apply. However, if the shopping mall is solely private in nature, the most recent Supreme Court opinion holds that the First Amendment would not be applicable. The Supreme Court also has ruled, however, that states may grant protection to free speech and association at privately-owned shopping malls. Several states currently grant free speech access to privately-owned facilities.

---

[34]*Amalgamated Food Employees Union v. Logan Valley Plaza*, 391 U.S. 308 (1968).
[35]*Loyd Corp. v. Tanner*, 407 U.S. 551 (1972).
[36]*Hudgens v. National Labor Relations Board*, 424 U.S. 507 (1976).
[37]*Pruneyard Shopping Center v. Robins*, 447 U.S. 74 (1980) (California's State Constitution prohibited the use of trespass laws by shopping center owners to exclude peaceful distribution of literature and petition in the mall area of the shopping center.)

Other Public Facilities

Other public facilities which do not fall into the category of parks, streets, or sidewalks, or which are not specifically mentioned above, can also be considered limited or designated public forums. Such facilities can be any public place that allows use by the community. This applies to buildings or nonbuildings. For example, a court ruled that a rotunda in a state capitol was a limited or designated public forum if expressive activities such as political, religious, or other varieties of symbolic speech had been permitted in the past.[38] A public fair may also be an ideal location for evangelization.[39]

NONPUBLIC FORUMS

Airports, Metros, Rails and Bus Stations

Airports, metros, rail stations, and bus stations are ideal places for First Amendment expressive activity. Millions of people traverse through these public transportation facilities every year, many of them from around the country, and many from around the world. Such places are ideal locations for distributing religious literature.

An airport does not fall into the category of a traditional public forum such as a public park, street, or sidewalk. Consequently, its facilities are not automatically deemed to be open to the public. Moreover, airports, like the other forms of public transportation facilities, generally do not intentionally open their facilities for expressive activity by outside organizations and therefore are not considered limited or designated public forums. The third type of a public forum is known as a nonpublic forum. In nonpublic forums, the government regulation "need only be reasonable, as long as the regulation is not an effort to suppress the speaker's activity due to disagreement with the speaker's view."[40]

A restriction on speech in a nonpublic forum is reasonable when it is consistent with the government's legitimate interest in preserving the property for the use to which it is lawfully dedicated.[41] With respect to the regulation of the distribution of literature at airport facilities or other transportation facilities, "the reasonableness inquiry is not whether the restrictions on speech are consistent with preserving the property for air travel, but whether they are reasonably related to maintaining the multipurpose that the authority has deliberately created."[42]

The Los Angeles International Airport formerly had a policy that pro-

---

[38]*Chabad-Lubavitch of Georgia v. Miller*, 5 F.3d 1383 (11th Cir. 1993) (en banc).

[39]*Heffron v. ISKCON*, 452 U.S. 640 (1981). This case involved a state fair which designated a specific location for the distribution or sales of literature for both secular and religious groups. The Krishna group wanted to be in a different location, but the court upheld the place regulation because it was applied evenly to secular and religious groups.

[40]*ISKCON v. Lee*, 112 S. Ct. 2711, 2705 (1992).

[41]*Id.* at 2712.

[42]*Id.* at 2713.

hibited all First Amendment activities within any of the airport facilities. When Jews for Jesus wanted to distribute religious literature, they were unable to do so because of this restriction. The United States Supreme Court ruled that this restriction on free speech was unreasonable and consequently violated the First Amendment.[43]

In a case involving the International Society for Krishna Consciousness, the United States Supreme Court ruled that the New York Airport Authority could prohibit solicitation of funds at the airport facilities, but could not prohibit the distribution of literature, because to do so would violate the First Amendment. The court noted that

> leafletting does not entail the same kinds of problems presented by face-to-face solicitation. Specifically, "[o]ne need not ponder the contents of a leaflet or pamphlet in order to mechanically take it out of someone's hand. . . . 'The distribution of literature does not require that the recipient stop in order to receive the message the speaker wishes to convey; instead the recipient is free to read the message at a later time.'" With the possible exception of avoiding litter, it is difficult to point to any problems intrinsic to the act of leafletting that would make it naturally incompatible with a large, multipurpose forum such as those at issue here.[44]

In ruling that airports cannot prohibit the distribution of religious literature, the Supreme Court looked at the nature and character of the airport. Airports are oftentimes, in a sense, like small cities. Many airports have restaurants, banking facilities, retail facilities, newspapers, and some even have hotel accommodations. These airports look, act, and sound like small cities. However, the Court did not classify modern airports as traditional public forums simply because they have not been around as long as traditional public parks, streets, or sidewalks. Yet the nature and character of these airports are very similar to traditional public forums. They provide a place for many people to meet, conduct business, and make transactions. They have sidewalks around the facilities and hallways for congregating. They have benches, restroom facilities, and for all practical purposes, operate like traditional public forums.

In one case which came to the attention of Liberty Counsel, the Orlando International Airport allowed literature distribution with certain strict and unreasonable requirements. The airport required that anyone seeking to distribute literature must fill out a lengthy application form and must wait at least three days prior to approval. The application form also required that the person distributing literature obtain $500,000.00 in liability insurance naming the City of Orlando and the Greater Orlando Aviation Authority as additional insureds, and wear a name badge identi-

---

[43]*Board of Airport Commissioners of Los Angeles v. Jews for Jesus*, 482 U.S. 569 (1987).
[44]*ISKCON v. Lee*, 112 S. Ct. at 2713-2714 (citing *United States v. Kokinda*, 497 U.S. 720, 734 (1990)).

fying their name, home address, height, age, weight, eye color, hair color, principal occupation, and organization affiliation, if applicable. During an international conference by the Gideon Bible Society, one particular Gideon was unable to obtain the $500,000.00 liability insurance policy. After correspondence between Liberty Counsel and the airport, the liability insurance policy was dropped from $500,000.00 to $100,000.00. However, other individuals seeking to distribute literature could not obtain this policy. Liberty Counsel then filed suit against the Orlando International Airport, and after the filing of the suit, the airport dropped these restrictive requirements. In one year, Orlando International Airport transports through its facilities approximately twenty-two million people. Many of these visitors to Orlando are from foreign countries visiting the entertainment facilities in central Florida. In order to understand the magnitude of twenty-two million, compare that to the total population of the state of Florida which is over thirteen million. In other words, almost two times the population of the state of Florida traverse through the Orlando International Airport every year. Religious literature given to these individuals literally goes around the entire world. The same can be true for other airports and other major locations for public transportation.

The same analysis applied to airports can be applied to metro or subway systems, railway systems, and bus stations. These facilities are very similar to airport facilities. In fact, one court ruled that literature distribution cannot be prohibited by the Massachusetts Bay Transportation Authority within the subway system.[45] The Authority prohibited the distribution of any printed materials for political or nonprofit purposes, prohibiting all noncommercial expressive activities from the paid areas of the subway stations and from the free areas of at least twelve stations. Within the free areas of the remaining stations, the Authority required prior authorization to engage in noncommercial speech. For many years, Jews for Jesus had distributed religious literature throughout the paid areas of the transit system. The new policy prohibited distribution in these particular areas, whereupon Jews for Jesus filed suit. The Authority argued that the ban on literature distribution was necessary for the public safety. The Authority argued that leafletting threatened public safety by disrupting passenger flow and creating litter. Litter, in turn, could cause accidents and fires or other disruptions, especially if paper clogged the switching devices on the tracks. The court remarked that the "Authority thus bears a heavy burden in justifying its absolute ban on leafletting, an activity that long has enjoyed the full protection of the First Amendment."[46] Noting that the Supreme Court had previously dismissed the danger to traffic congestion as a justification to ban leafletting, the court ruled that this flat ban in the subway area was unconstitutional.[47]

---

[45] *Jews for Jesus v. Massachusetts Bay Transportation Authority*, 984 F.2d 1319 (1st Cir. 1993).
[46] *Id.* at 1324, (citing *Lovell v. City of Griffin*, 303 U.S. 444, 450-52 (1938)).
[47] *Id.* at 1324-25.

In summary, nonpublic forums such as airports, metros, rail or subway systems, and bus stations are areas where First Amendment activity can occur. These are ideal areas for distributing religious literature because of the enormous amount of people passing through these transportation facilities.

9

Prayers at Public Assemblies

lthough prayer at public meetings predates our Constitution, and although it is replete throughout the historical documents of the early founders of this country, since the 1960s prayer at such meetings has taken on a somewhat checkered history. Prior to the early 1960s there was little controversy regarding prayer at public meetings. There had been no successful judicial challenge to prohibit prayer at any public meeting. However, in the past thirty years courts have come to differing conclusions regarding the constitutionality of prayer depending upon the circumstances surrounding the prayer. These circumstances include the particular event in question, the audience, and the participants. This chapter overviews prayers in public school classrooms, athletic events, graduation prayers, prayers in the courtroom, legislative prayers, and prayers offered before county or municipal board meetings.

PUBLIC SCHOOL CLASSROOMS

There are three types of public school classroom prayers. The first involves prayers composed by public school officials. The second deals with statutes authorizing a moment of voluntary prayer. The final type involves statutes, rules, or policies authorizing a moment of silence.

State-Composed or State-Led Prayers

The first case dealing with school prayer reached the United States Supreme Court in 1962. The case, known as *Engel v. Vitale*,[1] involved a prayer composed by the Board of Regents for the New York public schools. The prayer stated as follows: "Almighty God, we acknowledge our dependence upon thee, and we beg Thy blessings upon us, our parents, our teachers and our Country."[2] The parents of ten students brought suit against the public school and the Board of Regents arguing that the state-composed prayer

---

[1]370 U.S. 421 (1962).
[2]*Id.* at 422.

was a violation of the Constitution. The Supreme Court agreed by stating the following:

> [W]e think the constitutional prohibition against laws respecting an establishment of religion must at least mean that in this country it is no part of the business of government to compose official prayers for [students] to recite as part of a religious program carried on by government.[3]

From 1962 to the present, the United States Supreme Court has consistently ruled that state-composed and state-led prayers violate the First Amendment Establishment Clause.

In 1963 the United States Supreme Court considered a case involving state-required Bible readings and the recitation of the Lord's Prayer by a state official at the beginning of the school day. In *School District of Abington Township v. Schempp*,[4] the Supreme Court ruled that it was unconstitutional for state officials to read the Bible to public school students followed by the recitation of the Lord's Prayer at the beginning of each day.[5] School officials were charged with selecting various Bible verses and reading these verses at the beginning of each school day and then asking the students to recite the Lord's Prayer in unison. The Court ruled that both of these practices violated the First Amendment Establishment Clause.[6] However, the Court ruled that the Bible itself could be studied as literature and religion could be studied in a history of religions class.

Moment of Voluntary Prayer

The major case involving voluntary prayer decided by the Supreme Court is *Wallace v. Jaffree*.[7] In *Wallace*, the state of Alabama in 1978 passed a state law authorizing a one minute period of silence in all public schools "for meditation." In 1981, the state passed another law authorizing a period of silence "for meditation or voluntary prayer," and in 1982, the state amended the law to authorize teachers to lead "willing students" in a prescribed prayer to "almighty God . . . the Creator and Supreme Judge of the world."[8] Prior to reaching the United States Supreme Court, a federal court ruled that the statute allowing a time for meditation was constitutional.[9] This part of the decision was never appealed and, therefore, not before the Supreme Court for determination. The two parts of the statute which were before the Supreme Court involved the 1981 statute authorizing meditation or voluntary prayer and the 1982 statute authorizing teachers to lead willing students in a specific prayer.

---

[3]*Id.* at 425.
[4]374 U.S. 203 (1963).
[5]*Id.* at 211.
[6]*Id.* at 223.
[7]472 U.S. 38 (1985).
[8]*Id.* at 40.
[9]*Jaffree v. James*, 554 F. Supp. 727, 732 (S.D. Ala. 1982).

In reviewing this particular law, the Supreme Court considered the state legislative debates prior to the adoption of that law. Apparently Senator Donald Holmes was one of the main sponsors of the bill in question and stated on the legislative record that his intent behind the statute was an "effort to return voluntary prayer" to the public schools.[10] The Court, therefore, ruled that the Alabama state law was merely an attempt to get around its 1962 and 1963 opinions in *Engel* and *Abington Township* and struck down the laws in violation of the First Amendment Establishment Clause.

It is extremely important to note the exact parameters of the United States Supreme Court's opinion. The Supreme Court did not rule on the constitutionality of a moment of silence. The issue before the Supreme Court was a moment of "voluntary prayer" and another statute dealing with authorization of teachers to lead students in a specific state-composed prayer. Both of these statutes were struck down as unconstitutional.

Moment of Silence

Though the United States Supreme Court has never directly ruled on a moment of silence statute, its 1985 opinion in *Wallace v. Jaffree*[11] suggests that moment of silence statutes, rules, or policies will be held constitutional. Justice Stevens wrote the opinion in *Wallace v. Jaffree* striking down the state laws requiring a moment of voluntary prayer and a law authorizing teachers to lead students in a state-composed prayer. However, in a concurring opinon, Justice Powell stated that he fully agreed with Justice Sandra Day O'Connor's "assertion that some moment-of-silence statutes may be constitutional."[12]

In *Wallace v. Jaffree*, Justice O'Connor stated that the prior Supreme Court opinions of *Engel* and *Abington Township* were not dispositive of the constitutionality of moment of silence laws.[13] In this regard, she stated the following:

A state-sponsored moment of silence in the public schools is different from state-sponsored vocal prayer or Bible reading. First, a moment of silence is not inherently religious. Silence, unlike prayer or Bible reading, need not be associated with a religious exercise. Second, a pupil who participates in a moment of silence need not compromise his or her beliefs. During a moment of silence, a student who objects to prayer is left to his or her own thoughts, and is not compelled to listen to the prayers or thoughts of others. For these simple reasons, a moment of silence statute does not stand or fall under the Establishment Clause according to how the court regards vocal prayer or Bible reading.[14]

---

[10]*Wallace v. Jaffree*, 472 U.S. at 57.
[11]*Id.* at 38.
[12]*Id.* at 62.
[13]*Id.* at 71.
[14]*Id.* at 72.

Justice O'Connor cites Justice Brennan's concurring opinion in *Abington Township* as follows:

"[T]he observance of a moment of reverent silence at the opening of class" may serve "the solely secular purpose of the devotional activities without jeopardizing either the religious liberties of any members of the community or the proper degree of separation between the spheres of religion and government.[15]"

As noted above, the United States Supreme Court has never directly addressed a statute dealing with a moment of silence, but Justice O'Connor's opinion regarding the constitutionality of a moment of silence found support by a majority of the Court. In fact, Chief Justice William Rehnquist went so far as to suggest that the Supreme Court should recede from its 1962 and 1963 opinions which struck down state-led and state-composed prayers.[16]

In summary, presently state-composed and state-mandated prayers in public schools have been ruled unconstitutional. Moreover, moments of voluntary prayer have been ruled unconstitutional. However, a moment of silence statute or policy would be considered constitutional.

ATHLETIC EVENTS AND ASSEMBLIES

In 1989 a federal court of appeals ruled that prayer at a public high school football game was unconstitutional.[17] In this case a student was a member of the Douglas County High School marching band and objected to pregame invocations delivered at home football games. The invocations began with the words "Let us bow our heads" or "Let us pray," and the prayers frequently invoked reverence to Jesus Christ or closed with the words "In Jesus' name we pray."

From 1947 to 1986, an announcer would introduce the invocation speaker and usually identify the church affiliation. The student government originally invited the invocation speakers, but in 1950 local ministers began to give the invocations. In the early 1970s, an assistant football coach delegated the task of furnishing invocation speakers to a Presbyterian clergyman. From the early 1970s to 1986 the same clergyman recruited invocation speakers from the Douglas County Ministerial Association, whose membership consisted exclusively of Protestant Christian ministers. In 1986, in response to a complaint by a student, a so-called equal access plan was developed permitting the various school clubs and organizations to designate club members to give the invocation, including any student,

---

[15]*Id.* (quoting *Abington Township*, 374 U.S. at 281.)
[16]*Wallace v. Jaffree*, 472 U.S. at 91.
[17]*Jager v. Douglas County School District*, 862 F.2d 824 (11th Cir. 1989), *cert. denied*, 490 U.S. 1090 (1989).

parent, or school staff member. Under this plan, the student government was to randomly select the invocation speaker and no minister was to be involved in the selection process or in the delivering of the invocations. Notwithstanding this random selection process, the federal court of appeals still ruled that the prayers before high school football games violated the First Amendment Establishment Clause.[18]

Another federal court addressed the issue of prayer led by coaches of athletic teams and came to a similar conclusion as did the court regarding prayers before public high school football games. In *Doe v. Duncanville Independent School District*,[19] a girls' basketball coach regularly began and ended practice with a team recitation of the Lord's Prayer. At one of the first basketball games, the Lord's Prayer was recited in the center of the court at the end of the game, the girls on their hands and knees with the coach standing over them having their heads bowed. During away games, the coach would lead the team in prayer prior to leaving the school premises as well as before exiting the bus upon the team's return. A seventh grade basketball player objected to these prayers and filed suit. The court ruled that the recitation of the Lord's Prayer in this manner violated the First Amendment Establishment Clause because the coach, as an agent of the school, had actually "composed" a prayer.[20]

Another federal court ruled that the First Amendment did not permit the student counsel to open up assemblies with prayer.[21] In this case, the student counsel officers conducted various assemblies throughout the school year under the guidance and direction of the school principal. Students who did not wish to attend could report to a supervised study hall. With the permission of the principal, the student counsel was permitted to open their assemblies with prayer and Bible readings of their choosing. A time was set aside on the agenda, and the student counsel selected one member of the student body to say a prayer. Nevertheless, the court ruled that prayer in this context was unconstitutional.

When considering the above rulings, it is important to note the following. First, all of the above cases dealt with public secondary schools. The rulings may not apply to post-secondary schools in light of the age differences. When looking at the First Amendment Establishment Clause, courts have often looked at the age of the students involved. The older the student, the less risk the religious practice will be perceived as establishing a religion. Second, the case involving prayers before a public high school football game, and the prayer composed and led by a basketball coach, are similar in nature to the 1962 and 1963 Supreme Court rulings in *Engel* and *Abington Township*. The high school basketball coach composed the prayer

---

[18]*Id.* at 832-33.
[19]994 F.2d 160 (5th Cir. 1993).
[20]*Id.* at 164.
[21]*Collins v. Chandler Unified School District*, 644 F.2d 759 (9th Cir. 1981), *cert. denied*, 454 U.S. 863 (1981).

just like the State of New York did in the 1962 *Engel* case. Third, none of the above cases dealt with moments of voluntary silence. Moments of silence most probably would be found constitutional by the United States Supreme Court at these various events. Finally, if students were leading the prayer at these athletic events in conjunction with other student-initiated nonreligious speech, then to prohibit the students from the religious speech may well violate their First Amendment free speech rights. In other words, if students were allowed to speak at the athletic events or other assemblies, and if part of the content of the program were handed over to the guidance and direction of students, then presumably a student would be able to pray within this context. To prevent student speech because it is religious while allowing other student speech which is secular may well violate the student's First Amendment right to free speech and show hostility toward religion.

GRADUATION PRAYERS

We have already addressed prayers at public school graduations in Chapter Four. Briefly, prayers at public school graduations have been slightly restricted since 1992, but have not been completely prohibited. The Supreme Court in *Lee v. Weisman*[22] was concerned that school officials were actively involved in (1) placing prayer on the agenda, (2) inviting a religious clergyman to speak for the purpose of prayer, and (3) giving the clergyman specific guidelines for saying nonsectarian prayers. Prayer can still be conducted at public school graduations if school officials use secular criteria to invite the speaker, and once there, the speaker voluntarily prays. A valedictorian, salutatorian, or class officer can also voluntarily pray as part of the ceremony. The student body can elect a class chaplain or elect a class representative for the specific purpose of prayer. Part of the school program can be given over to the students and therefore be student-led and student-initiated. A parent and/or student committee can create and conduct part of the ceremony and, therefore, avoid state involvement. The ceremony can be conducted off the school premises by private individuals and therefore no state involvement would occur. Finally, private individuals can rent school facilities to conduct public school graduations on the public campus.[23]

COURTS

A North Carolina state court judge regularly opened his court saying: "Let us pause for a moment of prayer." The judge would then bow his head and recite aloud the following prayer:

---

[22]112 S. Ct. 2649 (1992).
[23]See *Jones v. Clear Creek Independent School District*, 977 F.2d 963 (5th Cir. 1992), *cert. denied*, 113 S. Ct. 2950 (1993). See also the discussion on public school graduation prayer in Chapter Four.

Oh Lord, our God, our Father in heaven, we pray this morning that You will place Your divine guiding hand on this courtroom and that with Your mighty outreached arm You will protect the innocent, give justice to those who have been harmed and mercy to us all. Let truth be heard and wisdom be reflected in the light of Your presence with us here today. Amen.[24]

The American Civil Liberties Union brought suit against this state court judge, and a federal court of appeals agreed that the judge violated the First Amendment Establishment Clause. The court reasoned that the prayer's primary purpose was religious, and it advanced and endorsed religion under the auspices of the state.[25]

Again, as noted in this chapter, a moment of silence would probably be ruled constitutional by the United States Supreme Court even within a courtroom setting.

LEGISLATIVE PRAYERS

The issue of legislative prayers came before the United States Supreme Court in 1983 in its landmark decision of *Marsh v. Chambers*.[26] This case dealt with a challenge to the Nebraska legislature opening up its sessions with a prayer offered by a paid chaplain who had been chosen by the Legislative Counsel. In finding the practice constitutional, the Court did not use its previous three-part test from the case of *Lemon v. Kurtzman*.[27] The so-called *Lemon* test requires that for a statute to be found constitutional and not a violation of the First Amendment Establishment Clause it (1) must have a secular purpose, (2) must not have a primary purpose of promoting religion, and (3) must not foster excessive governmental entanglement with religion. This test has caused great confusion among the federal courts.[28] Instead of

---

[24]*North Carolina Civil Liberties Union Legal Foundation v. Constangy*, 947 F.2d 1145 (4th Cir. 1991), *cert. denied*, 112 S. Ct. 3027 (1992).
[25]*Id.* at 1149-1152.
[26]463 U.S. 783 (1983).
[27]403 U.S. 602 (1971).
[28]Justices Scalia and Thomas have been very critical of the Supreme Court's use of the so-called *Lemon* test. The two joined in a stinging critique of the Court as follows:

> Like some ghoul in a late-night horror movie that repeatedly sits up in its grave and shuffles abroad, after being repeatedly killed and buried, *Lemon* stalks our Establishment Clause jurisprudence once again, frightening the little children and school attorneys. . . . Its most recently burial, only last Term [in *Lee v. Weisman*] was, to be sure, not fully six-feet under. . . . Over the years, however, no fewer than five of the currently sitting Justices have, in their own opinions, personally driven pencils through the creature's heart. . . .
>
> The secret of the *Lemon* test's survival, I think, is that it is so easy to kill. It is there to scare us (and our audience) when we wish it to do so, but we can command it to return to the tomb at will. . . . When we wish to strike down a practice it forbids, we invoke it. . . . Sometimes we take a middle ground of course, calling its three prongs "no more than helpful signposts." Such a docile and useful monster is worth keeping around, at least in a somnolent state; one never knows when one might need him.

Lamb's Chapel v. Center Moriches Union Free School District, 113 S. Ct. 2141, 2150 (1993). A number of Supreme Court Justices have criticized the *Lemon* test. *See Lee v. Weisman*, 112 S. Ct.

using this often criticized *Lemon* test, the Court looked at the original intent of the First Amendment by viewing history.

The Court began by stating the "opening of sessions of legislative and other deliberative public bodies with prayer is deeply imbedded in the history and tradition of this country."[29] Indeed, judicial proceedings are always begun by the announcement: "God save the United States and this Honorable Court."[30] In 1774, the Continental Congress adopted the tradition of opening its sessions with a prayer offered by a paid chaplain.[31] As one of its first items of business, the First Congress "adopted the policy of selecting a chaplain to open each session with prayer."[32] In 1789, the same year that the First Amendment was drafted, the Senate appointed a committee to consider the manner of electing chaplains and a similar committee was appointed in the House of Representatives. The first chaplain was elected in the Senate on April 25, 1789, and in the House on May 1, 1789.[33] On September 25, 1789, three days after Congress authorized the appointment of paid chaplains, a final agreement had been reached on the language of the Bill of Rights including the First Amendment. The Court gleaned from this early history that "the men who wrote the First Amendment Religion Clauses did not view paid legislative chaplains in opening prayers as a violation of that Amendment, for the practice of opening sessions with prayer has continued without interruption ever since that early session of Congress."[34]

In reviewing the history of legislative prayers, the Court went to the heart of the First Amendment's intent by stating the following:

> [H]istorical evidence sheds light not only on what the draftsmen intended the Establishment Clause to mean, but also on how they thought that Clause applied to the practice authorized by the First Congress—their actions reveal their intent.[35]

The Supreme Court concluded "that legislative prayer presents no more potential for establishment then the provision of school transportation, ben-

---

2649 (1992) (Scalia, J., joined by, *inter alios*, White, J., and Thomas, J., dissenting); *Allegheny County v. American Civil Liberties Union*, 492 U.S. 573, 655-57 (1989) (Kennedy, J., concurring in judgment in part and dissenting in part); *Corporation of the Presiding Bishop of the Church of Jesus Christ of Latter-Day Saints v. Amos*, 483 U.S. 327, 346-349 (1987) (O'Connor, J., concurring); *Wallace v. Jaffree*, 472 U.S. 38, 107-113 (1985) (Rehnquist, J., dissenting); *Id.* at 90-91 (White, J., dissenting); *School District of Grand Rapids v. Ball*, 473 U.S. 373, 400 (1985) (White, J., dissenting); *Widmar v. Vincent*, 454 U.S. 263, 282 (1981) (White, J., dissenting); *New York v. Cathedral Academy*, 434 U.S. 125, 134-135 (1977) (White, J., dissenting); *Roemer v. Maryland Board of Public Works*, 426 U.S. 736, 768 (1976) (White, J., concurring in judgment); *Committee for Public Education & Religious Liberty v. Nyquist*, 413 U.S. 756, 820 (1973) (White, J., dissenting).
[29] *Marsh*, 463 at 786.
[30] *Id.*
[31] *Id.* at 787.
[32] *Id.* at 787-88.
[33] *Id.*
[34] *Id.* at 788.
[35] *Id.* at 790.

eficial grounds for higher education, or tax exemptions for religious orga-nizations."[36] After reviewing the more than 200 years of unbroken history, the Court noted:

> [T]here can be no doubt that the practice of opening legislative sessions with prayer has become part of the fabric of our society. To invoke Divine guidance on a public body entrusted with making the laws is not, in these circumstances, an "establishment" of religion or a step toward establishment; it is simply a tolerable acknowledgment of beliefs widely held among the people of this country. As Justice Douglas observed, "[w]e are a religious people whose institutions presuppose a Supreme Being."[37]

BOARD MEETINGS

Prayers are frequently said at municipal and county board meetings includ-ing school board meetings or other meetings of public officials. In many respects, these prayers are very similar to prayers preceding legislative sessions.

A federal court of appeals ruled that a resolution of the County Board of St. Louis County in Minnesota providing for an invocation at its public meetings was not a violation of the First Amendment Establishment Clause.[38] Under this policy, a board of commissioners invited local clergy-men to offer prayers prior to the commencement of each board meeting. The chairman of the board would generally announce the following: "As is our practice, the Reverend John Doe will now give a prayer." The Court found that this practice was consistent with the First Amendment because the prayer had a "secular legislative purpose of setting a solemn tone for the transaction of governmental business" and assisted "toward the main-tenance of order and decorum."[39] The practice of opening these board meetings with prayers was not "an establishment of religion proscribed by the establishment clause of the First Amendment in any pragmatic, mean-ingful and realistic sense of that clause."[40] Similarly, the state Supreme

---

[36]*Id.* at 791, (citing *Everson v. Board of Education*, 330 U.S. 1 (1947)). *See also Tilton v. Richardson*, 403 U.S. 672 (1971); *Walz v. Tax Commission*, 397 U.S. 664 (1970).

[37]*Id.* at 792 (citing *Zorach v. Clauson*, 343 U.S. 306, 313 (1952)). A California appeals court ruled that a presidential proclamation for a national day of thanksgiving was constitutional. In an interesting turn of events, President Bush declared April 5-7, 1991, as National Days of Thanksgiving following the conclusion of the Persian Gulf War. In the state of California, the educational code required community colleges to close on every day appointed by the President as a public fast, thanksgiving, or holiday. Certain school employees requested the three days off as paid holidays, but the Governing Board refused, claiming that the presidential proclamation was unconstitutional. The California appeals court ruled that the presidential proclamation was consistent with the First Amendment. *California School Employees Ass'n. v. Marin Community College District*, 15 Cal. App. 4th 273 (Cal. Ct. App. 1993).

[38]*Bogen v. Doty*, 598 F.2d 1110 (8th Cir. 1979).

[39]*Id.* at 1114-115.

[40]*Id.* at 1115.

Court of New Hampshire ruled that inviting local ministers to open town meetings with an invocation was not prohibited by the First Amendment Establishment Clause.[41]

---

[41]*Lincoln v. Page,* 109 N.H. 30, 241 A.2d 799 (N.H. 1968).

10

The Right to Picket and Demonstrate

The ability of citizens to peacefully gather and demonstrate for a particular cause is an important aspect of maintaining liberty. The First Amendment prohibits the government from "abridging the freedom of speech" and from prohibiting "the right of the people peacefully to assemble." The Supreme Court has noted that

> [p]ublic places are of necessity the locus for discussion of public issues, as well as protest against arbitrary government action. At the heart of our jurisprudence lies the principle that in a free nation citizens must have the right to gather and speak with other persons in public places.[1]

Picketing is expressive activity protected by the First Amendment Free Speech Clause. The right to picket or demonstrate is, in part, dependent upon the location. Picketing in traditional public forums such as parks, streets, and sidewalks is clearly protected speech. Picketing may also occur outside of these areas in limited or designated public forums and may also occur in nonpublic forums.[2] When considering picketing, it is also important to determine whether the property site is privately or publicly owned. There may be certain noise level restrictions on picketing. Some courts have placed buffer zones around areas frequented by picketers to protect private business interests. Some pickets have turned violent, and courts have attempted to restrain this violence. The media is fond of showing pro-life demonstrators being dragged off to jail, and based upon this display, many people have a misconception that picketing may be prohibited activity. However, picketing and demonstrating pre-date the Constitution and are clearly protected by the First Amendment.

The act of picketing may include several factors, including carrying

---

[1] *ISKCON v. Lee*, 112 S. Ct. 2711, 2716-17 (1992).
[2] See Chapter Nine regarding definitions of public forums.

picket signs, wearing inscribed messages on clothing, speaking, distributing literature, or merely congregating. The Supreme Court has noted that direct one-on-one communication is probably "the most effective, fundamental, and perhaps economical avenue of political discourse."[3] The First Amendment protects the speakers' right "not only to advocate their cause but also to select what they believe to be the most effective means for doing so."[4]

The First Amendment limits the government's ability to restrict picketing because of the content of the speech. The Supreme Court stated:

> [T]he First Amendment means that the government has no power to restrict expression because of its message, its ideas, its subject matter, or its content. . . . Any restriction on expressive activity because of its content would completely undercut the "profound national commitment to the principle that debate on public issues should be uninhibited, robust, and wide-open."[5]

Indeed, "[r]egulations which permit the government to discriminate on the basis of the content of the message cannot be tolerated under the First Amendment."[6] Any "content-based restriction on political speech in a public forum . . . must be subjected to the most exacting scrutiny."[7] Restricting picketing or demonstrating based upon the content of the speech constitutes "censorship in a most odious form" which violates the First Amendment.[8] Rather than restricting speech, the government should continue to offer other avenues of speech. Speech should be combated with speech rather than censorship. Education is the proper and preferable alternative.[9]

A correlative of individual picketing and demonstration is the constitutional right to engage in such activity with others of similar beliefs. The "freedom to associate applies to the beliefs we share, and to those we consider reprehensible. It tends to produce the diversity of opinion that oils the machinery of democratic government and insures peaceful, orderly change."[10] Though freedom of association is not specifically set out in the First Amendment, "it has long been held to be implicit in the freedoms of speech, assembly, and petition."[11] The Supreme Court has declared that the

> freedom to speak, to worship, and to petition the Government for the redress of grievances could not be vigorously protected from interference

---

[3]*Meyer v. Grant*, 486 U.S. 414, 424 (1988).
[4]*Id.*
[5]*Police Department of Chicago v. Mosley*, 408 U.S. 92, 95-96 (1972) (quoting *New York Times Co. v. Sullivan*, 376 U.S. 254, 270 (1963)).
[6]*Simon & Schuster v. New York Crime Victims Board.*, 112 S. Ct. 501, 508 (1991).
[7]*Boos v. Barry*, 485 U.S. 312, 321 (1988).
[8]*Cox v. Louisiana*, 379 U.S. 536, 581 (1965).
[9]*Whitney v. California*, 274 U.S. 357 (1927).
[10]*Gilmore v. City of Montgomery*, 417 U.S. 556, 575 (1974).
[11]*Healy v. James*, 408 U.S. 169, 181 (1972).

by the State [if] a correlative freedom to engage in group effort toward those ends were not also guaranteed.[12]

Whether picketing is done individually or in a group, there would be "no conceivable government interest" that would justify a complete ban on this protected First Amendment activity.[13] Although some courts have attempted to restrict peaceful literature distribution, "a complete ban on handbilling would be substantially broader" than any necessary government interest.[14] Indeed, peaceful literature distribution cannot be prohibited under the concern that to allow such might block the flow of traffic on a public sidewalk, because one "need not ponder the contents of a leaflet or pamphlet in order to mechanically take it out of someone's hand."[15]

Some governmental entities have required picketers or demonstrators to notify public officials prior to the conducted activity. While this may be reasonable for a parade in terms of logistics and traffic control, it may not be reasonable for a peaceful demonstration on a public sidewalk. The requirement of giving advance notice to the government of one's intent to speak inherently inhibits free speech.[16] The Supreme Court has indicated that prior notification is "quite incompatible with the requirements of the First Amendment."[17] The "simple knowledge that one must inform the government of his desire to speak and must fill out appropriate forms and comply with applicable regulations discourages citizens from speaking freely."[18] The "delay inherent in advance notice requirements inhibits free speech by outlawing spontaneous expression."[19] It is clear that when "an event occurs, it is often necessary to have one's voice heard promptly, if it is to be considered at all."[20]

In addition to prior notice requirements, some governmental authorities have attempted to place financial burdens on free speech. Certainly the government may impose minimal financial burdens on the exercise of free speech such as permit fees, but these burdens are permitted only when the amount involved is reasonable and directly related to the accomplishment of legitimate governmental purposes.[21] A parade permit probably would be permissible, but a permit to picket on a sidewalk seems unreasonable. However, the government cannot make the requirements for the financial

---

[12]*Roberts v. United States Jaycees*, 468 U.S. 609, 622 (1984).

[13]*Board of Airport Commissioners of Los Angeles v. Jews for Jesus*, 482 U.S. 569, 575 (1987).

[14]*Ward v. Rock Against Racism*, 491 U.S. 781, 799 n.7. (1989).

[15]*ISKCON v. Lee*, 112 S. Ct. at 2713-14 (citing *United States v. Kokinda*, 497 U.S. 720, 734 (1990)).

[16]*NAACP v. City of Richmond*, 743 F.2d 1346 (9th Cir. 1984).

[17]*Thomas v. Collins*, 323 U.S. 516, 540 (1945).

[18]*NAACP v. City of Richmond*, 743 F.2d at 1455 (citing *Rosen v. Port of Portland*, 641 F.2d 1243 (9th Cir. 1981)).

[19]*NAACP v. City of Richmond*, 743 F.2d at 1355.

[20]*Shuttlesworth v. City of Birmingham*, 394 U.S. 147, 163 (1969).

[21]*Collin v. Smith*, 447 F. Supp. 676, 684 (N.D. Ill. 1978), *cert. denied*, 439 U.S. 916 (1978). *See also* *Cox v. New Hampshire*, 312 U.S. 569, 575-77 (1941); *Lubin v. Panish*, 415 U.S. 709 (1974); *Bullock v. Carter*, 405 U.S. 134 (1972); *United States Labor Party v. Codd*, 527 F.2d 118 (2d Cir. 1975).

cost of obtaining a parade permit so unreasonable as to restrict free speech activities. One federal court struck down an ordinance requiring groups to obtain a liability insurance policy in the amount of at least $300,000 and property damage insurance in the amount of at least $50,000. The court ruled that these requirements were unconstitutional since the activity involved free speech.[22] If a parade permit is necessary to picket or demonstrate on a public street, the cost should be minimal and the standards for requiring the permit must be objective and applied equally.[23] In the context of literature distribution, Liberty Counsel filed suit against the Orlando International Airport's requirement of obtaining $100,000 of liability insurance prior to the distribution of literature. After filing suit, the airport eliminated the financial requirement.

While some government entities have attempted to limit picketing and demonstrating activities by restricting the distribution of literature or by requiring the picketer to be publicly identified, courts have routinely struck down these restrictions. A regulation banning literature distribution while picketing would actually suppress "a great quantity of speech that does not cause the evils that it seeks to eliminate, whether they be fraud, crime, litter, traffic congestion or noise."[24] Neither the picketer nor the organization represented need be identified in the material used during the picket. The Supreme Court has consistently stated that "anonymous pamphlets, leaflets, brochures and even books have played an important role in the progress of mankind."[25] Moreover, the government may not compel members of groups involved in picketing to be publicly identified.[26] Any identification requirement "would tend to restrict freedom to distribute information and thereby freedom of expression."[27] Public identification is repugnant to the Constitution. The Supreme Court declared the following:

> Persecuted groups and sects from time to time throughout history have been able to criticize oppressive practices and laws either anonymously or not at all. The obnoxious press licensing law of England, which was also enforced on the Colonies was due in part to the knowledge that exposure of the names of printers, writers and distributors would lessen the circulation of literature critical of the government. The old seditious libel cases in England show the lengths to which government had to go to find out who was responsible for books that were obnoxious to the rulers. . . . Before the Revolutionary War colonial patriots frequently had to conceal their authorship or distribution of literature that easily could

---

[22]*Collin*, 447 F. Supp. at 676.
[23]*Forsyth County v. Nationalist Movement*, 112 S. Ct. 2395 (1992).
[24]*Ward*, 491 U.S. at 799 n.7. (citation omitted).
[25]*Talley v. California*, 362 U.S. 60, 64 (1960).
[26]*Bates v. City of Little Rock*, 361 U.S. 412 (1960); *NAACP v. Alabama* ex. re. Patterson, 357 U.S. 449 (1957).
[27]*Talley*, 362 U.S. at 64.

have brought down on them prosecutions. . . . Even the Federalist Papers, written in favor of adoption of our Constitution, were published under fictitious names. It is plain that anonymity has sometimes been assumed for the most constructive purposes. . . . [I]dentification and [its concomitant] fear of reprisal might deter perfectly peaceful discussions of public matters of importance.[28]

In the past, some states have attempted to obtain membership lists of organizations that are actively engaged in picketing or protest activities. This has often been done in an effort to restrict free speech, but it is clearly unconstitutional. Requiring organizations to identify their members engaged in First Amendment activities may cause fear in those members and thus prevent them from continuing association with the organization. Consequently, anonymity of those engaged in First Amendment speech and those associated with groups participating in such activities is constitutionally protected.[29]

The government cannot prohibit speech or expressive conduct "because of disapproval of the ideas expressed."[30] Courts cannot restrict picketing or demonstrating "simply because society finds the idea itself offensive or disagreeable."[31] Indeed, "the mere presumed presence of unwitting listeners or viewers does not serve automatically to justify curtailing all speech capable of giving offense."[32] The Supreme Court has noted that "[w]e are often captives outside the sanctuary of the home and subject to objectionable speech."[33] Merely because the speech is unwelcome "does not deprive it of protection."[34]

Picketing and demonstrating often create confrontation of the opposing views. However, even hostile audience reactions cannot justify the suppression of speech.[35] One federal court struck down a ban on "persisting in talking to or communicating in any manner with" a person or persons "against his, her or their will" in order to persuade that person to quit or refrain from seeking certain employment.[36] The First Amendment was

---

[28]*Id.* at 64-65.

[29]In *Bates*, the Court noted the chilling effect that would result from identification and disclosure requirements. "For example, a witness testified: 'Well, the people are afraid to join, afraid to join because the people—they don't want their names exposed and they are afraid their names will be exposed. . . . They will be intimidated and they are afraid to join.'" *Bates*, 361 U.S. at 416 n.6. The Court also highlighted the following testimony: "Well, I have—we were not able to rest at night or day for quite awhile. We had to have our phone number changed because they called at day and night. . . . I would tell them who is talking and they have throwed [sic] stones at my home. They wrote me—I got a—I received a letter threatening my life and they threatened my life over the telephone." *Id.* at 416 n.7.

[30]*R.A.V. v. City of St. Paul*, 112 S. Ct. 2538, 2542 (1992).

[31]*Simon & Schuster*, 112 S. Ct. at 509. *See also Cohen v. California*, 403 U.S. 15 (1971).

[32]*Cohen*, 403 U.S. at 21.

[33]*Id.*

[34]*United Food and Commercial Workers International Union v. I.B.P., Inc.*, 857 F.2d 422, 432 (8th Cir. 1988) (and cases cited).

[35]*Forsyth County*, 112 S. Ct. at 2404 (and cases cited).

[36]*United Food*, 857 F.2d at 425 n.4, 435.

meant to permit disputatious speech, speech that "may start an argument or cause a disturbance."[37] The Supreme Court has noted that

> free speech is not a right that is given only to be so circumscribed that it exists in principle but not in fact. Freedom of expression would not truly exist if the right could be exercised only in an area that a benevolent government has provided as a safe haven for crackpots.[38]

The First Amendment which requires that government may not abridge the right to free speech "means what it says."[39]

Like it or not, the First Amendment is strong medicine to those who attempt to suppress speech because the content is offensive. The Supreme Court declared:

> [T]he fact that society may find speech offensive is not a sufficient reason for suppressing it. Indeed, if it is the speaker's opinion that gives offense, that consequence is a reason for according it constitutional protection.[40]

PRIVATE VS. PUBLIC PROPERTY

The site of the picketing or demonstrating activity is important to determining its constitutionality. As stated in a previous chapter, the First Amendment protects individuals against state action on seeking to restrict First Amendment rights. The First Amendment consequently restrains only government action, not private action. Therefore, a private individual has no First Amendment right to picket on private property since the First Amendment does not restrain the private property owner. However, since the First Amendment restrains government activity, a citizen does have the right to picket within a traditional public forum or possibly within a designated, limited, or nonpublic forum.

Traditional public forums include parks, streets, and sidewalks. Access to traditional public forums or other similar public places "for the purpose of exercising First Amendment rights cannot constitutionally be denied broadly."[41] Public parks, streets, and sidewalks "have immemorially been held in trust for the use of the public."[42] "In [these] quintessential public forums, the government may not prohibit all communicative activity."[43]

Some protesters at abortion clinics have been arrested for trespassing on

---

[37]*Tinker v. Des Moines Independent School District*, 393 U.S. 503, 508 (1969).
[38]*Id.* at 513.
[39]*Id.*
[40]*FCC v. Pacifica Foundation*, 438 U.S. 726, 745 (1978), *quoted in Hustler Magazine, Inc. v. Falwell*, 485 U.S. 46, 55 (1988).
[41]*Grayned v. City of Rockford*, 408 U.S. 104, 117 (1972).
[42]*Frisby v. Schultz*, 487 U.S. 474, 481 (1988), (quoting *Hague v. CIO*, 307 U.S. 496, 515 (1939)). *See also Perry Education Ass'n. v. Perry Local Educators' Ass'n*, 460 U.S. 37 (1983).
[43]*Frisby*, 487 U.S. at 481 (quoting *Perry Education Ass'n*, 460 U.S. at 45 (1983)). *See also Heffron v. ISKCON*, 452 U.S. 640 (1981).

private property. These arrests generally arise out of situations involving picketers blocking ingress or egress of an abortion clinic or physically being on private rather than public property. Sometimes pro-life demonstrators have used what is known as the "necessity defense" to justify breaking the trespass laws. The so-called necessity defense was defined in the early 1900s. The defense involves the necessity of one person trespassing on the private property of another person in order to either avoid serious personal harm or to save the life of another. This defense grew out of a case known as *Ploof v. Putnam*,[44] which involved a boat dock on Lake Champlain. While sailing, a violent tempest arose, and in order to avoid personal and property damage to the sailing vessel, the owner of the vessel moored the sloop to a private dock. When the dock owner noticed the sloop moored to his dock, he untied the sloop and it was destroyed in the storm. The court ruled that the defense of necessity applied with special force to the preservation of human life and that one may sacrifice the personal property of another in order to save either his life or those lives around him. In another case known as *Vincent v. Lake Erie Transportation Company*,[45] a state court ruled that, because of necessity, it was lawful for a ship to maintain its tie to a dock even though the waves forcing the ship up and down destroyed the dock, but also indicated that the ship owner was responsible for repairing the dock.

Based on the defense of necessity, pro-life picketers have argued that it is permissible to break the law of trespass in order to save the life of an unborn child by blocking access to, or trespassing upon, the private property of an abortion clinic. So far this defense has met with very little success in relieving picketers from trespass laws.[46]

Residential picketing involves both public and private issues. Residences are certainly privately-owned, but the sidewalks in front of residential areas are public sidewalks and therefore traditional public forums. As stated in a previous chapter, the Supreme Court has ruled that peaceful picketing within a residential area is constitutionally protected so long as the picketing activities move throughout the neighborhood on the sidewalk and are not directly localized at one particular residential address.[47] Picketing in a residential area is permissible so long as the protesters move about on public sidewalks within the neighborhood. For example, courts have ruled that pro-life demonstrators may picket in a residential neighborhood where a physician who performs abortions resides so long as the protesters move about in the neighborhood and do not solely target one residential address.[48]

---

[44]81 Vt. 471, 71 A. 188 (Vt. 1908).

[45]109 Minn. 456, 124 N.W. 221 (Minn. 1910).

[46]*City of Wichita v. Tilson*, 855 P.2d 911 (Kan. 1993) (ruling that when the objective sought is to prevent by criminal activity a lawful, constitutional right of abortion, the defense of necessity is inapplicable and evidence of when life begins is irrelevant and should not be admitted at trial).

[47]*Frisby*, 487 U.S. at 479. See Chapter 11, Door-to-Door Witnessing.

[48]*Vittitow v. City of Arlington*, 830 F. Supp. 1077 (S.D. Ohio 1993). *See Madsen v. Women's Health Center, Inc.*, 114 S. Ct. 2516, 2529-30 (1994).

BUFFER ZONES

A buffer zone is a parameter set by either a court or legislative body around a particular facility where pickets frequently take place. These buffer zones have restricted the amount of picketers and the activity of picketing within a certain parameter. In light of the escalating activity around abortion clinics, some courts have placed buffer zones around clinics. Legislative attempts to create buffer zones around abortion clinics and other medical facilities have also occurred. These buffer zones are clearly a threat to free speech activities.

Polling Places

The concept of buffer zones may be traced back to voter intimidation around polling booths. The United States Supreme Court ruled that the state of Tennessee may place a 100-foot buffer zone around a polling place within which no literature distribution or display of campaign posters, sign, or other campaign material may occur on the day of elections.[49] In reaching this conclusion, the Supreme Court recognized that the First Amendment "'has its fullest and most urgent application' to speech uttered during a campaign for political office."[50] The Court also noted that First Amendment expression around the polling place in question occurred in a public forum where people were invited to be present. The Court further noted that the specific regulation on speech was content-based because only political speech was prohibited whereas other speech was not. Consequently, the Court ruled that such a buffer zone must be subjected to "exacting scrutiny" and could only survive constitutional challenge if a state had a "compelling interest" for the buffer zone.

To reach its conclusion, the Court reviewed extensive history. States clearly have a compelling interest to protect the rights of citizens to vote freely in an election conducted with integrity and reliability.[51] Indeed, the Court noted the following:

> No right is more precious in a free country than that of having a voice in the election of those who make the laws under which, as good citizens, we must live. Other rights, even the most basic, are illusory if the right to vote is undermined.[52]

Though a content-based regulation of speech in a public forum "rarely survives such scrutiny," based on the history involved, the buffer zone was constitutional.[53] This history dates back to the colonial period, when many

---

[49]*Burson v. Freeman*, 112 S. Ct. 1846 (1992).
[50]*Id.* at 1850, (quoting *UEU v. San Francisco Democratic Commission*, 489 U.S. 214, 223 (1989)).
[51]*Burson*, 112 S. Ct. at 1851. The Court noted that the "right to vote freely for the candidate of one's choice is the essence of a democratic society." *Reynolds v. Sims*, 377 U.S. 533, 555 (1964).
[52]*Wesberry v. Sanders*, 376 U.S. 1, 17 (1964).
[53]*Burson*, 112 S. Ct. at 1852.

government officials were elected *viva voce* or by the showing of hands. Voting was not a private affair, but, in fact, "an open, public decision witnessed by all and improperly influenced by some."[54] Approximately twenty years after the formation of the Union, most states had incorporated a paper ballot in the electoral process. The various political parties wishing to gain influence then began producing their own paper ballots in flamboyant colors. Persons taking these paper ballots to polling places were frequently met by "ticket peddlers" who tried to convince individuals to vote for a particular party ticket. These discussions often became heated and influenced the outcome of votes. This situation was not a "pleasant spectacle."[55]

Australia adopted an official ballot encompassing all candidates of all parties on the same ticket. The Australian system then incorporated the erection of polling booths. This system appeared to be a vast improvement and was eventually adopted in England in 1872. The polling booth concept failed after several attempts but eventually began in Louisville, Kentucky, and then moved to Massachusetts and the state of New York in 1888. The city of Louisville "prohibited all but voters, candidates or their agents, and electors from coming within fifty feet of the voting room enclosure."[56] The Massachusetts and New York laws placed a guard rail around the booths and excluded the general public from mingling within the guard rail areas. New York eventually adopted a 100-foot buffer zone around any polling place, and consequently, much of the intimidation and fraud encountered in earlier years had been cured. One commentator remarked, "We have secured secrecy; and intimidation by employers, party bosses, police officers, saloon keepers and others has come to an end."[57]

Today all fifty states limit access to areas in and around polling places. Even the National Labor Relations Board limits activities at or near its polling places during union elections. After reviewing this history, the Court concluded by stating the following:

> In sum, an examination of the history of election regulation in this country reveals a persistent battle against two evils: voter intimidation and election fraud. After an unsuccessful experiment with an unofficial ballot system, all 50 States, together with numerous other Western democracies, settled on the same solution: a secret ballot secured in part by a restricted zone around the voting compartments. We find that this widespread and time-tested consensus demonstrates that some restricted zone is necessary in order to serve the States' compelling interest in preventing voter intimidation and election fraud.[58]

---

[54]*Id.*
[55]*Id.* at 1852-53.
[56]*Id.* at 1854.
[57]*Id.*
[58]*Id.* at 1855.

Although buffer zones originally arose out of elections and polling booths, the significant history is important. It is improper to take buffer zones arising out of elections processes and, in turn, place buffer zones around other facilities. Buffer zones will rarely survive the First Amendment. The only reason buffer zones in the election process survived a First Amendment analysis is because of the fundamental right to vote which is probably the most important right of an American citizen. Moreover, buffer zone restrictions around polling places are deeply imbedded in American history.

Churches

Though somewhat unanticipated, one city in the state of Kansas passed an ordinance creating a no picketing, or buffer zone, around churches. An individual sought to picket around the church carrying a pro-life sign. Even though he was aware of the no picketing buffer zone ordinance around the church, he picketed anyway and was arrested. The Supreme Court of Kansas ruled that the picketer did not violate the buffer zone because the ordinance was read as prohibiting only targeted picketing of churches.[59]

Public Schools

An ordinance placing a 150-foot buffer zone around public schools but exempting from this buffer zone labor dispute picketing was found by the United States Supreme Court to be unconstitutional.[60] The Court primarily found this buffer zone unconstitutional because it treated different forms of speech unequally. No speech was allowed within the 150-foot buffer zone except labor picketing disputes, and based on that unequal treatment, the buffer zone was struck down.

Abortion Clinics

Abortion clinics have been the primary areas of controversy for an increasing number of decisions regarding buffer zones.[61] One court noted that pro-

---

[59]*City of Prairie Village v. Hogan,* 253 Kan. 424, 855 P.2d 949 (Kan. 1993).
[60]*Grayned,* 408 U.S. at 104; *Mosley,* 408 U.S. at 92.
[61]Though not a buffer zone case, the United States Supreme Court ruled in *Bray v. Alexandria Women's Health Clinic,* 113 S. Ct. 753 (1993), that 42 U.S.C. § 1985(3), the so-called Ku Klux Klan Act, could not be used to restrict picketing of abortion clinics. The Court ruled that abortion does not qualify as an individiously discriminatory animus directed toward women in general, that the incidental effect of abortion clinic demonstrations on some women's right to interstate travel was not sufficient to show a conspiracy to deprive those women of their protected interstate travel right, and that the deprivation of the right to an abortion could not serve as the basis for a purely private conspiracy. Though the Supreme Court ruled that the first part of section 1985(3), known as the "deprivation" clause, does not provide a federal cause of action against persons obstructing access to abortion clinics, the same Supreme Court left open the possiblity that the second part of section 1985(3), known as the "hindrance" clause, may provide a federal cause of action. The Tenth Circuit Court of Appeals has picked up on this idea and suggested that the "hindrance" clause may be used against abortion protestors. *National Abortion Federation v. Operation Rescue,* 8 F.3d. 680 (9th Cir. 1993). *See also* Nina Pillard, "Litigating § 1985(3) Claims After *Bray*

life advocates must "be permitted to articulate their belief that abortion should not be permitted because it involves the taking of human life."[62] One court correctly recognized that "although the words 'killings' or 'murder' are certainly emotionally charged, it is difficult to conceive of a forceful presentation of the anti-abortion viewpoint which would not assert that abortion is the taking of human life."[63] Abortion speech is certainly political speech and therefore should receive the highest protection under the First Amendment. "Indeed, abortion may be the political issue of the last twenty years."[64]

Some have reasoned that buffer zones are permissible because they do not prohibit all free speech and pro-life demonstrators may exercise their right to speak in another locale. However, the Supreme Court stated that one "is not to have the exercise of his liberty of expression in appropriate places abridged on the plea that it may be exercised in some other place."[65] The mere fact that pro-life demonstrators "remain free to employ other means to disseminate their ideas does not take their speech . . . outside the bounds of First Amendment protection."[66] Though some buffer zones restricting the blocking of access to and from an abortion clinic and limiting the amount of picketers present at a given time have been upheld by some state and federal courts, other courts have struck down such bans.[67]

---

v. Alexandria Women's Health Clinic," Civil Rights Litigation and Attorney Fees Annual Handbook, ed. Steve Saltzman and Barbara M.Wolvovitz, Vol. 9, (1993), p. 325.

[62]Planned Parenthood Shasta-Diablo v. Williams, 16 Cal. Rptr. 2d 540, 549 (Cal. 1st DCA 1993).

[63]Cannon v. City and County of Denver, 998 F.2d 867 (10th Cir. 1993).

[64]Planned Parenthood Shasta-Diablo, 16 Cal. Rptr. at 549.

[65]Schneider v. New Jersey, 308 U.S. 147, 163 (1939).

[66]Meyer v. Grant, 468 U.S. at 424.

[67]Cheffer v. McGregor, 6 F.3d 705 (11th Cir. 1993) (a 36-foot and 300-foot buffer zone and a ban on images violates free speech); Cannon v. City and County of Denver, 998 F.2d 867 (10th Cir. 1993) (ruling that arrest of abortion protestors violated the constitutional right to picket on a public sidewalk in front of an abortion clinic and further ruling that words such as "murder" or "The Killing Place" were not fighting words and could not be proscribed); Mississippi Women's Medical Clinic v. McMillan, 866 F.2d 788 (5th Cir. 1989) (ruling a 500-foot buffer zone around an abortion clinic unconstitutional); United Food, 857 F.2d at 430-32 (same); Howard Gault Company v. Texas Rural Legal Aid, Inc., 848 F.2d 544, 548-61 (5th Cir. 1988) (ruling unconstitutional a ban on more than two picketers within 50 feet of one another); Davis v. Francois, 395 F.2d 730 (5th Cir. 1968) (ban on more than two picketers at a building "patently unconstitutional"); Pro-Choice Network v. Project Rescue, 799 F. Supp. 1417 (W.D.NY. 1992) (a restriction allowing two protestors within a 15-foot buffer zone upheld); Town of West Hartford v. Operation Rescue, 726 F. Supp. 371 (D. Conn. 1992) and Town of West Hartford v. Operation Rescue, 792 F. Supp. 161 (D. Conn. 1992) (order upheld prohibiting blocking of clinic but not prohibiting other free speech or association activities), vacated in part, 991 F.2d 1039 (2d Cir. 1993); Jackson v. City of Markham, 773 F. Supp. 105 (N.D. Ill. 1991) (granting an injunction to protect the right to picket on a sidewalk outside of a roller rink); Thomason v. Jernigan, 770 F. Supp. 1195 (E.D. Mich. 1991) (ruling it unconstitutional to prohibit pro-life individuals in a public right of way); Northeast Women's Center, Inc. v. McMonagle, 939 F.2d 57 (3rd Cir. 1991) (a buffer zone allowing six protestors within a buffer zone was permissible but a 500-foot buffer zone in a residential area was unconstitutional); Southwestern Medical Clinics, Inc. v. Operation Rescue, 744 F. Supp. 230 (D. Nev. 1989) (order prohibiting blockading of clinic but allowing other free speech or free association activities upheld); National Organization for Women v. Operation Rescue, 726 F. Supp. 1483 (E.D. Va. 1989) (a restriction on activities tending to intimidate, harass or disturb patients by expression of views on the issue of abortion was ruled unconstitutionally overbroad), aff'd, 914 F.2d 582 (4th Cir. 1990), rev'd in part, vacated in part, Bray v. Alexandria Women's Health Clinic, 113 S. Ct. 753 (1993); National Organization for Women v. Operation Rescue, 726 F. Supp. 300

In the absence of illegal conduct, a flat ban on all peaceful picketing within a traditional public forum such as a park, street, or sidewalk, is patently unconstitutional. To prohibit all peaceful picketing having no history of violence in a traditional public forum, such as a sidewalk outside of an abortion clinic, is unconstitutional.[68]

In one interesting case, the District of Columbia prohibited the "display [of] any flag, banner, or device designed or adapted to bring into public notice any party, organization, or movement" in the United States Supreme Court building or on its grounds, which were defined to include the public sidewalks constituting the outer boundaries of the grounds.[69] A picketer was threatened with arrest when he distributed leaflets on the sidewalk in front of the courthouse regarding the removal of unfit judges from the bench. In addressing this situation, the United States Supreme Court indicated there was "no doubt that as a general matter peaceful picketing and leafletting are expressive activities involving 'speech' protected by the First Amendment."[70] The Court further noted that places such as streets, sidewalks and parks, without more, are considered public forums.[71] The Court went on to state the following:

> In such places, the government's ability to permissively restrict expressive conduct is very limited; the government may enforce reasonable time,

<hr>

(D.C. District 1989) (upholding an order blockading a clinic but not prohibiting or restricting other free speech activities); *Fargo Women's Health Organization, Inc. v. Lambs of Christ,* 488 N.W.2d 401 (N.D. 1992) (a buffer zone allowing only two protestors within 100 feet and prohibiting literature distribution and prohibiting speaking to abortion clinic staff was unconstitutional but the noise restriction was upheld); *Hirsch v. City of Atlanta,* 261 Ga. 22, 401 S.E.2d 530 (Ga. 1991), *cert. denied,* 112 S. Ct. 75 (1991) (upholding a restriction allowing only 20 protestors to use a sidewalk at any one given time within a 50-foot buffer zone); *Planned Parenthood v. Maki,* 478 N.W.2d 637 (Iowa 1991) (a prohibition against one individual from blocking entrance to and trespassing upon clinic property upheld because no other protestor's right to free speech was restricted); *Dayton Women's Health Center v. Enix,* 68 Ohio App. 3d 579, 589 N.E.2d 121 (Ohio App. 2d. 1991); *Planned Parenthood v. Project Jericho,* 52 Ohio St. 3d. 56, 556 N.E.2d 157 (Ohio 1990) (a buffer zone permitting picketing and literature distribution within reasonable limits for the purpose of expression of opinion upheld); *Planned Parenthood v. Operation Rescue,* 550 N.E.2d 1361 (Mass. 1990) (upholding a restriction blocking a clinic while allowing the right to pray, sing, and peacefully picket on public sidewalks); *Cousins v. Terry,* 721 F. Supp. 426 (N.D.N.Y. 1989) (prohibiting blocking access to an abortion clinic); *Zimmerman v. D.C.A. at Welleby, Inc.,* 505 So. 2d 1371 (Fla. 4th DCA 1987) (overturning an injunction against peaceful picketing at sales office of condominium project); *Bering v. Share,* 106 Wash.2d 212, 721 P.2d 918 (Wash. 1986), *cert. dismissed,* 479 U.S. 1060 (1987) (upholding a buffer zone restriction which did not prohibit picketing on a public sidewalk); *Planned Parenthood v. Cannizzaro,* 204 N.J. Super. 531, 499 A.2d 535 (N.J. Super. Ch. 1985) (a restriction allowing picketing in sidewalks or streets abutting the clinic but requiring five feet distance between picketers upheld); *Parkmed Company v. Pro-Life Counseling, Inc.,* 442 N.Y.S. 396 (N.Y. App. Div. 1981) (injunction on demonstrating in public areas outside and abortion business unconstitutional).

[68]*Madsen v. Women's Health Center, Inc.,* 114 S. Ct. 2516 (1994). Cf. *Thornhill v. Alabama,* 310 U.S. 88 (1940).

[69]40 U.S.C. § 13K.

[70]*United States v. Grace,* 461 U.S. 169, 176 (1983). See also *Carey v. Brown,* 447 U.S. 455, 460 (1980); *Gregory v. Chicago,* 394 U.S. 111, 112 (1969); *Jamison v. Texas,* 318 U.S. 413 (1943); *Thornhill v. Alabama,* 310 U.S. 88 (1940); *Schneider v. New Jersey,* 308 U.S. 147 (1939).

[71]*Grace,* 461 U.S. at 177.

place, and manner regulations as long as the restrictions "are content neutral, or narrowly tailored to serve a significant government interest, and leave open ample alternative channels of communication.". . . Additional restrictions such as an absolute prohibition on a particular type of expression will be upheld only if narrowly drawn to accomplish a compelling governmental interest.[72]

There might be rights of other persons to consider in picketing cases, but "the Supreme Court's First Amendment jurisprudence tilts the scale assessing threatened harm decisively in favor of the protesters."[73] Certainly the "First Amendment retains a primacy in our jurisprudence because it represents the foundation of a democracy—informed public discourse."[74]

Sometimes state courts enter injunctions creating their own buffer zones. In one case a state court entered a 300-foot buffer zone around white-owned businesses due to civil rights protesting activities. A federal court was requested to block enforcement of the state court injunction, and ruled that the 300-foot buffer zone was an unconstitutional violation of free speech.[75]

The leading case on buffer zones around abortion clinics is the landmark decision in *Madsen v. Women's Health Center, Inc.*[76] This case arose in Melbourne, Florida, when a state court judge entered an injunction placing a 36-foot buffer zone around three sides of an abortion clinic. Within this zone was a public highway and a public sidewalk. The injunction also contained a noise restriction and prohibited the display of any "images observable" from within the clinic. Additionally, a 300-foot buffer zone was placed around the clinic and around the private residential homes of any owner, employee, staff member, or agent of the clinic. Pro-life speech could occur within the 300-foot buffer zone only upon the consent of the listener. Violations of these buffer zones resulted in criminal prosecution. In addition to those named in the state court injunction, the buffer zone restriction applied to anyone "acting in concert with" those named in the injunction. After the injunction was entered on April 8, 1993, numerous pro-life picketers were arrested merely for being present on a public sidewalk. Many were arrested after kneeling down to pray on this sidewalk. However, pro-choice demonstrators were not arrested. Myrna Cheffer was not named in the state court injunction. She desired to peacefully picket at the clinic but feared arrest. On her behalf, Liberty Counsel filed suit in federal court against the state court judge who entered the buffer zone restriction. The federal court of appeals first noted that the buffer zone was content-based and pointed out the following:

---

[72]*Id.* (quoting *Perry Education Ass'n,* 460 U.S. at 45). *See also Hudgens v. NLRB,* 424 U.S. 507, 515 (1976); *Hague v. CIO,* 307 U.S. 496, 515 (1939).
[73]*McMillan,* 866 F.2d at 795.
[74]*Id.* at 796.
[75]*Machesky v. Bizzell,* 414 F.2d 283 (5th Cir. 1969).
[76]114 S. Ct. 2516 (1994)

That the speech restrictions at issue are viewpoint-based cannot seriously be doubted. The order enjoins Operation Rescue, Operation Rescue America, [O]peration Goliath, their officers, agents, members, employees and servants, and Ed Martin, Bruce Cadle, Pat Mahoney, Randall Terry, Judy Madsen, and Shirley Hobbs, and all persons acting in concert or participation with them or on their behalf. . . . Such a restriction is no more viewpoint-neutral than one restricting the speech of "the Republican Party, the state Republican Party, George Bush, Bob Dole, Jack Kemp and all persons acting in concert or participation with them or on their behalf." The practical effect of this section of the injunction was to assure that while pro-life speakers would be arrested, pro-choice demonstrators would not.[77]

The federal court of appeals went on to state the following:

A viewpoint-specific restriction in a traditional public forum is unconstitutional unless (1) it is necessary to serve a compelling state interest and (2) it is narrowly drawn to achieve that end. . . . The state court injunction does not seem to be either.[78]

The federal court in *Cheffer* proclaimed: "We protect much that offends in the name of free speech—we cannot refuse such protection to those who find abortion morally reprehensible."[79] The court ruled the buffer zone unconstitutional.

At the same time Liberty Counsel was representing Myrna Cheffer in a federal lawsuit against the judge who entered the buffer zone injunction, Liberty Counsel also appealed the judge's decision through the state courts on behalf of three pro-life sidewalk counselors who were named on the injunction. Eight days after the *Cheffer* opinion, the Florida Supreme Court ruled that the entire injunction was constitutional.[80] The case was appealed to the United States Supreme Court which rendered its decision in the case known as *Madsen v. Women's Health Center, Inc.*[81] Stating that an injunction may not "burden more speech than necessary," the court ruled that the 300-foot zone around residential property violated the First Amendment right to free speech.[82] The Court also ruled that the 300-foot buffer zone around the clinic was unconstitutional. The Court also stated that the injunction's requirement that pro-life picketers receive consent from those persons seeking access to the clinic was unconstitutional. The Court further struck down the ban on all images observable and two sides of the 36-foot

---

[77]*Cheffer v. McGregor*, 6 F.3d 705 (11th Cir. 1993).
[78]*Id.* (citation ommitted).
[79]*Id.* at 7. The *Cheffer* case recognizes that a nonparty may file suit in federal court against the state court judge who entered the injunction requesting the federal courts to intervene and block the state court proceeding.
[80]*Operation Rescue v. Women's Health Center, Inc.*, 626 So. 2d 664 (Fla. 1993).
[81]*Madsen*, 114 S. Ct. 2516.
[82]*Id.* at 2525.

speech buffer around the clinic. The *Madsen* Court upheld a ban on excessive noise which could be heard within the clinic and part of the 36-foot zone near the entrance and driveway to the clinic.

Under *Madsen*, before any injunction may be sought, there must be a showing that (1) the picketers have violated, or imminently will violate, some provision of statutory or common law, and (2) there is a cognizable danger of recurrent violation.[83] Moreover, *Madsen* also requires that before such a speech restrictive buffer zone can be instituted, a less restrictive injunction must first be tried. For example, if the two aforementioned prerequisites are met, an injunction may prevent blocking access to the clinic. If the protester violates that injunction, a more restrictive injunction may be applied against the individual protester, thus limiting the protester's free speech.

The *Madsen* test can be summarized as follows:

Injunctive relief affecting speech is permissible only upon a showing that: (1) the defendant has violated, or imminently will violate, some provision of statutory or common law;[84] (2) there is a cognizable danger of recurrent violation;[85] (3) a nonspeech-restrictive injunction preventing the repeated illegal conduct has proven ineffective to protect the significant government interests because the defendant has repeatedly violated the injunction;[86] and (4) a subsequent speech-restrictive injunction may not burden more speech than necessary to serve a significant government interest.[87]

The first two prongs of the above test are applicable to any injunction since injunctive relief is an equitable remedy.[88] Thus, prongs one and two must be met before the entry of any injunction, whether the injunction restricts speech or conduct. After prongs one and two are met, a court may restore law and order by a nonspeech-restrictive injunction, and once that injunction proves to be ineffective, a subsequent speech-restrictive injunction may be issued, but that injunction may not burden more speech than necessary to serve a significant government interest.[89] As a result of the *Madsen* decision, most buffer zones around abortion clinics will be considered unconstitutional.[90]

---

[83]*Id.* at n.3.
[84]*Madsen*, 114 S. Ct. at 2524 n.3.
[85]*Id.*
[86]*Id.* at 2527.
[87]*Id.* at 2525-26.
[88]*Id.* at 2524 n.3.
[89]The *Madsen* Court relied heavily on the assumption that the pro-life protestors repeatedly violated a nonspeech-restrictive injunction, and it is based on this reliance that the Court upheld a portion of the 36-foot buffer zone involving the speech-restrictive section of the second injunction. The *Madsen* Court suggested that individuals may have restrictions placed on their right to free speech if they repeatedly engage in illegal conduct. *See National Society of Professional Engineers v. United States*, 435 U.S. 679, 697-98 (1978).
[90]*See, e.g., Pro-Choice Network v. Schenk*, 34 F.3d 130 (2d Cir. 1994). Below is a diagram of the clinic and surrounding geography which was part of the record before the United States Supreme Court:

NOISE LEVELS

Noise levels, with or without sound amplification, have often become an issue in picketing or demonstrating activities. Noise ordinances must be precise and sometimes have been ruled unconstitutional either because they are vague or overbroad. Indeed,

> an enactment is void for vagueness if its prohibitions are not clearly defined. Vague laws offend several important values. First, because we assume that man is free to steer between lawful and unlawful conduct, we insist that laws give the person of ordinary intelligence a reasonable opportunity to know what is prohibited, so that he may act accordingly. Vague laws may trap the innocent by not providing fair warning. Second, if arbitrary and discriminatory enforcement is to be prevented, laws must provide explicit standards for those who apply them. A vague law impermissibly delegates basic policy matters . . . for resolution on an *ad hoc* and subjective basis, with the attendant dangers of arbitrary and discriminatory application. Third, but related, where a vague statute "abut[s] upon sensitive areas of basic First Amendment freedoms," it "operates to inhibit the free exercise of those freedoms."[91]

A noise ordinance would be unconstitutional if it "either forbids or requires the doing of an act in terms so vague that men of common intelligence must necessarily guess at its meaning and differ as to its application."[92] Certainly those expected to obey a noise ordinance must "be informed as to what the state commands or forbids."[93]

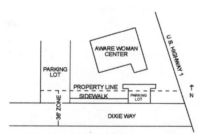

In upholding the portion of the 36-foot zone at the clinic entrance and driveway, the Court focused on two factors: (1) an assumption that the protestors had violated a prior nonspeech-restrictive injunction which was ineffective in maintaining free ingress and egress; and (2) the narrow confines of the clinic which included a strip of sidewalk approximately four feet wide and 37-feet long that connected the two parking lots. The road directly in front of the clinic, Dixie Way, was only 21 feet, four inches wide. Other than the narrow strip of sidewalk directly in front of the clinic, no other sidewalks existed in the residential area along Dixie Way or U.S. Highway 1. Clearly, if the first factor was absent, the Court would not have upheld the 36-foot zone at the clinic entrance and driveway. Additionally, if the second factor was absent, the Court may not have upheld this portion of the zone. In other words, if the confines of the clinic were not so narrow, leaving little other alternative but the imposition of the 36-foot zone, the Court more than likely would have stricken this portion of the injunction like it struck the majority of the injunction.

[91]*Grayned*, 408 U.S. at 108-109 (citations omitted).
[92]*Connally v. General Construction Co.*, 269 U.S. 385, 391 (1926).
[93]*Lanzetta v. New Jersey*, 306 U.S. 451, 453 (1939).

Sometimes noise ordinances are so broad that there is no clearly identifiable noise level which, when reached, would result in violating the ordinance. Ordinances which retain decibel levels are more specific than ordinances which simply prohibit loud noises. Oftentimes noise ordinances which do not have decibel levels require specific case-by-case evaluation to determine the facts and whether the protester willfully created a noise level incompatible with the area.[94] For example, in the city of Beaufort, South Carolina, city officials enacted a noise ordinance that prohibited any person from willfully disturbing any neighborhood or business in the city or making or continuing loud and unseemly noises. This ordinance was passed as a result of several years of street preaching on Saturdays in front of business establishments while standing on the sidewalk or in the bed of pickup trucks. The noise levels of these preachers were obviously loud, and their preaching was found to be in violation of the ordinance. The South Carolina Supreme Court ruled that the language was not vague and that adequate notice had been given to the preachers by the police authorities.[95]

VIOLENT MIXED WITH NONVIOLENT ACTIVITY

Many of the recent attempted restrictions, including buffer zones, on picketing activity in the context of abortion protests have arisen because of escalating violent activity. While courts do have a right to restrict violent activity, which is not protected by the First Amendment, any restriction on picketing or protesting must be precise so as to separate the violent from the nonviolent activity. Indeed, a "free society prefers to punish the few who abuse rights of speech *after* they break the law than to throttle them and all others beforehand."[96]

The classic case involving violent activity mixed with nonviolent activity is *NAACP v. Claiborne Hardware*.[97] The facts of *Claiborne Hardware* are quite interesting. In March of 1966, several hundred black demonstrators implemented a boycott of white merchants following racial abuses in Claiborne County, Mississippi. The business merchants sued for an injunction against the demonstrators and Charles Evers, a leader of the movement who "sought to persuade others to join the boycott through pressure and the 'threat' of social ostracism."[98] Mr. Evers and other active participants of the boycott furthered their cause by seeking to embarrass nonparticipants and "coerce them into action" and conformity.[99]

Some of the demonstrators, acting for all others, became involved in "acts of physical force and violence" against potential customers and used

---

[94]*Kovacs v. Cooper*, 336 U.S. 77 (1949).
[95]*City of Beaufort v. Baker*, 432 S.E. 2d 470 (S.C. 1993).
[96]*Southeastern Promotions, Ltd. v. Conrad*, 420 U.S. 546, 559 (1975).
[97]458 U.S. 886 (1982).
[98]*Id.* at 909-10.
[99]*Id.* at 910.

"[i]ntimidation, threats, social ostracism, vilification, and traduction" in order to achieve their desired results.[100] "Enforcers" known as "black hats" were stationed in the vicinity of the white-owned business to record the names of the boycott violators and those violators were later disclosed in a pamphlet entitled the *Black Times*, which was published by the organization.[101] "In two cases, shots were fired at a house; in a third, a brick was thrown through a windshield; . . . and a group of young blacks apparently pulled down the overalls of an elderly black mason known as 'Preacher White' and spanked him for not observing the boycott."[102] Momentum was added to the boycott following the assassination of Dr. Martin Luther King, Jr., on April 4, 1968, and "[t]ension in the community neared a breaking point." On April 18, 1969, a local civil rights leader was shot and killed.[103] Mr. Evers was quoted as saying: "If we catch any of you going into any of them racist stores, we're going to break your d— neck."[104] Nevertheless, coinciding with the escalation in activities was the continuous "uniformly peaceful and orderly" picketing of the white-owned businesses which often involved small children and occurred "primarily on weekends."[105]

After hearing all of the above evidence, the Mississippi Supreme Court entered a permanent injunction restricting the demonstrators from stationing "store watches" at the merchants' business premises, from "persuading" any person to withhold his patronage from the merchants, and from "using demeaning and obscene language to or about any person," and finally, from "picketing or patrolling" the premises of any of the merchants.[106] However, the United States Supreme Court overruled the Mississippi Supreme Court decision, stating that every element of the boycott was "a form of speech or conduct that is ordinarily entitled to protection under the First and Fourteenth Amendments."[107] The Supreme Court also stated that when restricting free speech activities, there must be "precision of regulation" when "conduct occurs in the context of constitutionally protected activity."[108] The Court further noted that "only unlawful conduct and the persons responsible for conduct of that character" may be restrained.[109]

In another case, a court ruled that it is improper to lump together protected peaceful activity with violent unprotected activity and to prohibit both forms of activity because one is unlawful.[110] In a similar but unrelated situation, the United States Supreme Court ruled that a university could not prohibit the presence of a student group simply because its parent or

---

[100]*Id.* at 894.
[101]*Id.* at 904-05.
[102]*Id.* at 904-05.
[103]*Id.* at 901-02.
[104]*Id.* at 902.
[105]*Id.* at 903.
[106]*Id.* at 893.
[107]*Id.* at 907.
[108]*Id.* at 916.
[109]*Id.* at 927 n.67.
[110]*Machesky*, 414 F.2d at 283.

national affiliate organization had displayed violent and disruptive behavior.[111] It is, therefore, impermissible to use violent activities to justify prohibiting peaceful picketing activities around abortion clinics or any other facility. There must be a distinction made between the violent and nonviolent activities. While violent activities can be prohibited as not being protected by the Free Speech Clause, legitimate peaceful demonstration cannot be restrained under the guise that someone else became violent. Moreover, simply because an individual is a member of an organization known for its violent activities is not sufficient to restrict that individual's free speech activities. Only if the individual has demonstrated violent disruptive activities can that individual be restricted.

It is unconstitutional for one person to lose his or her First Amendment free speech rights because someone else acted unseemly. Indeed, the "right to associate does not lose all constitutional protection merely because some members of the group may have participated in conduct or advocated doctrine that itself is not protected."[112] The Supreme Court has firmly held that "peaceful assembly for lawful discussion cannot be made a crime."[113] If "absolute assurance of tranquillity is required, we may as well forget about speech."[114] While dissidents elsewhere face legal sanctions for every stripe, in the United States the right to free speech belongs to the politically correct and incorrect, the disaffected as well as the loyal, the obnoxious as well as the sensitive, the vociferous as well as the meek.[115]

---

[111]*Healy*, 408 U.S. at 169.

[112]*Claiborne Hardware*, 458 U.S. at 908. *See also Citizens Against Rent Control/Coalition for Fair Housing v. City of Berkeley*, 454 U.S. 290, 294 (1981) (the "practice of persons sharing common views banning together to achieve a common end is deeply embedded in the American political process"); *Scales v. United States*, 367 U.S. 203, 229 (1961) (a "'blanket prohibition of association with a group having both legal and illegal aims' would present 'a real danger that legitimate political expression or association would be impaired'"); *NAACP v. Alabama ex. rel. Patterson*, 357 U.S. 449, 460 (1958) ("Effective advocacy of both public and private points of view, particularly controversial ones, is undeniably enhanced by group association.").

[113]*De Jonge v. Oregon*, 299 U.S. 353, 365 (1937).

[114]*City of Houston v. Hill*, 482 U.S. 451, 462 n.11 (1987) (quoting *Spence v. Washington*, 418 U.S. 405, 416 (1974) (editing remarks and citations omitted).

[115]*See e.g., Forsyth County v. Nationalist Movement*, 112 S. Ct. 2395 (1992) (racist march); *Texas v. Johnson*, 491 U.S. 397 (1989) (flag burning); *Hustler Magazine, Inc. v. Falwell*, 485 U.S. 46 (1988) (lewd parody); *NAACP v. Claiborne Harware Co.*, 458 U.S. 886 (1982) (aggressive boycott enforced with threats of ostracism).

11

Door-to-Door Witnessing

The right to witness in private residential neighborhoods going door-to-door is an important right protected by the Constitution. Most of the door-to-door witnessing cases have dealt with Jehovah's Witnesses. In one case, a city attempted to impose a licensing scheme essentially banning Jehovah's Witnesses from witnessing door-to-door in predominantly Roman Catholic neighborhoods. The Jehovah's Witnesses were also playing records attacking the Roman Catholic church as an "enemy" and stating that the church was of the devil. This licensing scheme attempted to prohibit the door-to-door witnessing activities of the Jehovah's Witnesses, but the United States Supreme Court ruled that this was unconstitutional.[1] The *Cantwell* opinion was the landmark opinion first ruling that the Free Exercise Clause of the First Amendment was applicable to the states. The regulation at issue allowed the city officials to determine who would be permitted to engage in solicitation or distribution of literature based upon the content of the message.

The United States Supreme Court has also ruled unconstitutional a municipal "license tax" that was imposed upon door-to-door solicitation and witnessing by Jehovah's Witnesses. The Court noted the following:

> Those who can tax the privilege of engaging in this form of missionary evangelism can close its doors to all those who do not have a full purse. Spreading religious beliefs in this ancient and honorable manner would thus be denied the needy. Those who can deprive religious groups of their colporteurs can take from them a part of the vital power of the press which has survived from the Reformation.[2]

In one case, the Supreme Court considered the constitutionality of a city ordinance that made it unlawful for any person distributing literature "to ring the doorbell, sound the door knocker, or otherwise summon the

---

[1]*Cantwell v. Connecticut*, 310 U.S. 296 (1940); *Church of Scientology Flag Service Organization, Inc. v. City of Clearwater*, 2 F.3d 1514 (11th Cir. 1993).
[2]*Murdock v. Pennsylvania*, 319 U.S. 105, 112 (1943).

inmate or inmates of any residence to the door for the purpose of receiving" such literature. The United State Supreme Court ruled that this type of ordinance was unconstitutional and stated the following:

> Freedom to distribute information to every citizen wherever he desires to receive it is so clearly vital to the preservation of a free society that, putting aside reasonable police and health regulations of time and manner of distribution, it must be fully preserved.[3]

The right to distribute literature door-to-door is an important First Amendment right. Oftentimes other forms of communication are too costly. The Supreme Court has recognized that "[d]oor to door distribution of circulars is essential to the poorly financed causes of little people."[4]

A federal district court in New York ruled that an ordinance requiring the consent of a householder before approaching the home was unconstitutional. Interestingly named, the *Town of Babylon* court ruled that to require "consent of householders before approaching their homes constitutes, in effect, an indirect unconstitutional imposition of a licensing fee; it generates costs which burden the exercise of first amendment rights in direct proportion to the number of persons the speaker wants to reach."[5]

In addition to the above, many other federal courts have ruled that cities may not flatly and unreasonably prohibit door-to-door witnessing.[6]

Picketing in residential neighborhoods is also constitutionally protected. Most residential neighborhoods have public sidewalks and these public sidewalks are considered traditional public forums.[7] As the Supreme Court has noted, public sidewalks "have immemorially been held in trust for the use of the public."[8] Notwithstanding the fact that the public sidewalks are in residential neighborhoods, they still are classified as traditional public forums and therefore are open to expressive activity by the public.

One difference between residential and business areas containing public sidewalks is the fact that in residential areas, the government has an interest in protecting "the well-being, tranquility, and privacy of the home."[9] In this regard, the Supreme Court has stated that the home is the "last citadel of the tired, the weary, and the sick."[10] In order to protect residential privacy, a city may pass an ordinance that restricts targeted picketing of a sin-

---

[3] *Martin v. City of Struthers*, 319 U.S. 141, 146-67 (1943).
[4] *Id.*
[5] *Troyer v. Town of Babylon*, 483 F. Supp. 1135 (E.D.N.Y. 1980), aff'd 628 F.2d 1346 (2nd Cir. 1980), aff'd, 449 U.S. 998 (1980).
[6] *See eg. Largent v. Texas*, 318 U.S. 418 (1943); *Jamison v. Texas*, 318 U.S. 413 (1943); *Weissman v. City of Alamogordo*, 472 F. Supp. 425 (D.N.M. 1979); *McMurdie v. Doutt*, 468 F. Supp. 766 (N.D. Ohio 1979); *Levers v. City of Tullahoma*, 446 F. Supp. 884 (E.D. Tenn. 1978); *Murdock v. City of Jacksonville*, 361 F. Supp. 1083 (M.D. Fla. 1973).
[7] *Frisby v. Schultz*, 487 U.S. 474, 481 (1988). *See also Perry Education Ass'n v. Perry Local Educators' Ass'n*, 460 U.S. 37 (1983); *Hague v. CIO*, 307 U.S. 496, 515 (1939).
[8] *Frisby*, 487 U.S. at 481 (quoting *Hague*, 307 U.S. at 515).
[9] *Frisby*, 487 U.S. at 484.
[10] *Id.*

gle residential address. Focused "picketing taking place solely in front of a particular residence" may be prohibited, but the government may not ban the general "marching through residential neighborhoods, or even walking around in front of an entire block of houses."[11] In other words, while the government may prohibit picketing targeted at a single residential address, it may not prohibit general picketing throughout a neighborhood. Individuals may protest a particular residence, but must do so by marching on the public sidewalk throughout the neighborhood. Congregating solely in front of a single residential home can be restricted, but marching generally throughout the neighborhood protesting an individual location is constitutionally protected.

---

[11]*Frisby*, 487 U.S. at 477, 483. *See also Madsen v. Women's Health Center, Inc.*, 114 S. Ct. 2516, 2529-30 (1994).

12

The Right to Display Religious Signs

The display of religious signs is another area of religious liberty that has come under attack. In a Wisconsin case, Liberty Counsel worked with an individual who wanted to display 4,000 crosses on his private property. Local city officials argued that the display of crosses was not permitted by the sign ordinance and was, therefore, unlawful. This allegation was clearly incorrect.

In another case brought to Liberty Counsel's attention, a person erected a sign on his private property with a pro-life message. One day he noticed that the sign was gone. He then erected another sign at the same location. To his surprise, he saw a crew of people dismantling the sign, and when he approached, he realized they were city officials. Though other commercial signs were allowed in the area, city officials attempted to remove his sign because it had a pro-life message.

Another instance brought to Liberty Counsel's attention involved a church sign. This sign included crosses on the church property in memorial to those unborn children who lost their lives through abortion. In the middle of the crosses, the church erected a sign explaining the meaning of the crosses as a memorial. City officials interpreted the crosses to meet the requirements of the sign ordinance but wanted to remove the sign in the midst of the crosses. The church argued that without the sign in the midst of the crosses, passersby would not know the meaning of the multiple crosses. In response, city officials determined that in order to prohibit the display of the religious sign, the city would pass an ordinance prohibiting the display of all religious signs. An attorney on behalf of Liberty Counsel attended a city council meeting on this issue and warned that if the city chose this route, it would face a federal lawsuit. The city then requested the assistance of Liberty Counsel to draft a new sign ordinance.

The above examples illustrate the many conflicts that have arisen over signs. When considering whether government can restrict the display of a religious or pro-life sign, several factors must be considered including the location of the display, the size of the display, and whether the government allows other commercial signs such as advertising or real estate signs to be displayed.

The Supreme Court has clearly stated that noncommercial speech receives higher First Amendment protection than commercial speech.[1] An ordinance allowing commercial signs, such as those involving advertising or real estate, but disallowing religious or pro-life signs, would clearly be a content-based regulation and therefore presumptively invalid.[2] It is impermissible to restrict signs simply because of the content of the speech. Therefore, it is impermissible to allow commercial signs while disallowing noncommercial signs.[3] Courts have ruled that an ordinance permitting commercial signs and some other forms of signs, but banning political or issue-related messages, violates the First Amendment.[4]

Based upon the above, it is evident that a city cannot allow commercial billboards while restricting the use of noncommercial billboards.[5] The Supreme Court has noted the following in this regard:

> The fact that the city may value commercial messages relating to on-site goods and services more than it values commercial messages relating to off-site goods and services does not justify prohibiting an occupant from displaying its own ideas or those of others. . . . Insofar as the city tolerates [signs] at all, it cannot choose to limit their contents to commercial messages; the city may not conclude that the communication of commercial information concerning goods and services connected with a particular site is of greater value than the communication of noncommercial messages.[6]

Since the Supreme Court has noted that noncommercial speech retains greater First Amendment protection than commercial speech, a government entity cannot award more protection to commercial signs than is afforded noncommercial signs.

Certainly government entities can regulate signs in the interest of aesthetics and traffic safety.[7] "[A]esthetic judgments are necessarily subjective, defying objective evaluation, and for that reason must be carefully scruti-

---

[1]*Metromedia, Inc. v. City of San Diego*, 453 U.S. 490 (1981); *Matthews v. Town of Needham*, 596 F. Supp. 932, 934 (D. Mass. 1984) ("Noncommercial speech is afforded more protection than commercial speech."). In *City of Cincinnati v. Discovery Network, Inc.*, 113 S. Ct. 1505 (1993), the Supreme Court seems to have narrowed the distinction between commercial and noncommercial speech.
[2]*R.A.V. v. City of St. Paul*, 112 S. Ct. 2538, 2542 (1992).
[3]*Runyon v. Fasi*, 762 F. Supp. 280, 284 (D. Haw. 1991).
[4]*City of Ladue v. Gilleo*, 114 S. Ct. 2038 (1994); *Tauber v. Town of Longmeadow*, 695 F. Supp. 1358, 1362 (D. Mass. 1988) (city bylaws banning posting of political signs but allowing others constituted impermissible content-based restriction on speech).
[5]*Messer v. City of Douglasville*, 975 F.2d 1505 (11th Cir. 1992).
[6]*Metromedia*, 453 U.S. at 513. See also *John Donnelly & Sons v. Campbell*, 639 F.2d 6 (1st Cir. 1980).
[7]*Messer*, 975 F.2d at 1505; *Citizens United for Free Speech II v. Long Beach Township Board of Commissioners*, 802 F. Supp. 1223 (D.N.J. 1992).

nized to determine if they are only a public rationalization of an impermissible purpose."[8] Moreover, aesthetic interests are never "sufficiently compelling to justify a content-based restriction on . . . freedom of expression."[9] In other words, in the interest of aesthetics, a government entity may not place differing restrictions on noncommercial versus commercial signs. Restrictions on the basis of aesthetics must be equally applied to religious as well as to secular speech. However, simply because there is equal treatment between religious and secular speech does not necessarily mean that all aesthetic restrictions are constitutional.

Another interest that a government entity may have in regulating signs deals with traffic safety. Sometimes aesthetics and traffic safety may combine in terms of limiting the size of signs. However, when considering "the universe of distractions that face motorists" on city streets, noncommercial signs "are not sufficiently significant to justify so serious a restriction upon expression."[10]

It is an important principle that the Constitution protects the display of noncommercial religious, pro-life, or political signs. If individuals were not allowed to display signs, then they may not be able to speak at all to the general public. One court noted that other options of speaking through television and radio "involve substantially more cost and less autonomy and reach a significant number of nonlocal persons who [may] likely not have the interest or inclination to receive or act on such information."[11] Indeed, many citizens cannot afford to spend large sums of money to exercise their First Amendment rights.[12] In this regard, one court noted:

> [M]any messages advocating religious, social, or political views are greatly restricted from dissemination if they must primarily or solely rely upon costly print and electronic means for exposure; the expense and ineffectiveness in using either of these two forms of communication is often prohibitive, and signage remains an important alternative.[13]

Indeed, a long standing principle of constitutional law is that "one is not to have the exercise of his liberty of expression in appropriate places abridged on the plea that it may be exercised in some other place."[14] Therefore, it is insufficient to restrict the usage of signs simply because there might be alternative means of disseminating the message.

---

[8]*Metromedia*, 453 U.S. at 510.
[9]*Loftus v. Township of Lawrence Park*, 764 F. Supp. 354 (W.D. Pa. 1991). *See also Signs, Inc. v. Orange County*, 592 F. Supp. 693, 697 (M.D. Fla. 1983).
[10]*Arlington County Republican Committee v. Arlington County*, 790 F. Supp. 618, 624 (E.D. Va. 1992), *aff'd in part, rev'd in part, vacated in part*, 983 F.2d 587 (4th Cir. 1993).
[11]*Burkhart Advertising, Inc. v. City of Auburn*, 786 F. Supp. 721, 733 (N.D. Ind. 1991).
[12]*Arlington County Republican Committee*, 790 F. Supp. at 627 (citing *Martin v. City of Struthers*, 319 U.S. 141 (1943) ("Door-to-door distribution of circulars is essential to the poorly financed causes of little people.")).
[13]*Burkhart Advertising*, 786 F. Supp. at 733.
[14]*Schneider v. New Jersey*, 308 U.S. 147, 163 (1939).

Though not often encountered, it is clearly impermissible to require the daily removal of signs or displays because such a requirement would result in the denial of free speech. In one such case, the city of Cincinnati passed an ordinance prohibiting the presence of any display, exhibit, or structure in Fountain Square between the hours of 10:00 P.M and 6:00 A.M.. Though not strictly a sign ordinance, the case involved the Congregation of Lubavitch which had regularly displayed an eighteen-foot menorah in Fountain Square in preceding years. The requirement of having no displays between certain specified hours appeared to be content-neutral, but in reality, it would have required the Jewish organization to dismantle its menorah every single day. It took approximately six hours to assemble and disassemble the structure. This unreasonable burden would have prohibited the display of the menorah. In this context, a federal appeals court rightfully struck down the ordinance because of its unconstitutionality.[15] Since "communication by signs and posters is virtually pure speech,"[16] the government may not easily restrict this form of expression.

SUMMARY

In summary, the display of religious, political, and pro-life signs is constitutionally protected speech. Clearly, if a governmental entity allows commercial signs, then it may not restrict the presence of noncommercial signs. Most residential neighborhoods allow commercial signs in the form of real estate signs. As such, religious, political, and pro-life speech may be displayed on signs in such neighborhoods. Commercial signs are found throughout many business districts, and consequently, governmental entities may not restrict the presence of noncommercial signs. Certain restrictions may be placed on the display of signs for aesthetic purposes or traffic control. These restrictions primarily involve regulations pertaining to the distance in which the sign may be displayed in proximity to the street or the size of the display. However, simply because an aesthetic or traffic display restriction applies to both commercial and noncommercial speech does not necessarily mean the restriction is constitutional. The regulation may not be so restrictive as to essentially prohibit First Amendment activity.

---

[15]*Congregation Lubavitch v. City of Cincinnati*, 997 F.2d 1160 (6th Cir. 1993).
[16]*Baldwin v. Redwood*, 540 F.2d 1360, 1366 (9th Cir. 1976), *cert. denied sub nom., Leipzig v. Baldwin*, 431 U.S. 913 (1977).

13

Religious Discrimination in Employment

The Civil Rights Act of 1964 is a fairly broad-reaching civil rights act. Title II applies to discrimination in places of public accommodation based on race or religion. Titles III and IV ban racial and religious segregation in public facilities and in public education. Title VI requires that federal assistance recipients not be discriminated against on the basis of race, and Title VII, the subject of this chapter, applies to nondiscrimination in employment.

The wording applicable to religious discrimination in employment states as follows:

(a) It shall be an unlawful employment practice for an employer
  (1) to fail or refuse to hire or to discharge any individual, or otherwise to discriminate against any individual with respect to his compensation, terms, conditions, or privileges of employment, because of such individual's race, color, religion, sex, or national origin; or
  (2) to limit, segregate, or classify his employees or applicants for employment in any way which would deprive or tend to deprive any individual of employment opportunities or otherwise adversely affect his status as an employee, because of such individual's race, color, religion, sex, or national origin.[1]

This ban on discrimination applies to all employers, including religious organizations, which engage in any industry or activity "affecting commerce" and which employ fifteen or more employees for each working day in each of the twenty or more calendar weeks in the current or preceding calendar year.[2] Part-time employees can be counted in computing an orga-

[1] 42 U.S.C. § 2000e-2(a).
[2] 42 U.S.C. § 2000e-2.

nization's total number of employees.[3] Courts are without authority to consider employment discrimination suits against employers under Title VII if the employer has fewer than fifteen employees.[4]

Before proceeding, two other points should be noted. First, in addition to having the prerequisite fifteen employees for the specified time period, the employer must be engaged in an industry or activity "affecting commerce." In general, churches which are not engaged in commercial enterprises would have few interstate business transactions and may be considered as not affecting commerce even if the fifteen requisite employees have been employed for the requisite time period. However, even very little activity can be construed by courts as affecting commerce. For example, the sale of cassette tapes across state lines, or the broadcasting of church services across state lines, would be considered "affecting commerce."

Second, there are various other exemptions to Title VII. Religious educational institutions are exempt under Title VII as follows:

> [I]t shall not be an unlawful employment practice for a school, college, university, or other educational institution or institution of learning to hire and employ employees of a particular religion if such school, college, university, or other educational institution or institution of learning is, in whole or in substantial part, owned, supported, controlled, or managed by a particular religion or by a particular religious corporation, association, or society, or if the curriculum of such school, college, university, or other educational institution or institution of learning is directed toward the propagation of a particular religion.[5]

It should be noted that the exemption for religious educational institutions is an exemption from religious discrimination but not from the other forms of discrimination. Another exemption is the "bona fide occupational qualification." This exemption is as follows:

> Notwithstanding any other provision of this subchapter . . . it shall not be an unlawful employment practice for an employer to hire and employ employees . . . on the basis of his religion, sex, or national origin in those certain instances where religion, sex, or national origin is a bona fide occupational qualification reasonably necessary to the normal operation of that particular business or enterprise. . . .[6]

This exemption applies to religion, sex, or national origin. For example, the Moroccan Pavilion at EPCOT Center may hire only those of Moroccan descent because of the necessity to create a Moroccan atmo-

---

[3]*Pedreyra v. Cornell Prescription Pharmacies, Inc.*, 465 F. Supp. 936 (D. Colo. 1979).
[4]*Bonomo v. National Duck Pin Bowling Congress, Inc.*, 469 F. Supp. 467 (D. Md. 1979).
[5]42 U.S.C. § 2000e-2(e)(2).
[6]42 U.S.C. § 2000e-2(e).

sphere. Finally, religious organizations are exempt from the religious discrimination requirement as follows:

> This subchapter shall not apply to . . . a religious corporation, association, educational institution, or society with respect to the employment of individuals of a particular religion to perform work connected with the carrying on by such corporation, association, educational institution, or society of its activities.[7]

In 1972, Congress amended Title VII to enable religious organizations to discriminate on the basis of religion in all employment decisions. Therefore, a Baptist church may hire all Baptists and a Catholic church may hire all Catholics.[8]

For other employers who are covered by Title VII, the employer is restricted from discriminating on the basis of religion. The employee must first have a sincerely held religious belief that is negatively impacted or burdened by a particular employment practice. The employee then has the obligation to notify the employer of the belief and of the negative impact on that belief. The burden then shifts to the employer to provide reasonable accommodation to that belief unless doing so would result in an undue hardship to the employer. Take an example that was brought to the attention of Liberty Counsel. A Seventh-day Adventist had a sincerely held religious belief that Saturday is the seventh day Sabbath upon which no work should be conducted. This employee was a salesperson who had worked for the same employer for some time. During the week, the employer required a sales meeting to be conducted. For an unexplained reason, the employer then required the sales meeting to be conducted on Saturday. In this case, the employer already knew of the salesperson's religious belief. The employee brought his belief to the attention of the employer again and requested that the sales meeting be held on some other day or possibly even Sunday. The employer did not accommodate this religious belief even though accommodation was clearly possible. In this situation, the employer discriminated on the basis of religion.

When discrimination does occur after following the above steps, the employee should contact the Equal Opportunity Employment Commission (EEOC) and should also contact the state human rights commission. Contact with these commissions is extremely important because of short time limits. Failure to contact these commissions may result in the inability to use either the state discrimination law or the federal Title VII law as a basis for a discriminatory claim. The employee should document in writing a request to the employer stating the religious belief, noting the adverse impact on that belief, and requesting an accommodation of the belief. The

---

[7]42 U.S.C. § 2000e-1.
[8]*Corporation of the Presiding Bishop of the Church of Jesus Christ of Latter-Day Saints v. Amos,* 483 U.S. 327 (1987).

employer should attempt to accommodate this religious belief, but if it does result in an undue hardship, the employer should document this undue hardship and both parties should seek competent counsel.

14

Free Exercise Rights

The Bill of Rights contains what many refer to as the Establishment Clause and the Free Exercise Clause. In pertinent part, the First Amendment states, "Congress shall make no law respecting the establishment of religion or prohibiting the free exercise thereof. . . ."[1] The first part of the Amendment is referred to as the Establishment Clause while the second part is referred to as the Free Exercise Clause.

Like the Establishment Clause, the Free Exercise Clause restricts certain activities of governmental entities. The Free Exercise Clause limits only the government from restricting religion. In order for the Free Exercise Clause to apply, there must be a governmental entity involved. One party must be acting under governmental authority while the other party must be private. The free exercise right under the Constitution is an affirmative right of all individuals and private institutions, limiting governmental restrictions on the free exercise of religion. One individual cannot restrict the free exercise of another individual's religion. However, a governmental entity is limited in its ability to restrict the free exercise of religion without a compelling governmental interest to do so. Clearly, the First Amendment is a limitation on governmental power.

The interpretation of the Free Exercise Clause remained fairly stable during the mid-1900s. However, in 1990, the United States Supreme Court handed down the decision of *Employment Division v. Smith*[2] in which the Court severely limited the free exercise rights of all citizens. In 1993, Congress reacted to this dramatic shift in constitutional interpretation by passing what is known as the Religious Freedom Restoration Act (hereinafter referred to as the "Act").[3] This Act restores free exercise rights as they existed prior to the 1990 *Smith* decision.

---

[1]U.S. Const. amend. I. For discussion on the origins and historical understanding of the free exercise of religion, see McConnell, *The Origins and Historical Understanding of Free Exercise of Religion,* 103 Harv. L. Rev. 1409 (1990).
[2]494 U.S. 872 (1990).
[3]42 U.S.C. § 2000bb. See Appendix G for complete text.

This chapter is divided into free exercise rights prior to *Smith*, free exercise rights during the *Smith* era between 1990 and 1993, and free exercise rights after the *Smith* era. Free exercise rights after the *Smith* era, from late 1993 forward, are the same as the free exercise rights prior to *Smith*. The only time period in which free exercise rights dramatically changed was from 1990 to 1993, a period of history during which many individuals had their religious freedoms trampled by the government.

PRE-*SMITH* ERA

Prior to 1990, the Free Exercise Clause found its apex in two cases decided by the United States Supreme Court. The first was a 1963 case known as *Sherbert v. Verner*[4] dealing with unemployment compensation, and the second was *Wisconsin v. Yoder*[5] dealing with compulsory education laws.

In *Sherbert*, the South Carolina Employment Security Commission denied unemployment benefits to a Seventh-day Adventist because the claimant refused to perform a job search on Saturday. Seventh-day Adventists have sincerely held religious beliefs that the Sabbath is to be observed on the seventh day of the week, beginning Friday evening at sundown and concluding Saturday evening at sundown. Because of this sincerely held religious belief, Adell Sherbert refused to work on Saturday and, therefore, was denied unemployment benefits on the grounds that her refusal to work on Saturday precluded her from obtaining suitable employment. The Supreme Court ruled that this denial was a violation of her free exercise rights. First, the Court ruled that Ms. Sherbert had a sincerely held religious belief not to do any work on the Sabbath. Second, the state requirement to receive unemployment benefits burdened her sincerely held religious belief by causing her to choose between receipt of unemployment benefits or violating her religious convictions. Third, because of this conflict between the state requirement for unemployment benefits and the claimant's free exercise rights, the Court ruled that the state must have a compelling governmental interest in order to succeed. The Court found that there was no compelling governmental interest. The interest at stake was to preserve the unemployment compensation fund from dilution by false claims, but the state could clearly achieve that interest in a less restrictive manner. Consequently, to deny unemployment benefits to a claimant who refuses to work on the Sabbath was a violation of the Free Exercise Clause.[6]

In *Yoder*, the Supreme Court ruled that the Wisconsin compulsory attendance law requiring children to attend school until age sixteen violated

---

[4]374 U.S. 398 (1963).
[5]406 U.S. 205 (1972).
[6]*See also Thomas v. Review Board, Indiana Employment Security Division*, 450 U.S. 707 (1981); *Hobbie v. Unemployment Appeals Commission of Florida*, 480 U.S. 136 (1987) (a state cannot withhold unemployment benefits from a Seventh-day Adventist who refuses to work on the seventh-day Sabbath).

the free exercise rights of the Old Order Amish faith. Wisconsin, like all fifty states, had a compulsory education law that required students to attend school until age sixteen. However, the religious tenets of the Old Order Amish conflicted with this compulsory attendance law. The Old Order Amish believed that by sending their children to high school, they would not only expose themselves to danger of censorship by the church community, but they would also endanger their own salvation and the salvation of their children. According to the Old Order Amish heritage, salvation requires life in a church community separate and apart from the world and worldly influence.[7] The Supreme Court observed the following:

> Formal high school education beyond the eighth grade is contrary to Amish beliefs, not only because it places Amish children in an environment hostile to Amish beliefs with increasing emphasis on competition in classwork and sports and with pressure to conform to the styles, manners, and ways of the peer group, but also because it takes them away from their community, physically and emotionally, during the crucial and formative adolescent period of life.[8]

The Court ruled that: (1) the Amish had a sincerely held religious belief which was contrary to compulsory education past the eighth grade; (2) the compulsory state education law placed a significant burden on this sincerely held religious belief; and (3) there was no compelling governmental interest strong enough to violate this sincerely held religious belief. Indeed, "a State's interest in universal education, however highly we rank it, is not totally free from a balancing process when it impinges on the fundamental rights and interests, such as those specifically protected by the Free Exercise Clause of the First Amendment."[9] In reaching its conclusion, the Court reviewed the history of the Amish religion and noted that one or two years of formal high school education for an Amish student would do little in view of the informal vocational education long practiced by the Amish community. The Amish formed a very self-sufficient community with no evidence that lack of one or two more years of education would result in the students becoming burdens on society. Consequently, this compulsory education law was unconstitutional as applied to the Amish religion.

Though not every claim was successful under the Free Exercise Clause,[10] prior to 1990 the test for free exercise rights required two find-

---

[7]*Yoder*, 406 U.S. at 210.

[8]*Id.* at 211.

[9]*Id.* at 214.

[10]*Reynolds v. United States*, 98 U.S. 145 (1879) (rejecting a claim that criminal laws were unconstitutional as applied against the religious practice of polygamy); *Gillette v. United States*, 401 U.S. 437 (1971) (rejecting a claim that the military selective service system violated the free exercise of religion by conscripting persons who oppose a particular war on religious grounds); *United States v. Lee*, 455 U.S. 252 (1982) (rejecting a claim that the payment of social security tax violated the free exercise rights of the Amish religion); *Bowen v. Roy*, 476 U.S. 693 (1986) (rejecting a claim that obtaining a social security number for the benefit of the applicant's daughter violated

ings: (1) a sincerely held religious belief (2) that is burdened by some governmental action. In light of these two findings, the government must show a compelling governmental interest in order to restrict free exercise rights. In the absence of a compelling interest, free exercise prevails and the government restriction on religion must fail. The Court has already stated that if the compelling interest test means what it says, "many laws will not meet the test."[11]

THE *SMITH* ERA, 1990–1993

On April 17, 1990, the United States Supreme Court drastically altered its interpretation of the Free Exercise Clause. In *Employment Division v. Smith*,[12] the Court essentially abolished the compelling governmental interest test in free exercise cases. In its place, the Court fashioned a different test that stated if a religious practice is burdened by a general law of neutral applicability, the religious claim will fail and the governmental intrusion on free exercise rights will succeed. Prior to 1990, anyone showing a sincerely held religious belief which had been burdened by some governmental activity would be afforded the compelling interest test. If the compelling interest test "means what it says . . . many laws will not meet the test."[13] The compelling interest test meant that most laws under the strict scrutiny standard would be presumptively invalid. The government must show a compelling governmental interest in order to intrude on free exercise rights. In order for the test to be utilized, the only showing was that the individual had a sincerely held religious belief that was burdened by some governmental action.

In 1990, the United States Supreme Court changed its interpretation. Specifically, the Court stated "we cannot afford the luxury of deeming presumptively invalid as applied to the religious objective, every regulation of conduct that does not protect an interest of the highest order."[14] In other words, the Supreme Court felt that the past quarter of a century of free exercise rights was a "luxury" which the country could no longer afford. Under the *Smith* test, any law that specifically did not single out religion as its object of regulation would be held valid in the face of a free exercise claim.

---

free exercise rights); *Lyng v. Northwest Indian Cemetary Protective Association*, 485 U.S. 439 (1988) (ruling that the government's logging and road construction activities took precedence over traditional Indian religious practices); *Goldman v. Weinberger*, 475 U.S. 503 (1986) (rejecting a claim that the prohibition of wearing a yarmulke pursuant to a military dress regulation violated free exercise rights); *O'Lone v. Estate of Shabazz*, 482 U.S. 342 (1987) (sustaining a prison's refusal to excuse inmates from work requirements to attend religious worship services); *Hernandez v. Commissioner*, 109 S. Ct. 2136 (1989) (rejecting a free exercise challenge to payment of income taxes alleged to make religious activities more difficult). In *Lyng, Goldman*, and *O'Lone*, the Court did not apply the *Sherbert* free exercise test.
[11]*Smith*, 494 U.S. at 888.
[12]*Id.* at 872.
[13]*Id.* at 888.
[14]*Id.*

So long as the law applied across the board to religious and nonreligious activities, the law would prevail over the religious objector. Ironically, in 1972 the United States Supreme Court believed exactly the opposite when it stated the following: "A regulation neutral on its face may, in its application, nonetheless offend the constitutional requirement for governmental neutrality if it unduly burdens the free exercise of religion."[15] In other words, in 1972 the Supreme Court stated that a neutral law could still violate free exercise rights, but in 1990, the Supreme Court stated that a neutral law would not violate free exercise rights. Using the example noted above regarding the unemployment case of *Sherbert*, if that case had been decided between 1990 and 1993, Ms. Sherbert would have lost her free exercise claim. This is because the unemployment law requiring a job search on the seventh-day Sabbath would be a neutral law of general applicability. This law was not made for the purpose of singling out religion. On the contrary, this law applies equally to religious and nonreligious activities. As such, between 1990 and 1993, neutral laws were constitutional, whereas prior to 1990, if law in application burdened a sincerely held religious belief, that law would be unconstitutional. Similarly, the compulsory attendance laws ruled unconstitutional in *Yoder* may have been found constitutional between 1990 and 1993 because compulsory attendance laws are neutral laws of general applicability.

From 1990 to 1993, free exercise rights were dealt a devastating blow. Though the Minnesota Supreme Court ruled that an Amish person's refusal to place an orange triangle on the back of a buggy violated free exercise rights, the United States Supreme Court vacated that decision in light of *Smith*.[16] After *Smith*, many religious rights were lost in cases involving immigration,[17] landmarking,[18] religious clothing of a Muslim teacher,[19] workers' compensation,[20] home education,[21] zoning,[22] jurisdiction of the National Labor Relations Board over religious schools,[23] the applicability of the Age Discrimination and Employment Act over religious organizations,[24] religious objections to autopsies,[25] and many others.

According to one court, the Supreme Court's decision in *Smith* "cut back, possibly to minute dimensions, the doctrine that requires government to accommodate, at some cost, minority religious preferences."[26] The

---

[15]*Yoder*, 406 U.S. at 220.

[16]*Minnesota v. Hershberger*, 462 N.W.2d 393 (Minn. 1990).

[17]*Intercommunity Center for Justice and Peace v. INS*, 910 F.2d 42 (2nd Cir. 1990).

[18]*St. Bartholomew's Church v. City of New York*, 914 F.2d 348 (2nd Cir. 1990).

[19]*United States v. Board of Education for the School District of Philadelphia*, 911 F.2d 882 (3rd Cir. 1990).

[20]*South Ridge Baptist Church v. Industrial Commission of Ohio*, 911 F.2d 1203 (6th Cir. 1990).

[21]*Vandiver v. Hardin County Board of Education*, 925 F.2d 927 (6th Cir. 1991).

[22]*Cornerstone Bible Church v. City of Hastings*, 948 F.2d 648 (8th Cir. 1990).

[23]*NLRB v. Hanna Boys Center*, 940 F.2d 1295 (9th Cir. 1991).

[24]*Lukaszewski v. Nazareth Hospital*, 764 F. Supp. 57 (E.D. Pa. 1991).

[25]*Montgomery v. County of Clinton*, 743 F. Supp. 1253 (W.D. Mich. 1990); *You Vang Yang v. Sturner*, 728 F. Supp. 845 (D.R.I. 1990).

[26]*Hunafa v. Murphy*, 907 F.2d 46 (7th Cir. 1990).

United States Supreme Court in *Smith* belittled free exercise rights. Though the term "free exercise" specifically occurs in the First Amendment, the Supreme Court stated that in order to obtain the protection of free exercise rights that existed prior to 1990, any free exercise claim must meet either of the following: (1) the law impacting the religious practice is not a neutral law of general applicability but is one that specifically targets religion,[27] or (2) the free exercise right must be combined with some other implicit or explicit constitutional right. In other words, in order for the compelling interest test to be applicable after *Smith*, the law must specifically target religion, or the free exercise right must be combined with some other constitutional right such as free speech, privacy, or parental rights. This hybrid combination would then equate to the same standard utilized by the Court prior to 1990. This simply belittled free exercise rights by requiring free exercise to be combined with some other constitutional recognition. In reaction to this limitation on free exercise rights, Congress took action in 1993 by enacting the Religious Freedom Restoration Act.

POST-*SMITH* ERA

Because religious freedom rights were dealt a devastating blow by the *Smith* decision that reigned between 1990 and 1993, Congress passed what is known as the Religious Freedom Restoration Act (hereinafter referred to as the "Act").[28] The major portion of the act states as follows:

(a) IN GENERAL—Government shall not burden a person's exercise of religion even if the burden results from a rule of general applicability, except as provided in subsection (b).
(b) EXCEPTION—Government may substantially burden a person's exercise of religion only if it demonstrates that application of the burden to the person—
  (1) is in furtherance of a compelling governmental interest; and
  (2) is the least restrictive means of furthering that compelling governmental interest.[29]

The Act recreates the constitutional standard that existed prior to the 1990 *Smith* decision. Thus, all of the Supreme Court's decisions noted above involving free exercise rights prior to the *Smith* decision will again be applicable. The three-year reign of terror of *Smith* is now over, and free exercise rights are again recognized as deserving specific protection. Unfortunately, the First Amendment to the United States Constitution specifically recognizes and protects free exercise rights, but this was ignored

---

[27]*Church of the Lukumi v. City of Hialeah*, 113 S. Ct. 2217 (1993)(a law specifically enacted against the Santeria religion violated free exercise rights because it was required to meet a compelling interest test since the law was not neutral and of general applicability).
[28]42 U.S.C. § 2000bb. See Appendix G for full text.
[29]42 U.S.C. § 2000bb-1.

by the Supreme Court in 1990. Now these rights are protected by legislative enactment rather than the Constitution. The standard again requires the showing of (1) a sincerely held religious belief, (2) which is burdened by some governmental action. If these two factors are present, the government must show a compelling governmental interest and must further show that the restriction on the religious practice is the least restrictive means of achieving that compelling governmental interest. Remember, once the compelling governmental interest test is applicable, the Supreme Court has already recognized that "many laws will not meet the test."[30] Prior to the passage of the Religious Freedom Restoration Act, the National Right to Life Committee opposed the Act unless it contained an abortion-neutral amendment. Specifically, National Right to Life argued that the amendment would be used to justify abortion. Though some courts have been requested to grant an abortion in the face of governmental restrictions to the contrary, based on a free exercise right,[31] the United States Supreme Court specifically rejected such a claim under the Free Exercise Clause of the Constitution.[32]

SUMMARY

Prior to 1990, the Free Exercise Clause was a powerful constitutional protection for religious freedom. If an individual had (1) a sincerely held religious belief, (2) which was burdened by some governmental regulation, then the government had to show a compelling governmental interest in order to limit the free exercise of religion. If the government had a compelling governmental interest to restrict religion, then it had the burden to show that the limitation of religion was the least restrictive means of achieving the compelling interest. If there was no compelling governmental interest, then the individual free exercise right won. If there was a compelling governmental interest, but there was a less restrictive means to achieve that interest, again, the individual's free exercise of religion would triumph. According to the Supreme Court, if the compelling interest test means what it says, "many laws will not meet the test."[33] In other words, once an individual showed that a sincerely held religious belief was burdened by a governmental regulation, most governmental regulations would fail in light of the Free Exercise Clause.

In 1990, the interpretation of the Free Exercise Clause was drastically altered by the *Smith* decision. The Supreme Court ruled in 1990 that individual free exercise would fail if the governmental regulation was a neutral law of general applicability. In other words, if the governmental regulation applied equally to religious as well as nonreligious practices, the free exer-

[30]*Smith*, 494 U.S. at 888.
[31]*McCrae v. Califano*, 491 F. Supp. 630 (E.D.N.Y. 1980).
[32]*Harris v. McCrae*, 100 S. Ct. 2671 (1980). *See* Bopp, *Will There Be a Constitutional Right to Abortion After the Reconsideration of Roe v. Wade?*, 15 J. Contemporary L. 131 (1989).
[33]*Smith*, 494 U.S. at 888.

cise right would lose. The only time the compelling governmental interest test would arise is if (1) the regulation specifically singled out religion for special treatment or (2) the free exercise right was combined with some other implicit or explicit constitutional protection. Thus, by combining two constitutional provisions, free exercise with some other constitutional provision, the free exercise right would then reach the level of protection it enjoyed prior to 1990. Free exercise in and of itself no longer demanded the strict compelling governmental interest. Consequently, any governmental regulation on religion only needed to be reasonable, and since most laws would have a reasonable basis for existence, free exercise rights were dealt a devastating blow between 1990 and 1993.

Reacting to this drastic change in the interpretation of the Free Exercise Clause, the Religious Freedom Restoration Act was passed in late 1993. This federal law grants free exercise rights to the status as they existed prior to 1990. Thus, if an individual has (1) a sincerely held religious belief, (2) which is burdened by some governmental regulation, then the government must have a compelling interest to restrict the religious exercise and must achieve that compelling governmental interest in the least restrictive manner. Fortunately, free exercise rights are again protected by federal law, but unfortunately, this protection is not constitutionally-based but is now statutorily-based. It is unfortunate that Congress had to act to protect the free exercise of religion when the very first amendment to the Bill of Rights clearly grants strong constitutional protection to religious exercise and practices.

15

Political Activity of
Nonprofit Organizations

The extent to which churches and nonprofit organizations may engage
in lobbying and political campaigns is illusive and often misunderstood.[1] Pastors and leaders of nonprofit corporations are frequently
leery about becoming too vocal on political matters for fear of jeopardizing the organization's nonprofit status. Paralyzed by this fear, many leaders refuse to address political issues. This is why it is so important to know
the parameters imposed on nonprofit corporations, because only when
these parameters are known can the organization truly be free to communicate without jeopardizing its tax structure.

The information presented below can be summarized as follows: (a) a
501(c)(3) nonprofit organization and a church are permitted to engage in
lobbying activities so long as no substantial part of their overall activities
are directed toward lobbying, but these organizations are strictly prohibited from endorsing or opposing a candidate for public office; (b) a
501(c)(4) organization is permitted to engage in lobbying activities without
any limitation, but is prohibited from endorsing or opposing a political candidate for public office; (c) a 501(h) organization is permitted to engage in
lobbying activities without limitation if the activities are performed by volunteer services or with certain specified monetary limitations if expenditures
are directed toward lobbying activities, but this type of an organization is
prohibited from endorsing or opposing a candidate for public office; (d) a
political action committee may engage in lobbying activities without limitation and may endorse or oppose a candidate for public office with the only
limitation being that which is imposed by state or federal law pertaining to
the amount of contributions permissible per candidate; and (e) as long as a
pastor or representative is not purporting to speak for the church or
501(c)(3) organization, but is, instead, expressing views as an individual cit-

---

[1]Since churches are exempt from federal income tax, they are treated as nonprofit organizations
exempt from income tax under the Internal Revenue Code § 501(c)(3).

izen, there are no lobbying limitations on the pastor or representative, and the only political limitations would be the amount of money allowed by state or federal law to contribute to a political candidate.

Prior to 1934, there were no lobbying limitations imposed upon non-profit organizations by the Internal Revenue Code. However, without benefit of Congressional hearings, an amendment was added to the Revenue Act of 1934, which was designed to prohibit tax exemption for organizations that attempt to influence legislation.[2] In 1954, then Senator Lyndon B. Johnson proposed an amendment to what later became the Internal Revenue Code of 1954, which specifically prohibited nonprofit organizations from endorsing or opposing a candidate for public office.[3] Senator Johnson, who later became President Johnson, apparently proposed this amendment to counteract a nonprofit organization which opposed his candidacy for senator.

To determine the extent of political activity of a nonprofit organization, an important distinction must be made between (1) legislative or lobbying activities, and (2) intervention in a political campaign. Nonprofit organizations are permitted to engage in legislative or lobbying activities, but are strictly prohibited from endorsing or opposing a candidate for public office. An organization will be regarded as attempting to influence legislation if the organization (a) contacts, or urges the public to contact, members of the legislative body for the purpose of proposing, supporting, or opposing legislation; or (b) advocates the adoption or rejection of legislation.[4] The term "legislation" includes any action by Congress, any state legislature, any local council or similar governing body, or by the public in a referendum, initiative, constitutional amendment, or similar procedure. However, *a 501(c)(3) tax-exempt organization may attempt to influence legislation so long as it only devotes an insubstantial part of its activities to the adoption or rejection of such legislation.* Consistent with this distinction, the following guideline will be divided between legislative activity and political campaigns.[5] An organization cannot be tax-exempt if it has the following characteristics: (a) its main or primary objective(s) (as distinguished from its incidental or secondary objectives), may be obtained only by legislation or a defeat of proposed legislation; and (b) it advocates, or campaigns for, the obtainment of such main or primary objective(s) as distinguished from engaging in a nonpartisan analysis, study, or research, and making the results thereof available to the public.[6] The ban against engaging in a political campaign on behalf of any candidate for public office "is an absolute

---

[2]Bruce Hopkins, *The Law of Tax-Exempt Organizations*, 1991 Cum. Supp. pp. 14-15; Douglas Kirk, *Cases and Materials on Nonprofit Tax-exempt Organizations*, 1992 § 5-10.
[3]Bruce Hopkins, *The Law of Tax-Exempt Organizations*, 281 (5th Edition 1987).
[4]Treas. Reg. § 1.501(c)(3)-1(c)(3)(ii).
[5]*Id.* at § 1.501(c)(3)-1(c)(3)(ii)(b).
[6]*Id.* at § 1.501(c)(3)-1(c)(3)(iii). *See also Cammarano v. United States*, 358 U.S. 498 (1959); *Christian Echoes National Ministry, Inc. v. United States*, 470 F.2d 849 (10th Cir. 1972), *cert. denied*, 414 U.S. 864 (1973).

prohibition. There is no requirement that political campaigning be substantial."[7]

ORGANIZATIONAL STRUCTURES
501(c)(3) Organizations

A nonprofit organization that elects 501(c)(3) status under the Internal Revenue Code is afforded (1) federal tax-exempt status and (2) tax deductibility on behalf of the donors who contribute to the organization. One of the main advantages of 501(c)(3) is that the donors under § 170 of the Internal Revenue Code can claim a federal tax deduction on their contributions.

Churches organized exclusively for religious or charitable purposes are automatically exempt from federal taxes. The church may apply for exemption but is not required to do so. However, other nonprofit organizations seeking federal tax-exempt status must apply for exemption, utilizing Form 1023. The advantage of being recognized as a 501(c)(3) organization is obvious, but there are some restrictions. A 501(c)(3) organization is described as one in which "no substantial part of the activities . . . is carrying on propaganda, or otherwise attempting, to influence legislation . . . and which does not participate in or intervene in (including the publishing or distributing of statements), any political campaign on behalf of any candidate for public office."[8]

The "substantial part" wording was enacted by Congress in 1934. The Internal Revenue Service (IRS) has stated that an organization will be regarded as attempting to influence legislation if the organization: (1) contacts or urges the public to contact members of the legislative body for the purpose of proposing, supporting, or opposing legislation; or (2) advocates the adoption or rejection of legislation.[9]

The IRS has further noted that an organization may not be considered exempt if: (1) its primary objective may be obtained only by legislation or defeat of proposed legislation; and (2) it advocates or campaigns for the attainment of such main or primary objective as distinguished from engaging in nonpartisan analysis, study, or research, and making the results thereof available to the public.[10] Furthermore, the IRS has stated that attempts to influence legislation are not limited to direct appeals to members of the legislature but may include indirect appeals to legislators through the electorate or the general public.[11]

---

[7]*Internal Revenue Manual* § 3(10)1. *See also United States v. Dykema*, 666 F.2d 1096, 1101 (7th Cir. 1981), *cert. denied*, 456 U.S. 983 (1982); 696 F.2d757 (10th Cir. 1982)*Hutchinson Baseball Enterprises, Inc. v. Commissioner*, 696 F.2d 757,760 (10th Cir. 1982); *Association of the Bar of the City of New York v. Commissioner*, 858 F.2d 876 (2d Cir. 1988).
[8]I.R.C. § 501(c)(3).
[9]Treas. Reg. § 1.501(c)(3)-1(c)(3)(ii).
[10]*Id.* at § 1.503(c)(3)-1(c)(3)(iii).
[11]*Internal Revenue Manual* §§ 392-394 (1989).

The *Internal Revenue Manual*[12] recognizes that "there is no simple rule" as to what constitutes a "substantial" portion of the total activities of the organization, and has further recognized that the determination is a "factual one."[13]

In one case, a court found that legislative activity is not substantial if it does not exceed 5 percent of the organization's total activities. This so-called 5 percent rule was originally taken from the case of *Seasongood v. Commissioner*.[14] Since the so-called substantial part test looks at the organization's overall activities, one federal court of appeals indicated that in addition to time spent "writing, telegraphing, or telephoning" legislators and testifying before legislative committees, the time spent within the organization "formulating, discussing and agreeing upon the positions," which are to be advocated must be taken into account in order to determine substantiality.[15] While the so-called 5 percent test is still used by some as the benchmark, the IRS has rejected that test and instead indicated that the determination is a factual one and is "more often one of characterizing the various activities as attempts to influence legislation."[16]

Generally speaking, a 501(c)(3) organization may: (1) educate on social issues which have political ramifications; (2) urge the general public to become involved in the democratic political process, so long as it is non-partisan; (3) publish neutral voting records of political candidates so long as there is no endorsement; (4) provide education about the political process; (5) lobby, if the legislation directly affects the tax-exempt status of the organization or directly impacts the operation of the organization; and (6) influence legislation so long as such activity does not constitute more than a "substantial" part of the organization's total activities.

A 501(c)(3) organization may lose its tax-exempt status if its legislative activities exceed more than a "substantial" part of its total activities. Moreover, a 501(c)(3) organization is prohibited from engaging in any political campaign on behalf of any candidate for public office. This is an absolute prohibition, and thus a 501(c)(3) organization is prohibited from directly endorsing or opposing a candidate for public office. Having said this, it should be noted that only a few organizations have ever lost their tax-exempt status for engaging in political activity, none of which have been churches.

501(h) Organizations

In 1976, Congress provided a new option for 501(c)(3) organizations that wish to engage in lobbying activity. The Internal Revenue Code created a

---

[12]*Id.*
[13]*Id.*
[14]*Seasongood v. Commissioner*, 227 F.2d 907 (6th Cir. 1955) (The organization in this case was neither a church nor a religious organization.)
[15]*Kuper v. Commissioner*, 332 F.2d 562 (3rd Cir. 1964), *cert. denied*, 379 U.S. 920 (1964). *See also* League *of Women Voters of United States v. United States*, 180 F. Supp. 379 (Ct. Cl. D.C. 1960).
[16]*Internal Revenue Manual* §§ 392-394 (1989).

501(h) election for 501(c)(3) organizations; and instead of using the "substantial" part test of a 501(c)(3) organization, a 501(h) organization uses an "expenditure test." The 501(h) election is not available for all 501(c)(3) organizations. Churches, integrated auxiliaries of churches, conventions, and associations of churches may not elect 501(h) coverage.[17] Private foundations and government units are also prohibited from electing the 501(h) provision.

An eligible 501(c)(3) organization may, therefore, file IRS Form 5768 to elect 501(h) status. The election is made on Form 5768, known as "Elections/Revocation of Election by Eligible § 501(c)(3) Organization to Make Expenditures to Influence Legislation." In 1976, Congress enacted an alternative to the substantial part test. If an eligible organization elects the expenditure test of §§ 501(h) and 4911, specific statutory dollar limits on the organization's lobbying expenditures apply. "In contrast to the substantial part test, the expenditure test imposes no limit on lobbying activities that do not require expenditures, such as certain unreimbursed lobbying activities conducted by *bona fide* volunteers."[18]

Under the 501(h) election, the measuring factor is not the *activities* of the organization, but the *expenditures* of the organization directed toward lobbying. There are two types of lobbying: (1) grass roots expenditures, which include attempts to influence the public attitudes or to encourage the public to contact their legislators regarding legislatio; and (2) direct lobbying, which involves any attempt to influence legislation through communication with a member or employee of the legislative body or any government official or employee. A grass roots communication will be considered a lobbying communication only if it refers to a specific piece of legislation, advocates a view on such legislation, or encourages the recipient of the communication to take action on the legislation. A direct lobbying communication will only be so considered if it refers to a specific piece of legislation and advocates a view on that legislation.

The limitation on direct lobbying expenditures is based on a sliding scale as follows: (1) 20 percent of the first $500,000 of the organization's exempt expenditures, plus (2) 15 percent of the second $500,000, plus (3) 10 percent of the third $500,000, plus (4) 5 percent of any additional exempt purpose expenditures. The expenditures may not exceed $1,000,000 for any one year period.

Grass roots lobbying expenditures may not exceed 25 percent of the above figures. For example, if an organization has $500,000 in exempt purpose expenditures, it may spend up to $100,000 in direct lobbying (20 per-

---

[17]Several major denominations lobbied Congress not to permit churches the option to elect 501(h) status. The philosophical reasoning behind this unusual request was that the churches argued they should not be subject to any lobbying limitations at all. To concede that the churches needed a 501(h) status would be, in a sense, to concede that the lobbying limitations imposed in the first place were legitimate. Unfortunately, therefore, churches may not presently elect 501(h) status.

[18]Treas. Reg. § 1.501(h)-1 *et seq.*; § 56.4911-0 *et seq.*

cent of $500,000 = $100,000). It may spend either the entire $100,000 toward direct lobbying, or it may spend up to 25 percent of that figure for grass roots lobbying, resulting in $75,000 for direct lobbying and $25,000 for grass roots lobbying. A $17,000,000 organization may spend up to $1,000,000 on direct lobbying expenditures (20 percent of first $500,000; 15 percent of second $500,000; 15 percent of the third $500,000; and 5 percent of the remaining $15,500,000 of which $750,000 may go toward direct lobbying and $250,000 may go toward grass roots lobbying).

Volunteer activities are not considered expenditures if there are no funds expended on such activities. For a 501(c)(3) organization that has not made the 501(h) election, volunteer activities are considered part of the total activities of said organization, but a 501(h) organization is only concerned with actual money spent on lobbying activities.

If a 501(h) organization exceeds the expenditure limitation, there is a penalty excise tax imposed equal to 25 percent of the amount of the excess lobbying expenditures. If the organization's lobbying expenditures normally exceed the limits by 50 percent, then the organization will jeopardize its tax-exempt status, but this is based on a four year cycle. Thus, an organization may exceed its expenditure limit in one year by more than 50 percent, but the next year may not exceed the expenditure limit. However, if the average of the four years is more than 50 percent of the expenditure limits, the organization may have to pay an excise tax or may lose its tax-exempt status, but only for the years in which the limits were exceeded. Therefore, a 501(h) has more mobility to engage in lobbying activities, but is still prohibited from directly endorsing or opposing a political candidate for public office.

501(c)(4) Organizations

The Internal Revenue Code also recognizes a third type of organization known as a 501(c)(4) organization, or sometimes referred to as a social welfare organization.

A 501(c)(4) organization is afforded tax-exempt status, but unlike a 501(c)(3) or 501(h), does not have the advantage of tax-deductible contributions. Because it does not allow donors to deduct contributions from federal income tax, 501(c)(4) organizations do not have the prohibition from engaging in efforts to influence legislation. In *Regan v. Taxation with Representation*,[19] the United States Supreme Court recognized that a 501(c)(3) organization could establish a separate organization under 501(c)(4) for the purpose of lobbying activities. The court noted that "the IRS apparently requires only that the two groups be separately incorporated and keep records adequate to show that tax deductible contributions are not used to pay for lobbying."[20]

---

[19] 461 U.S. 540 (1983).
[20] *Id.* at 554 n.6.

A 501(c)(4) organization may therefore directly lobby, either by volunteer activity or by expenditures. However, a 501(c)(4) is still prohibited from directly opposing or supporting a political candidate for public office.

Summary of Organizations

In summary, a 501(c)(3) organization is tax-exempt, and the contributions are tax-deductible. Such an organization is prohibited from expending more than a "substantial" part of its activities toward lobbying (which includes volunteer and expenditure activities). A 501(c)(3) organization which is not a church, integrated auxiliary of a church, association or convention of churches, private foundation or government unit, is allowed to elect a 501(h) status and thus use an expenditure test. Under an expenditure test, only money spent toward lobbying is considered. A nonprofit organization may incorporate as a 501(c)(3) and separately incorporate as a 501(c)(4) organization. There are no lobbying limitations on 501(c)(4) organizations.

Neither a 501(c)(3), a 501(h) election, nor a 501(c)(4) may directly oppose or support a political candidate for public office. To directly oppose or support a candidate for public office, a state or federal political action committee (PAC) must be established. Though PACs are governed by the strict reporting requirements, the advantage is that PACs can directly support or oppose a candidate for public office. Contributions to a PAC are not tax-deductible.

PASTORS AND REPRESENTATIVES OF NONPROFIT ORGANIZATIONS

In January of 1992, the IRS published a statement regarding Jimmy Swaggart Ministries. Jimmy Swaggart Ministries had apparently endorsed Pat Robertson for President in 1988. Jimmy Swaggart stated at a worship service that Pat Robertson would most probably announce his candidacy for President and that he would lend his support to Mr. Robertson. Jimmy Swaggart then wrote an article entitled "From Me to You" in the church's official magazine known as *The Evangelist* in which he stated: "We are supporting Pat Robertson for the office of President of the United States" and "we are going to support him prayerfully and put forth every effort we can muster in his behalf." The magazine indicated on its masthead that it was "The voice of Jimmy Swaggart Ministries." According to the IRS, "when a minister of a religious organization endorses a candidate for public office at an official function of the organization, or when an official publication of a religious organization contains an endorsement of a candidate for public office by the organization's minister, the endorsement will be considered an endorsement of the organization since the acts and statements of a religious organization's minister at official functions of the organization and its official publications are the principal means by which a religious organization communicates its official views to its members and supporters."[21]

Though the publicized IRS statement may be an exaggeration and may not be supportable if challenged in court, it is nonetheless the IRS's view that when a minister speaks at an official church function, the expression of that minister will be considered the expression of the church. Prior to this news release, most assumed that a minister could appear in a pulpit during a worship service and state personal views so long as a disclaimer was made that the church was not endorsing or opposing those views. The IRS has apparently taken a different position on this matter. Presumably, a minister should be able to express personal views outside of an official church function so long as a disclaimer is made that the church is not endorsing or opposing a specific candidate for public office.

After the IRS finished with Jimmy Swaggart, it focused on Jerry Falwell. Rev. Jerry Falwell's "Old Time Gospel Hour" was ordered to pay the IRS $50,000 in back taxes for improperly engaging in political activities in 1986 and 1987. The settlement resulted in the IRS revoking Old Time Gospel Hour's tax-exempt status for both years. The IRS found that OTGH, which broadcasts Mr. Falwell's sermons, devoted both personal and other church assets to political fundraising efforts.[22]

KEY TO ABBREVIATIONS

The following key will be used to designate each organization or entity in order to illustrate permissible political activity:

Pastor	(or representative)
501(c)(3)	(or church; tax-exempt and tax-deductible)
501(h)	(tax-exempt and tax-deductible)
501(c)(4)	(tax-exempt but not tax-deductible)
PAC	(not tax-exempt and not tax-deductible)

LEGISLATIVE OR LOBBYING ACTIVITY

	Pastor	501(c)(3)	501(h)	501(c)(4)	PAC
1. Lobbying on issues unrelated to the organization's function or tax exempt status.	Y	Y*	Y**	Y	Y

* except that the lobbying activities cannot exceed a substantial part of the overall activities of the organization.
** if the lobbying activity is done through volunteer services; otherwise, an expenditure test must be utilized.

[21]Richard Hammer, ed., "Political Activities by Churches," *Church, Law and Tax Report,* Vol. VI, No. 5, September/October 1992, pp. 7-8.
[22]*Nonprofit Alert,* May 1993; Lynn Buzzard, ed., *Religious Freedom Reporter,* Vol. 13, No. 4, April 1993, p. 140.

	Pastor	501(c)(3)	501(h)	501(c)(4)	PAC
2. Lobbying on issues directly related to the existence, powers and duties, exempt status, or the deductibility of contributions to the organizations.	Y	Y	Y	Y	Y
3. Educating the members of the organization orally or through written communication regarding the status of legislation in a nonpartisan, objective manner without advocating a specific view on such legislation.[23]	Y	Y	Y	Y	Y
4. Educating the members of the organization orally or through written communication regarding the status of legislation and advocating a specific view on such legislation.	Y[24]	Y*	Y**	Y	Y

* except that such activities cannot exceed a substantial part of the organization's overall activities.
** if done by volunteer services; otherwise the expenditure test must be unitilized.

	Pastor	501(c)(3)	501(h)	501(c)(4)	PAC
5. Provide education regarding the political process and encourage members in a nonpartisan manner to become involved in the political process.	Y	Y	Y	Y	Y
6. Petition drives.	Y	Y*	Y**	Y	Y

* except that such activity should not exceed a substantial part of the organization's overall activities unless the petition drive directly relates to legislation affecting the function of the organization or the tax-exempt status of said organization.
** without limitation if performed by volunteer services; otherwise, the expenditure test should be utilized.

	Pastor	501(c)(3)	501(h)	501(c)(4)	PAC
7. Rental of organization's mailing list.	N/A	Y*	Y*	Y*	Y

* if rented at fair market value. Said list could be loaned to a legislative group such as a 501(c)(4) organization since the Federal Election Campaign Act[25] applies only to political campaigns.

POLITICAL CAMPAIGN ACTIVITY

	Pastor	501(c)(3)	501(h)	501(c)(4)	PAC
1. Endorsement of political candidates.	Y[26]	N	N	N	Y

---

[23]The IRS has indicated that an organization which objectively studies legislation in a nonpartisan manner and which compiles this information for distribution to the general public but neither proposes specific legislation or advocates the passage or defeat of any pending legislation is not attempting to influence legislation. Rev. Rul. 64-195, 1964-2 C.B. 138.

[24]See above section on pastors and representatives of nonprofit organizations.

[25]2 U.S.C. § 431.

[26]See above section on pastors and representatives of nonprofit organizations.

		Pastor	501(c)(3)	501(h)	501(c)(4)	PAC
2.	Contributions to political campaigns.	Y	N	N	N	Y
3.	In-kind and independent expenditures for or against political candidates.	Y	N	N	N	Y
4.	Fundraising for candidates.	Y[27]	N	N	N	Y
5.	Introduction of political candidates at organization meetings.	Y[26]	Y*	Y*	Y*	Y
	* but no endorsement					
6.	Political candidates to speak at organization functions.	N/A	Y[29]	Y[30]	Y[31]	Y
7.	Nonpartisan voter registration.	Y	Y	Y	Y	Y
8.	Distribution of candidate surveys and incumbent voting records which *do not* contain editorial opinions endorsing or opposing candidates.	Y	Y	Y	Y	Y

The following two situations, as proposed by the IRS, would be permissible distribution of voter guides by a 501(c)(3), 501(h) or 501(c)(4) organization:

Situation 1:
   Organization A has been recognized as exempt under section 501(c)(3) of the Code by the Internal Revenue Service. As one of its activities, the organization annually prepares and makes generally available to the public a compilation of voting records of all members of Congress on major legislative issues involving a wide range of subjects. The publication contains no editorial opinion, and its contents and structure do not imply approval or disapproval of any members or their voting records.
   The "voter education" activity of Organization A is not prohibited political activity within the meaning of section 501(c)(3) of the Code.

---

[27]*Id.*
[28]*Id.*
[29]A political candidate could speak at this organization so long as the candidate was speaking on issues that directly affected the organization and did not attempt to campaign at the organization. Based on Rev. Rul. 74-547, this type of an organization should be free to have political candidates address the members so long as (1) overt campaigning activities are avoided, (2) the same opportunity is afforded to other qualified candidates, and (3) the attendees are informed before or after the speech that the organization does not endorse any candidate for public office. However, a candidate could certainly preach at a church or address a nonprofit organization without the organization having to invite the candidate's opponent if no endorsements or campaigning activities occurred.
[30]*Id.*
[31]*Id.*

Situation 2:

Organization B has been recognized as exempt under section 501(c)(3) of the Code by the Internal Revenue Service. As one of its activities in election years, it sends a questionnaire to all candidates for governor in State M. The questionnaire solicits a brief statement of each candidate's position on a wide variety of issues. All responses are published in a voters' guide that it makes generally available to the public. The issues covered are selected by the organization solely on the basis of their importance and interest to the electorate as a whole. Neither the questionnaire nor the voters' guide, in content or structure, evidences a bias or preference with respect to the views of any candidate or group of candidates.

The "voter education" activity of Organization B is not prohibited political activity within the meaning of section 501(c)(3) of the Code.[32]

	Pastor	501(c)(3)	501(h)	501(c)(4)	PAC
9. Distribution of candidate surveys and incumbent voting records which *do* contain editorial opinions endorsing or opposing candidates.	Y	N	N	N	Y

The following two situations, as proposed by the IRS, would not be permissible voter guides by a 501(c)(3), 501(h) or 501(c)(4) organization:

Situation 3:

Organization C has been recognized as exempt under section 501(c)(3) of the Code by the Internal Revenue Service. Organization C undertakes a "voter education" activity patterned after that of Organization B in Situation 2. It sends a questionnaire to candidates for major public offices and uses the responses to prepare a voters' guide which is distributed during an election campaign. Some questions evidence a bias on certain issues. By using a questionnaire structured in this way, Organization C is participating in a political campaign in contravention of the provisions of section 501(c)(3) and is disqualified as exempt under that section.

Situation 4:

Organization D has been recognized as exempt under section 501(c)(3) of the Code. It is primarily concerned with land conservation matters. The organization publishes a voters' guide for its members and others concerned with land conservation issues. The guide is intended as a compilation of incumbents' voting records on selected land conservation issues of importance to the organization and is factual in nature. It contains no express statements in support of or in opposition to any can-

---

[32]Rev. Rul. 78-248.

didate. The guide is widely distributed among the electorate during an election campaign.

While the guide may provide the voting public with useful information, its emphasis on one area of concern indicates that its purpose is not nonpartisan voter education.

By concentrating on a narrow range of issues in the voters' guide and widely distributing it among the electorate during an election campaign, Organization D is participating in a political campaign in contravention of the provisions of section 501(c)(3) and is disqualified as exempt under that section.[33]

	Pastor	501(c)(3)	501(h)	501(c)(4)	PAC
10. Maintaining a nonpartisan bulletin board regarding legislative and political campaign issues.	Y	Y*	Y*	Y*	Y

* if the organization allows all viewpoints to be presented in a non-partisan manner without the organization's endorsement.

11. Distribution of political statements and political endorsements in lobbies or parking lots.	Y	Y*	Y*	Y*	Y

* if the distribution is not controlled or organized by the organization and distribution is also permitted for opposing viewpoints.

12. Use of the organization's facilities by political candidates.	N/A	Y*	Y*	Y*	Y

* if provided on a nonpartisan basis.[34]

13. Political forum where candidates are invited to discuss political viewpoints.	N/A	Y*	Y*	Y*	Y

* if done on a nonpartisan basis.[35]

14. Nonprofit radio or television media providing reasonable air time equally to all legally qualified candidates without endorsing a particular candidate.	N/A	Y[36]	Y	Y	Y

---

[33]*Id.*

[34]See above under Political Campaign Activity, example 6.

[35]*Id.*

[36]In 1974, the IRS stated that providing broadcasting facilities to "legally qualified candidates for elected public office furthers the education of the electorate by providing a public forum for the exchange of ideas and the debate of public issues which instructs them on subjects useful to the individual and beneficial to the community." The IRS stated that if the organization makes its facilities equally available to the candidates for public office, then this activity "does not make the expression of political views by the candidates the acts of the broadcasting station within the intendment of section 501(c)(3) of the Code." Rev. Rul. 74-574, 1974-2 C.B. 160.

	Pastor	501(c)(3)	501(h)	501(c)(4)	PAC
15. Supporting or opposing judicial appointments[37] to state or federal court or to the United States Supreme Court.	Y	Y*	Y*	Y*	Y

* because such an appointee is not involved in a political campaign, but such activity may be construed as lobbying.

SUMMARY

It is important to note the difference between legislative activities and political campaigns. The IRS does not prohibit all involvement in lobbying or legislative activities, but this activity is somewhat restricted depending upon the nature of the organization. According to the United States Supreme Court, an organization could divide its activities by incorporating as a 501(c)(3) tax-exempt and tax-deductible organization with certain lobbying limitations and by separately incorporating as a 501(c)(4) tax-exempt but not tax-deductible organization which has no lobbying limitations.[38]

There is no lobbying limit on a 501(c)(4) organization but there are lobbying limits on a 501(c)(3) and a 501(h) organization. It should be noted that since the amendments to the IRS Code in 1934 on lobbying activities and 1954 on political campaign activities, only a handful of organizations have ever lost their tax-exempt status for engaging in too much political activity. However, no church has ever lost its nonprofit status for engaging in political or lobbying activity.[39] One case challenging nonprofit status involved Christian Echoes National Ministry.[40] When the court looked at Christian Echoes Ministry, it found that it encouraged the public to: (1) write their Congressmen to influence political decisions; (2) work in politics at the precinct level; (3) support the Becker Amendment; (4) maintain the McCarrin Immigration Law; (5) contact their congressmen to oppose interference with the freedom of speech; (6) purge the American press of its responsibility for misleading its readers; (7) inform congressmen that the House Committee on Un-American Activities must be retained; (8) oppose an Air Force Contract to disarm the United States; (9) dispel the mutual mistrust between North and South America; (10) demand an investigation of the biased reporting of major television networks; (11) support the Dirksen Amendment; (12) demand that Congress limit foreign aid spending; (13) discourage support for the World Court; (14) support the Connally Reservation; (15) cut off diplomatic relations with Communist Countries; (16) reduce the federal payroll by discharging needless job holders and bal-

---

[37]This only applies to *appointments*, not to *elective* judicial positions.
[38]*Regan v. Taxation With Representation*, 461 U.S. 540 (1983).
[39]Richard Hammer, ed., "Political Activities by Churches," *Church Law and Tax Report*, Vol. VI, No. 5, September/October 1992, p.2.
[40]*Christian Echoes National Ministry, Inc. v. United States*, 470 F.2d 849 (10th Cir. 1972), *cert. denied*, 414 U.S. 864 (1973).

ance the budget; (17) stop federal aid to education and socialized medicine as well as housing; (18) abolish the federal income tax; (19) end American diplomatic recognition of the Soviet Union; (20) withdraw from the United Nations; (21) outlaw the Communist Party in the United States; and (22) restore immigration laws. The organization also endorsed Senator Barry Goldwater. Since the organization's activities were *primarily* political, it lost its tax-exempt status.

Another nonprofit organization lost its tax-exempt status because of its campaign activities.[41] Nearly 76 percent of this particular organization's total budget was spent on legislative activities. Again, since its activities were *primarily* political, it lost its tax-exempt status. Only a few organizations have ever lost their tax-exempt status and clearly their overall activity excessively involved legislative and political activities, but again, no church has ever lost its tax-exempt status for engaging in too much political activity.

A 501(c)(3) organization is permitted to engage in certain lobbying activities so long as a substantial part of the organization's overall activities are not devoted to lobbying. A 501(c)(3) organization that makes a 501(h) election is permitted to engage in lobbying activities. The extent to which this type of organization may engage in lobbying activities is more clearly defined because an expenditure test is utilized. Volunteer services which are not reimbursed are not considered lobbying activities, thus there would be no limit upon a 501(h) organization's lobbying activities if it used volunteers. A 501(c)(4) organization is specifically designed to engage in lobbying and there are no restrictions on its lobbying activities. The main tax difference between a 501(c)(4) as compared to a 501(c)(3) and a 501(h) is that the former is tax-exempt but contributions are not tax-deductible, while the latter are tax-exempt and contributions to these organizations are tax-deductible.

In terms of intervening in political campaigns, there is a strict prohibition against endorsing or opposing political candidates for public office. This strict prohibition applies to 501(c)(3), 501(c)(4), and 501(h) organizations. However, these organizations can still distribute literature designed to educate regarding candidate voting records or viewpoints. The main proviso is that these voter education guides should be nonpartisan and should not specifically endorse or oppose candidates. These cards should avoid indicating favorable or unfavorable ratings and be presented in an objective manner.

Since pastors and representatives of nonprofit organizations are individuals, there are no restrictions regarding the amount of activity they may engage in with regards to legislative or political campaign issues. When endorsing a political candidate, the pastor or representative should avoid the appearance that the organization is giving the endorsement.

---

[41]*IRS General Counsel Memorandum* 39811.

Finally, Political Action Committees may engage in unrestricted legislative activities or political campaigns with the only limitation being state or federal reporting requirements.

Pastors, churches, and other nonprofit organizations can clearly be involved in the political process. It would be literally impossible for such organizations not to be involved in the political process because the viewpoints and issues advocated by churches and nonprofit organizations naturally have political consequences. To avoid the political process is to limit the effectiveness of churches and nonprofit organizations. The United States Supreme Court has recognized that "churches frequently take strong positions on public issues including . . . vigorous advocacy of legal or constitutional positions. Of course, churches as much as secular bodies and private citizens have that right."[42]

---

[42]*Walz v. Tax Commission,* 397 U.S. 664, 670 (1970).

16

Religion and the Future
of America

When the early pioneers of this country landed on the shores of what later became called America, they brought with them a vision. Though certainly not all were Christian, a large portion of the pioneers clearly operated under a Judeo-Christian worldview. This worldview taught them that history is not the simple repetitive cycle that the Greeks held, but that history had a purpose. While certain events of history repeat themselves, this Judeo-Christian worldview taught the pioneers that history was moving to a conclusion. These pioneers were part of this conclusion. The role that many of them played was to bring the gospel of Jesus Christ to a new land. In a real sense, these pioneers were missionaries to America.

It is no wonder that when these pioneers landed they erected crosses and staked out the land for Jesus Christ. It is also no wonder that when they framed their colonial documents, they expressed the view that their purpose in life was to spread the gospel, that laws should be consistent with the Bible, and, in reality, that they derived their laws from the Bible. In creating what is now known as the federal government, the founders drew from two primary sources. First, they were familiar with the monarchy from which they came and did not want to repeat the mistakes of their motherland. Second, they realized human frailty and the inevitable conclusion that power corrupts, and absolute power corrupts absolutely. In response, they formed a federal government with limited powers, having checks and balances between three branches of government. In setting up this government, many of the founders realized that if God did not build this house of America, those who labored did so in vain.

The founders recognized the importance of religion in their everyday lives. By and large, they did not schizophrenically separate their religious views from public life. Since the Judeo-Christian ethic was the primary worldview, public schools naturally taught students how to read using biblical verses, and biblical stories often taught points of morality. Probably the average student who did not claim to be Christian knew more about the Bible than many of today's young people who regularly attend Sunday school class. Many of the founders knew the original languages of the Bible. It was not unusual to study Greek and Latin. Today many students graduating from public schools do not even understand English.

Freedom and autonomy were important to the early founders. They established the federal government to be a government of certain limited and prescribed powers, primarily banding the colonies together for the purpose of national defense and security. The individual colonies did not want the federal government to intrude into matters of the states, particularly with matters of religion and education. The founders realized that with the increase of bureaucracy there was a concomitant decrease in liberties. As the federal government would grow, freedom, and specifically religious freedom, would wane.

Many of the individual states took on characteristics different from one another primarily because they were inhabited by either predominant religions or people of ethnic background. The individual states were not afraid to take on peculiarities different from their neighbors, and yet, they all attempted to coexist and to assist one another in certain areas. As transportation increased, migration from one state to the next increased. The federal government continued to increase in size and power, and along with this increase, bureaucracy continued to mount, and uniformity became the rule of the day. Today, multiculturalism is in vogue and political correctness is the rule. Many people have merged into a melting pot with differing religious backgrounds or no religious backgrounds. Today, some have the goal of making this country totally secular.

There is a struggle going on for the heart and soul of America. This struggle involves the Judeo-Christian heritage of this country and religious freedom. A growing bureaucratic federal government is not necessarily compatible with freedom—particularly religious freedom. To some extent, this country mirrors the history of Egypt. In Egypt, the pharaohs believed that they were God. As God, the pharaohs etched their names on monuments throughout the land. Many Egyptian pharaohs chipped off the previous pharaohs' names and inscribed their own as though they were the ones who had built the stone relics. Today, the same thing is taking place in America. As bureaucracy continues to grow, and the trend toward secularism and political correctness continues to mount, there comes a clash between a seculaistic mindset and Judeo-Christian worldview. As secularism triumphs, the god of the state eats away the religious symbols of yesteryear.

As the federal government continues to gain power, and as secularism continues to be the rule of the day, the symbols of our founders are being removed one-by-one. For many years, the city of St. Cloud, Florida, had erected a cross atop its water tower. Someone objected and filed suit. The cross is now gone. Only a bald water tower top remains. Corpus Christi, a city whose name means "the body of Christ," had for approximately four decades erected Latin crosses to commemorate Easter and the resurrection of Jesus Christ. Now it no longer does so. The crosses are gone. The city officials removed them out of fear of litigation, and the town became a victim of judicial terrorism.

The city of Zion chose the Star of David as part of its city seal. The star was synonymous with the city's name, but someone objected. The city was taken to court, and now the city's seal has been altered. The Star of David has been removed.

Another city, also named Zion, had a Latin cross in its city seal consisting of a seal draped with a ribbon that read "God Reigns." The seal was divided into four sections, one section containing a Latin cross, one with a dove carrying a branch, one with a scepter and one with a crown. This seal was designed in the early 1900s by the founder of Zion, the Reverend John Alexander Dowie, who was also the founder of the Christian Catholic Church. The city of Zion was established for "the purpose of the extension of the Kingdom of God upon earth." The city was taken to court and now the seal has been altered. The cross has been removed.

A painting of Jesus was donated to a Michigan school and placed in the school cafeteria. This painting had hung on the wall for many years, but one of the parents objected and took the school to court. Although it was like any other painting of a great leader, because Jesus was the founder of the Christian religion, the court stated that the painting must be removed. When you walk through this particular school today, the painting is gone. Another victim of judicial terrorism.

For many years a Latin cross stood on the memorial ground of a military cemetery. Someone was offended by this cross and took action in court. A court forced the removal of this historic Judeo-Christian symbol and now, on this military cemetery, the Latin cross is gone.

The Illinois town of Rolling Meadows had a city seal with a cross in one quadrant of the seal. After a school art assignment asking students to draw a potential city seal, one eighth-grade student designed a seal with a cross in one of the quadrants to depict the many churches in the area. In 1960, the city adopted the seal designed by the eighth-grade student. The seal actually consisted of a four leaf clover. Inside the clover were pictures of a school, industrial buildings, a church, a leaf, and a Latin cross. Someone objected to this cross and a federal court forced its removal. The city seal has now irrevocably been changed and the cross is gone.

In Wicker Memorial Park in Highland, Indiana, stood a 20-foot crucifix erected by the Knights of Columbus in 1955 as a memorial to fallen World War II veterans. The figure of Jesus hung from this crucifix for 38 years overlooking the public park. Five residents objected to the crucifix and brought suit in federal court claiming that the display violated the Constitution. After a very long legal battle, the appellate court ruled that the crucifix was unconstitutional. Bringing their cranes to the park, the city officials lowered the cross to the ground—a scene reminiscent of when the real cross and the real Jesus were lowered to the ground after His death. The crucifix is now gone, and the city of Highland became another victim of judicial terrorism.

When I attended public school, I remember class being opened each day with a prayer and the Pledge of Allegiance. Opening class with prayer today is now foreign to all public school students. My public school used to have Christmas holidays, but now public school students have winter holidays. Whenever public schools had Christmas concerts, it was natural to sing religious Christmas carols. Now, school officials are jittery about putting religious Christmas carols in public school music. I remember the day President John F. Kennedy was assassinated. The teachers gathered all of our classes into a big auditorium, and we watched the news on television. We were led by our teachers to pray on behalf of our fallen president. Today, prayer probably would not have been part of that event which was so vividly impressed on my mind.

In 1990, I traveled to Moscow in the then Soviet Union. I was part of a delegation of attorneys traveling to Russia to participate in a constitutional conference whereby there would be interchange between the USSR and the USA. The purpose of this interchange was to give ideas to the Soviet Union regarding the adoption and formation of a new constitutional form of government. While in the Kremlin, I was able to visit the church museums with their beautiful gold onion domes. Inside these beautiful structures every inch of the walls, including the ceilings and the enormous pillars, was painted with religious themes. Everywhere the eye could see were pictures of early New Testament events and other great Christian leaders throughout history. I was awed by these massive structures and also somewhat saddened. These churches had actually been thriving centers for religious worship in the very heart of the Kremlin. When the Soviet atheistic government took over, these churches lost their religious worship. Interestingly, the structures remained as relics to a bygone era and were used only as museums. I thought, had these museums been in America through this transition, these museums/churches may well have been ruled unconstitutional because of their religious heritage. In America, I wonder whether we will even have religious relics or whether we will continue to push all religious history and memory from existence.

During one of the meetings, a Soviet attorney sitting across the aisle stood up and announced to those that were assembled how thankful he was to be able to sit in a room with Americans. He expressed that in 1976, America celebrated its 200th anniversary of the Constitution, and he congratulated us. He hoped that the Soviet Union could do the same as it was moving through those days of transition. He stated he was so proud and privileged to be able to sit beside an American.

The words of this Soviet attorney have been etched forever in my mind. I am proud to be an American, but it is certainly a different America than what our founders envisioned. When Alexis de Tocqueville traveled this country in the 1830s, he stated that "the religious aspect of the country was the first thing that struck my attention."[1] If Alexis de Tocqueville returned

---

[1]*Democracy in America*, (New York: Vintage Books, 1945) 1:319.

to America today in the 20th century, I wonder what would impress him now? When he visited our public schools, would he be impressed by the religious influence? When the class began, would he hear a prayer? Would he look at an instructional book and see religious influences? When he talked to our representative leadership, on either a state or federal level, would he be impressed by their desire to serve this country out of a sense of mission? Or, instead, would he be impressed with the rising tide of teenage pregnancy, suicide, teenage abortion, juvenile crime, and indiscriminate killing? Would he feel safe when he entered our nation's capitol, one of the leading crime areas in the world? What would really impress Alexis de Tocqueville today? Would it be the religious aspect of this country, or would it be its secularistic trend? Would it be the fact that we are one of the most illiterate countries in the world, that we are in hopeless debt, that we are removing our nativity scenes from public property, or that we are erasing all of our religious heritage?

Yes the early founders did have a vision. This vision was inspired by their Judeo-Christian worldview. They came to this country for a purpose— to advance the gospel. Our country is slowly losing its religious vision, slowly losing the concept of its place in history. As the United States begins to merge into a one-world system form of government, we lose our uniqueness which is our contribution to the world. Without a religious cohesiveness and religious worldview, what happened in Los Angeles after the Rodney King verdict is not unusual. After that verdict was handed down, it appeared that society had erupted and lost all its cohesive underpinnings. Having no Judeo-Christian worldview or no religious heritage, a society left with only secularism will disintegrate and destroy itself. Having to answer to no higher power and recognize no other world existence, society left with no absolutes will come unglued at the seams.

The struggle for this country is a real one. The contents of this book are not simply theoretical and are not just legal jargon. The issue of religious freedom in the public square is really the battle for the heart and soul of America. If we lose religious freedom in the public square, then we have lost America forever. As religion goes, so goes America. The early founders knew the importance of religion in society, and they were willing to forsake their homes, their comfort, their families and even sacrifice their lives for freedom.

Today we have grown complacent, having graciously inherited the freedom of our forefathers. If we do not catch the vision that they once held, if we let the flame of freedom that they carried throughout this country die out, if we are not willing to sacrifice and put our lives on the line for freedom in whatever battle we face, then this country, as we now know it, will come to an end. Like an avalanche of snow tumbling down a mountain, it will crumble as surely as the world governments have crumbled in the past decades. I love this country too much to sit by and let that happen.

Appendix A

The Bill of Rights

AMENDMENT I

Congress shall make no law respecting an establishment of religion, or prohibiting the free exercise thereof; or abridging the freedom of speech, or of the press; or the right of the people peaceably to assemble; and to petition the Government for a redress of grievances.

AMENDMENT II

A well-regulated militia, being necessary to the security of a free State, the right of the people to keep and bear arms shall not be infringed.

AMENDMENT III

No soldier shall, in time of peace be quartered in any house, without the consent of the owner, nor in time of war, but in a manner to prescribed by law.

AMENDMENT IV

The right of the people to be secure in their persons, houses, papers, and effects, against unreasonable searches and seizures, shall not be violated, and no warrants shall issue, but upon probable cause, supported by oath or affirmation, and particularly describing the place to be searched, and the persons or things to be seized.

AMENDMENT V

No person shall be held to answer for a capital, or otherwise infamous crime, unless on a presentment or indictment of a Grand Jury, except in cases arising in the land or naval forces, or in the militia, when in actual service in time of war or public danger; not shall any person be subject for the same offense to be twice put in jeopardy of life or limb; nor shall be compelled in any criminal case to be a witness against himself, nor be deprived of life, liberty, or property, without due process of law; nor shall private property be taken for public use, without just compensation.

AMENDMENT VI

In all criminal prosecutions, the accused shall enjoy the right to a speedy and public trial, by an impartial jury of the State and district wherein the crime shall have been committed, which district shall have been previously ascertained by law, and to be informed of the nature and cause of the accusation; to be confronted with the witnesses against him; to have compulsory process for obtaining witnesses in his favor, and to have the assistance of counsel for his defense.

AMENDMENT VII

In suits at common law, where the value in controversy shall exceed twenty dollars, the right of trial by jury shall be preserved, and no fact tried by jury, shall be otherwise reexamined in any Court of the United States, than according to the rules of the common law.

AMENDMENT VIII

Excessive bail shall not be required, nor excessive fines imposed, nor cruel and unusual punishment inflicted.

AMENDMENT IX

The enumeration in the Constitution, of certain rights, shall not be construed to deny or disparage others retained by the people.

AMENDMENT X

The powers not delegated to the United States by the Constitution, nor prohibited by it to the States, are reserved to the States respectively, or to the people.

Appendix B

School Board Policy Regarding Religion

Symbols, Music, Art, Drama, and Literature

A. It is the intent of this policy to promote tolerance and understanding among students, faculty and staff. It is further the intent of this policy to neither promote nor to denigrate religion or religious practices. Students and staff members should be excused from participating in practices which are contrary to their religious beliefs unless there are compelling reasons that would prevent excusal.

1. The several holidays throughout the year which have a religious and secular basis may be observed in the public schools.
2. The historical and contemporary values and the origin of religious holidays may be explained in an unbiased and objective manner without sectarian indoctrination.
3. Music, art, drama, and literature having religious themes or bases are permitted as part of the curriculum for school-sponsored activities and programs if presented in a prudent and objective manner and as a traditional part of the cultural and religious heritage of the particular holiday.
4. The use of religious symbols such as a cross, menorah, crescent, Star of David, crèche, symbols of Native American religions, or other symbols that are part of a religious holiday are permitted as a teaching aid or resource provided such symbols are displayed as an example of the cultural and religious heritage of the holiday and are temporary in nature. Among these holidays are included Christmas, Easter, Passover, Hanukkah, St. Valentine's Day, St. Patrick's Day, Thanksgiving and Halloween.
5. The district's calendar should be prepared so as to minimize conflicts with religious holidays of all faiths.

B. Religious institutions and orientations are central to human experience, past and present. An education excluding such a significant aspect would be incomplete. It is essential that the teaching about and not of religion be conducted in a factual, objective and respectful manner.

1. The School Board supports the inclusion of religious literature, music, drama, and the arts in the curriculum and in school activities provided it is intrinsic to the learning experience in the various fields of study and is presented objectively. The Bible or other religious literature may be used as an appropriate study of history, civilization, ethics, or comparative religions so long as it is presented in an objective manner without promoting belief or nonbelief.

2. The emphasis on religious themes in the arts, literature and history should be only as extensive as necessary for a balanced and comprehensive study of these areas. Such studies should never foster any particular religious tenets or demean any religious beliefs.

3. Student-initiated expressions to questions or assignments which reflect their beliefs or non-beliefs about a religious theme shall be accommodated. Students are free to express religious belief or nonbelief in compositions, art forms, music, speech and debate.

Speech, Literature Distribution and Clothing

C. It is the intent of this policy to recognize the free speech rights of students in public school. Students on public school campuses have the right to express their ideas verbally and through the distribution of literature so long as their speech does not disrupt the ordinary operation of the school.

1. Students may verbally express their ideas during class so long as their verbal expressions are consistent with the subject matter being taught.

2. Students may verbally express their ideas to other students during noninstructional time so long as their speech is not disruptive to the ordinary operation of the school and does not infringe on the rights of other students.

3. Students may distribute literature during noninstructional time so long as the distribution is not disruptive to the ordinary operation of the school and does not infringe on the rights of other students.

4. Students may wear symbols or articles of clothing which contain written or symbolic expressions so long as such symbols or clothing is not obscene and does not infringe on the rights of other students.

5. As used in this section, the term "noninstructional time" means before or after school hours, between classes, during lunch or recess times.

6. As used in this section, the term "does not disrupt the ordinary operation of the school" means that the speaker be the initiator and cause of disruption. It does not mean that other students must agree with the speaker. Disruption by other students in response to the student's expressions should not be construed to mean that the speaker is causing disruption. "Disruptive to the ordinary operation of the school" includes littering, forcing other students to listen by shouting or preventing passage, and engaging in speech activities during instructional time which is not consistent with the subject matter being taught.

7. As used in this section, the term "infringe on the rights of other students" means defamatory expressions against another student.

Graduation Ceremonies

D. It is the intent of this policy to recognize the solemnity of graduation ceremonies. It is also the intent to recognize the delicate balance between free speech rights and establishment of religion concerns.

1. School officials shall not invite a clergyman for the specific purpose to pray at graduation, place the prayer on the agenda, and give the clergyman guidelines for saying the prayer.

2. School officials may use secular criteria to invite a speaker for the graduation ceremony, and if the speaker voluntarily chooses to pray, school officials should not prevent the prayer.

3. Schools may rent out their facilities to outside organizations to conduct graduation at which a clergyman or other person is invited to pray and where prayer is placed on the agenda so long as school officials do not organize, conduct, promote or prescribe the content of the graduation ceremony.

4. Schools may turn over part or all of the graduation ceremony to a parent and/or student committee to organize part or all of the ceremony at which the inclusion of prayer shall rest within the discretion of the graduating senior class. The prayer, if used, shall be given by a student or other person who is not an employee of the school.

Alternative Section Regarding Graduation Ceremonies

1. The use of a brief opening and/or closing message, not to exceed two minutes, at high school graduation exercises shall rest within the discretion of the graduating senior class.

2. The opening and/or closing message shall be given by a student volunteer, in the graduating senior class, chosen by the graduating senior class as a whole.

3. If the graduating senior class chooses to use an opening and/or closing message, the content of that message shall be prepared by the student volunteer and shall not be monitored or otherwise reviewed by the school board, its officers, or employees.

Student Clubs

E. It is the intent of this policy to recognize noncurriculum-related student clubs as being a traditional and vital part of a student's educational process within the public school system. It is further the intent to provide nondiscriminatory guidelines for the continued operation of student-initiated clubs.

1. Any public secondary school which receives federal financial assistance and which has a limited open forum shall not deny equal access or a fair opportunity to, or discriminate against, any students who wish to conduct a meeting within that limited open forum on the basis of the religious, political, philosophical, or the content of the speech at such meetings.

2. A public secondary school is a limited open forum whenever such school grants an offering to or opportunity for one or more noncur-

riculum-related student groups to meet on school premises during noninstructional time.

3. Schools shall be deemed to offer a fair opportunity to students who wish to conduct a meeting within its limited open forum if such school uniformly provides that—

   (a) the meeting is voluntary and student-initiated;

   (b) there is no sponsorship of the meeting by the school, the government, or its agents or employees;

   (c) employees or agents of the school or government are present at religious meetings only in a nonparticipatory capacity;

   (d) the meeting does not materially and substantially interfere with the orderly conduct of educational activities within the school; and

   (e) nonschool persons may not direct, conduct, control, or regularly attend activities of student groups.

4. Nothing in this section shall be construed to limit the authority of the school, its agents or employees, to maintain order and discipline on school premises, to protect the well-being of students and faculty, and to assure that attendance of students at meetings is voluntary.

5. The term "sponsorship" includes the act of promoting, leading, or participating in a meeting. The assignment of a teacher, administrator, or other school employee to a meeting for custodial purposes does not constitute sponsorship of the meeting.

6. The term "meeting" includes those activities of student groups which are permitted under a school's limited open forum and are not directly related to the school curriculum.

7. The term "noninstructional time" means time set aside by the school before actual classroom instruction begins or after actual classroom instruction ends.

Release Time

F. It is the intent of this policy to recognize that schools may offer a release time for students to leave the public school facilities for off-site instruction, including religious instruction.

1. Any school may provide a designated time during the school week for students to leave the public school facilities in order to obtain off-site instruction, which may include religious instruction.

2. Students shall not be required to attend off-site religious instruction, nor may students be required to leave the public school facilities during the designated time of this off-site instruction.

3. Any religious instruction that occurs during the release time shall not be on school premises, shall not be conducted by school personnel, and no academic credit shall be given for such instruction.

Use of School Facilities

G. It is the intent of this policy to recognize that school facilities are often made available for noncurriculum-related purposes to students as well as to nonstudents, and it is further the intent of this policy that such use shall be offered on an equal and nondiscriminatory basis.

1. Any school which makes available use of its facilities to any nonstudent as a meeting place before or after the official school day shall offer use of the school facilities on an equal and nondiscriminatory basis without regard to the content of the requested meeting.

2. Any school which offers use of its facilities to any nonstudent may charge a rental or use fee so long as such rental or use fee is required for any meeting requested by any nonstudent on an equal and nondiscriminatory basis without regard to the content of the requested meeting.

3. Notwithstanding any use made available to any nonstudent, the school may prohibit continued use of the school as a meeting place to any nonstudent if there is particularized evidence to show that the nonstudent user has and will continue to cause disruption or violence to the ordinary operation of the school.

4. In the request made by a student to use school facilities as a meeting place during school hours shall be governed by Section E of this policy relating to Student Clubs.

Severability

H. If any provision of this policy or the application thereof to any person or circumstances is judicially determined to be invalid, the provisions of the remainder of the section and the application to other persons or circumstances shall not be affected thereby.

SIGNIFICANT CASES SUPPORTING SCHOOL BOARD POLICY REGARDING RELIGION
Symbols, Music, Art, Drama, and Literature

Sections A and B of the policy are taken verbatim from the Eighth Circuit Court of Appeals case of *Florey v. Sioux Falls School District 49-5,* 619 F.2d 1311 (8th Cir.), *cert. denied,* 449 U.S. 987 (1980). This Eighth Circuit Court of Appeals case found that the policy as outlined in Sections A and B was constitutional. The United States Supreme Court denied review and therefore this case establishes the most authoritative ruling on this policy regarding symbols, music, art, drama, and literature. Sections A and B are also supported by the United States Supreme Court decision in *School District of Abington Township v. Schempp,* 374 U.S. 203 (1963).

Speech, Literature Distribution, and Clothing

Section C is supported by several cases. Foremost is the United States Supreme Court decision in *Tinker v. Des Moines Independent School District,* 393 U.S. 503 (1969). This was the landmark decision regarding free speech rights on public school campuses. The test for limiting student free speech is taken almost verbatim from the *Tinker* case and is outlined in Section C2. As it relates to the distribution of religious literature, several federal court cases have been used to outline this portion of the policy. *Rivera v. East Otero School District R-1*, 721 F. Supp. 1189 (D. Colo. 1989) and *Burch v. Barker*, 861 F.2d 1149 (9th Cir. 1988).

Graduation Ceremonies

Section D pertaining to graduation ceremonies is based upon the United States Supreme Court ruling in *Lee v. Weisman*, 112 S. Ct. 2649 (1992). Section D1 essentially states the ruling of the *Lee* decision. The remainder of Section D is based upon the Fifth Circuit Court of Appeals decision in *Jones v. Clear Creek Independent Schools*, 977 F.2d 963 (5th Cir. 1992), cert. denied, 113 S. Ct. 2950 (1993). This case cites *Lee v. Weisman* and outlines an exception as it relates to student prayer. Section D also utilizes the case of *Verbena United Methodist Church v. Chilton County Board of Education*, 765 F. Supp. 704 (M.D. Ala. 1991). In this particular case involving the rental of school facilities to outside organization for the purpose of conducting graduation services, there would be no constitutional concerns as raised in *Lee v. Weisman*. To prohibit such activities could be construed as a violation of free speech rights. The alternative section regarding graduation ceremonies is based on the cases of *Harris v. Joint School District No. 241*, 821 Supp. 638 (D. Idaho 1993) and *Adler v. Duval County School Board*, 851 F. Supp. 446 (M.D. Fla. 1994).

Student Clubs

Section E deals with the federal law known as the Equal Access Act found at 20 U.S.C. §§ 4071-74. The Equal Access Act was upheld by the United States Supreme Court in *Board of Education v. Mergens*, 110 S. Ct. 2356 (1990).

Release Time

Section F pertaining to release time is governed by the United States Supreme Court decision in *Zorach v. Clauson*, 343 U.S. 306 (1952). Other cases used for this section include *Lanner v. Wimmer*, 662 F.2d 1349 (10th Cir. 1981), *Doe v. Shenandoah County School Board*, 737 F. Supp. 913 (W.D. Va. 1990), and *Minnesota Federation of Teachers v. Nelson*, 740 F. Supp. 694 (D. Minn. 1990).

Use of School Facilities

Section G pertaining to use of public school facilities is governed by the United States Supreme Court decision in *Lamb's Chapel v. Center Moriches Union Free School District*, 113 S. Ct. 2141 (1993). This is the landmark United States Supreme Court case holding that use of school facilities must be offered on a nondiscriminatory basis even if the requester is a religious organization. The section dealing with rental value is governed by *Fairfax Covenant Church v. Fairfax County School Board*, 811 F. Supp. 1137 (E.D. Va. 1993), which ruled that a school may not require higher rent of a religious organization for use of its school facilities than as required of secular organizations.

Appendix C

The Equal Access Act

The Equal Access Act is a federal law that is applicable to all the states. The Act, passed by Congress and published at 20 U.S.C. §§ 4071-74, states as follows:

Sec. 4071
(a) It shall be unlawful for any public secondary school which receives federal financial assistance and which has a limited open forum to deny equal access or a fair opportunity to, or discriminate against, any students who wish to conduct a meeting within that limited open forum on the basis of the religious, political, philosophical, or the content of the speech at such meetings.

(b) A public secondary school has a limited open forum whenever such school grants an offering to or opportunity for one or more noncurriculum-related student groups to meet on school premises during noninstructional time.

(c) Schools shall be deemed to offer a fair opportunity to students who wish to conduct a meeting within its limited open forum if such school uniformly provides that—
    (1) the meeting is voluntary and student-initiated;
    (2) there is no sponsorship of the meeting by the school, the government, or its agents or employees;
    (3) employees or agents of the school or government are present at religious meetings only in a nonparticipatory capacity;
    (4) the meeting does not materially and substantially interfere with the orderly conduct of educational activities within the school; and
    (5) nonschool persons may not direct, conduct, control, or regularly attend activities of student groups.

(d) Nothing in this subchapter shall be construed to authorize the United States or any State or political subdivision thereof—
    (1) to influence the form or content of any prayer or other religious activity;
    (2) to require any person to participate in prayer or other religious activity;
    (3) to expend public funds beyond the incidental cost of providing the space for student-initiated meetings;

    (4) to compel any school agent or employee to attend a school meeting if the content of the speech at the meeting is contrary to the beliefs of the agent or employee;

    (5) to sanction meetings that are otherwise unlawful;

    (6) to limit the rights of groups of students which are not of a specified numerical size; or

    (7) to abridge the constitutional rights of any person.

(e) Notwithstanding the availability of any other remedy under the Constitution or the laws of the United States, nothing in this subchapter shall be construed to authorize the United States to deny or withhold federal financial assistance to any school.

(f) Nothing in this subchapter shall be construed to limit the authority of the school, its agents or employees, to maintain order and discipline on school premises, to protect the well-being of students and faculty, and to assure that attendance of students at meetings is voluntary.

Definitions of Common Terms

Sec. 4072. As used in this subchapter—

    (1) The term "secondary school" means a public school which provides secondary education as determined by State law.

    (2) The term "sponsorship" includes the act of promoting, leading, or participating in a meeting. The assignment of a teacher, administrator, or other school employee to a meeting for custodial purposes does not constitute sponsorship of the meeting.

    (3) The term "meeting" includes those activities of student groups which are permitted under a school's limited open forum and are not directly related to the school curriculum.

    (4) The term "noninstructional" time means time set aside by the school before actual classroom instruction begins or after actual classroom instruction ends.

Severability

Sec. 4073. If any provision of this subchapter or the application thereof to any person or circumstances is judicially determined to be invalid, the provisions of the remainder of the subchapter and the application to other persons or circumstances shall not be affected thereby.

Construction

Sec. 4074. The provisions of this subchapter shall supersede all other provisions of federal law that are inconsistent with the provisions of this subchapter.

Appendix D

Student Club Constitution

[TEENS FOR LIFE][1] CONSTITUTION

Article I

The name of this club shall be known as [Teens for Life].[2]

Article II

General Purposes

The general purpose of [Teens for Life][3] is to provide an opportunity for students to meet together during noninstructional time to study and promote the [sanctity of human life from the moment of conception until natural death. Teens for Life is a pro-life, nondenominational student club which seeks to promote the following purposes:
1. To provide education opposing abortion and infanticide.
2. To provide education on abortion alternatives such as adoption.
3. To provide education on euthanasia.][4]

Article III

Membership

Any student desiring to participate in the study of [pro-life issues][5] may be a member of [Teens for Life].[6] However, only members professing to be [pro-life],[7] as that term may be defined from time-to-time by the officers of this organization, are entitled to vote. A quorum for voting purposes shall consist of not less than four students eligible to vote. If school policy requires a sponsor for

---

[1]Insert name of club.
[2]Insert name of club.
[3]Insert name of club.
[4]Insert description of purpose of club.
[5]Insert type of issues.
[6]Insert name of club.
[7]Insert profession.

each noncurricular organization, then the club sponsor shall not be entitled to vote and the appointment of said sponsor shall not be construed as a school endorsement of the club. The officers of the organization shall be as follows:

1. President, Vice-President, Secretary and Treasurer.
2. Secretary and Treasurer may be combined offices.
3. Any student holding office must believe in and be committed to [pro-life][8] principles, as that term shall be defined by the next preceding officers of this organization.

Article IV
Meetings and Election of Officers

Meetings shall be conducted weekly consistent with school policy for other noncurricular organizations and not inconsistent with state or federal law. There shall be at least one annual meeting for the purpose of electing officers to be held in [January][9] of each year unless otherwise agreed upon by a vote of the membership. One week before the annual meeting, nominations may be made by the membership for officers to be placed on the slate of membership the following week. Nomination of officers may also be made from the floor at the time of the annual meeting. All votes must be cast by secret ballot and the candidates receiving the most votes of those members eligible to vote shall be instated as officers which term shall take effect immediately. Any vacancy in any office occurring before the next annual meeting shall be filled within two weeks pursuant to the same procedures outlined herein.

Article V
Duties and Responsibilities

The duties and responsibilities of the officers shall be as follows:

Section I - President

The president or the president's designee shall preside at all meetings and shall insure that all meetings are conducted properly.

Section II - Vice President

The vice president shall assist the president. If at any time the president is unable to perform the duties of president by reason of illness, incompetence, absence, or resignation, the vice president shall temporarily act as president until such time as an election occurs to fill the vacancy of president.

Section III - Secretary

The secretary shall be responsible for posting any time or place of any meeting. The secretary or the secretary's designee shall also be responsible for count-

---

[8]Insert type of principles.
[9]Insert month elections will be held.

ing ballots during the annual election. The secretary shall also be responsible for keeping any records or minutes.

Section IV - Treasurer

The treasurer shall be responsible for any monies under the direction, control or possession of the club.

Article VI

Adoption

This constitution shall be adopted by two-thirds majority vote of those members eligible to vote.

Article VII

Amendments

This constitution may be amended at any regular or annual meeting provided that the specific amendment is read or posted two consecutive weeks prior to the vote on the amendment. The amendment must be adopted by two-thirds majority vote of the membership entitled to vote. Any amendment shall take effect immediately unless a motion otherwise specifies a time certain.

Appendix E

Protection of Pupil Rights— The Hatch Amendment

20 U.S.C. § 1232H

The following is the federal law often referred to as the Hatch Amendment.

Inspection by parents or guardians of instructional material.

(a) All instructional material, including teacher's manuals, films, tapes, or other supplementary instructional material which will be used in connection with any research or experimentation program or project shall be available for inspection by the parents or guardians of the children engaged in such program or project. For the purpose of this section "research or experimentation program or project" means any program or project in any applicable program designed to explore or develop new or unproven teaching methods or techniques.

Psychiatric or psychological examinations, testing, or treatment.

(b) No student shall be required, as part of any applicable program, to submit to psychiatric examination, testing, or treatment, or psychological examination, testing, or treatment in which the primary purpose is to reveal information concerning:
   (1) political affiliations;
   (2) mental and psychological problems potentially embarrassing to the student or his family;
   (3) sex behavior and attitudes;
   (4) illegal, anti-social, self-incriminating and demeaning behavior;
   (5) critical appraisals of other individuals with whom respondents have close family relationships;
   (6) legally recognized privileged and analogous relationships, such as those of lawyers, physicians, and ministers; or

(7) income (other than that required by law to determine eligibility for participation in a program or for receiving financial assistance under such program); without the prior consent of the student (if the student is an adult or emancipated minor), or in the case of unemancipated minor, without the prior written consent of the parent.

STUDENT RIGHTS IN RESEARCH, EXPERIMENTAL PROGRAMS AND TESTING 34 CFR PART 98

The following is the federal regulation implementing the federal law often referred to as the Hatch Amendment.

§ 98.1 Applicability of part

This part applies to any program administered by the Secretary of Education that:

(a) (1) Was transferred to the Department by the Department of Education Organization Act (DEOA); and

    (2) Was administered by the Education Division of the Department of Health, Education and Welfare on the day before the effective date of the DEOA; or

(b) Was enacted after the effective date of the DEOA, unless the law enacting the new Federal program has the effect of making section 439 of the General Education Provisions Act inapplicable.

§ 98.3 Access to instructional material used in a research or experimental program.

(a) All instructional material—including teachers' manuals, films, tapes, or other supplementary instructional material—which will be used in connection with any research or experimentation program or project shall be available for inspection by the parents or guardians of the children engaged in such program or project.

(b) For the purpose of this part "research or experimentation program or project means any program or project in any program under § 98.1 (a) or (b) that is designed to explore or develop new or unproven teaching methods or techniques.

(c) For the purpose of this section "children" means persons not above age 21 who are enrolled in a program under § 98.1 (a) or (b) not above the elementary or secondary education level as determined under State law.

§ 98.4 Protection of students' privacy in examination, testing or treatment.

(a) No student shall be required as part of any program specified in § 98.1 (a) or (b) to submit without prior consent to psychiatric examination, testing or treatment, or psychological examination, testing or treatment, in which the primary purpose is to reveal information concerning one or more of the following:

(1) Political affiliations;

(2) Marital and psychological problems potentially embarrassing to the student or his or her family;

(3) Sex behavior and attitudes;

(4) Illegal, anti-social, self-incriminating and demeaning behavior;

(5) Critical appraisals of other individuals with whom the student has close family relationships;

(6) Legally recognized privileged and analogous relationships, such as those of lawyers, physicians, and ministers; or

(7) Income, other than that required by law to determine eligibility for participation in a program or for receiving financial assistance under a program.

(b) As used in paragraph (a) of this section, "prior consent" means:

(1) Prior consent of the student, if the student is an adult or emancipated minor; or

(2) Prior written consent of the parent or guardian, if the student is an unemancipated minor.

(c) As used in paragraph (a) of this section:

(1) "Psychiatric or psychological examination or test" means a method of obtaining information, including a group activity, that is not directly related to academic instruction and that is designed to elicit information about attitudes, habits, traits, opinions, beliefs or feelings; and

(2) "Psychiatric or psychological treatment" means an activity involving the planned systematic use of methods or techniques that are not directly related to academic instruction and that is designed to affect behavioral, emotional, or attitudinal characteristics of an individual or group.

§ 98.5 Information and Investigation office.

(a) The Secretary has designated an office to provide information about the requirements of section 439 of the Act, and to investigate, process, and review complaints that may be filed concerning alleged violations of the provisions of the section.

(b) The following is the name and address of the office designated under paragraph (a) of this section: Family Educational Rights and Privacy Act Office, U.S. Department of Education, 400 Maryland Avenue, S.W., Washington, D.C. 20202, (202) 708-5366.

§ 98.6 Reports.

The Secretary may require the recipient to submit reports containing information necessary to resolve complaints under section 439 of the Act and the regulations in this part.

§ 98.7 Filing a Complaint.

(a) Only a student or a parent or guardian of a student directly affected by a violation under section 439 of the Act may file a complaint under this part. The complaint must be submitted in writing to the Office.

(b) The complaint filed under paragraph (a) of this section must:

   (1) Contain specific allegations of fact giving reasonable cause to believe that a violation of either § 98.3 or § 98.4 exists; and

   (2) Include evidence of attempted resolution of the complaint at the local level (and at the State level if a State complaint resolution process exists), including the names of local and State officials contacted and significant dates in the attempted resolution process.

(c) The Office investigates each complaint which the Office receives that meets the requirements of this section to determine whether the recipient or contractor failed to comply with the provisions of section 439 of the Act.

§ 98.8 Notice of the Complaint.

(a) If the Office receives a complaint that meets the requirements of § 98.7, it provides written notification to the complainant and the recipient or contractor against which the violation has been alleged that the complaint has been received.

(b) The notice to the recipient or contractor under paragraph (a) of this section must-

   (1) Include the substance of the alleged violation; and

   (2) Inform the recipient or contractor that the Office will investigate the complaint and that the recipient or contractor may submit a written response to the complaint.

§ 98.9 Investigation and findings.

(a) The Office may permit the parties to submit further written and oral arguments or information.

(b) Following its investigations, the Office provides to the complainant and recipient or contractor written notice of its findings and the basis for its findings.

(c) If the Office finds that the recipient or contractor has not complied with section 439 of the Act, the Office includes in its notice under paragraph (b) of this section:

   (1) A statement of the specific steps that the Secretary recommends the recipient or contractor take to comply; and

   (2) Provides a reasonable period of time, given all of the circumstances of the case, during which the recipient or contractor may comply voluntarily.

§ 98.10 Enforcement of the Findings.

(a) If the recipient or contractor does not comply during the period of time set under §98.9 (c), the Secretary may either:

   (1) For a recipient, take an action authorized under 34 CFR Part 78 including:

      (i) Issuing a notice of intent to terminate funds under 34 CFR 78.21;

      (ii) Issuing a notice to withhold funds under 34 CFR 78.21 200.94(b) or 298.45(b), depending upon the applicable program under which the notice is issued; or

    (iii) Issuing a notice to cease and desist under 34 CFR 78.31, 200.94(c) or 298.45(c) depending upon the program under which the notice is issued; or

(2) For a contractor, direct the contracting officer to take an appropriate action authorized under the Federal Acquisition Regulations, including either:

    (i) Issuing a notice to suspend operations under 48 CFR 12.5; or

    (ii) Issuing a notice to terminate for default, either in whole or in part under 48 CFR 49.102.

(b) If, after an investigation under § 98.9, the Secretary finds that a recipient or contractor has complied voluntarily with section 439 of the Act, the Secretary provides the complainant and the recipient or contractor written notice of the decision and the basis for the decision.

Appendix F

Title VII
Employment Discrimination

42 U.S.C. § 2000e-1 FOREIGN AND RELIGIOUS EMPLOYMENT

(a) Inapplicability of subchapter to certain aliens and employees of religious entitles

This subchapter shall not apply to an employer with respect to the employment of aliens outside any State, or to a religious corporation, association, educational institution or society with respect to the employment of individuals of a particular religion to perform work connected with the carrying on by such corporation, association, educational institution, or society of its activities.

42 U.S.C. § 2000e-2. UNLAWFUL EMPLOYMENT PRACTICES

Employer practices

(a) It shall be an unlawful employment practice for an employer—
   (1) to fail or refuse to hire or to discharge any individual, or otherwise to discriminate against any individual with respect to his compensation, terms, conditions, or privileges of employment, because of such individual's race, color, religion, sex, or national origin; or
   (2) to limit, segregate, or classify his employees or applicants for employment in any way which would deprive or tend to deprive any individual of employment opportunities or otherwise adversely affect his status as an employee, because of such individual's race, color, religion, sex, or national origin.

Employment agency practices

(b) It shall be an unlawful employment practice for an employment agency to fail or refuse to refer for employment, or otherwise to discriminate against, any individual because of his race, color, religious, sex, or national origin, or to classify or refer for employment any individual on the basis of his race, color, religious, sex, or national origin.

Labor organization practices

(c) It shall be an unlawful employment practice for a labor organization—
   (1) to exclude or to expel from its membership, or otherwise to discriminate against, any individual because of his race, color, religion, sex, or national origin;
   (2) to limit, segregate, or classify its membership or applicants for membership, or to classify or fail or refuse to refer for employment any individual, in any way which would deprive or tend to deprive any individual of employment opportunities, or would limit such employment opportunities or otherwise adversely affect his status as an employee or as an applicant for employment, because of such individual's race, color, religion, sex, or national origin; or
   (3) to cause or attempt to cause an employer to discriminate against an individual in violation of this section.

Training programs

(d) It shall be an unlawful employment practice for any employer, labor organization, or joint labor-management committee controlling apprenticeship or other training or retraining, including on-the-job training programs to discriminate against any individual because of his race, color, religion, sex, or national origin in admission to, or employment in, any program established to proved apprenticeship or other training.

Business or enterprises with personnel qualified on basis of religion, sex, or national origin; educational institutions with personnel of particular religion

(e) Notwithstanding any other provision of this subchapter—
   (1) it shall not be an unlawful employment practice for an employer to hire and employ employees, for an employment agency to classify, or refer for employment any individual, for a labor organization to classify its membership or to classify or refer for employment any individual, or for an employer, labor organization, or joint labor-management committee controlling apprenticeship or other training or retraining programs to admit or employ any individual in any such program, on the basis of his religion, sex, or national origin is a bona fide occupational qualification reasonably necessary to the normal operation of that particular business or enterprise; and
   (2) it shall not be an unlawful employment practice for a school, college, university, or other educational institution or institution of learning to hire and employ employees of a particular religion if such school, college, university, or other educational institution or institution of learning is, in whole or in substantial part, owned, supported, controlled,

or managed by a particular religion or by a particular religious corporation, association, or society, or if the curriculum of such school, college, university, or other educational institution or institution of learning is directed toward the propagation of a particular religion.

Members of Communist Party or Communist-action or Communist-front organizations

(f) As used in this subchapter, the phrase "unlawful employment practice" shall not be deemed to include any action or measure taken by an employer, labor organization, joint labor-management committee, or employment agency with respect to an individual who is a member of the Communist Party of the United States or of any other organization required to register as a Communist-action or Communist-front organization by final order of the Subversive Activities Control Board pursuant to the Subversive Activities Control Act of 1950.

National security

(g) Notwithstanding any other provision of this subchapter, it shall not be an unlawful employment practice for an employer to fail or refuse to hire and employ any individual for any position, for an employer to discharge any individual from any position, or for an employment agency to fail or refuse to refer any individual for employment in any position, or for a labor organization to fail or refuse to refer any individual for employment in any position, if—
(1) the occupancy of such position, or access to the premises in or upon which any part of the duties of such position is performed or is to be performed, is subject to any requirement imposed in the interest of the national security of the United States under any security program in effect pursuant to or administered under any statute of the United States or any Executive Order of the President; and
(2) such individual has not fulfilled or has ceased to fulfill that requirement.

Seniority or merit system; quantity or quality of production; ability test; compensation based on sex and authorized by minimum wage provisions

(h) Notwithstanding any other provision of this subchapter, it shall not be an unlawful employment practice for an employer to apply different standards of compensation, or different terms, conditions, or privileges of employment pursuant to a bona fide seniority or merit system, or a system which measures earnings by quantity or quality of production or to employees who work in different locations, provided that such differences are not the result of an intention to discriminate because of race, color, religion, sex, or national origin, nor shall it be an unlawful employment practice for an employer to give and to act upon the results of any professionally developed ability test provided that such test, its administration or action upon the results is not designed, intended or used to discriminate because of race, color, religion, sex or national original. It shall not be an unlawful employment practice under this subchapter for any employer to differentiate upon the basis of sex in determining the amount of the wages or compensation paid or to be paid to employees of such employer if such differentiation is authorized by the provisions of section 206(d) of Title 29.

Businesses or enterprises extending preferential treatment to Indians

(i) Nothing contained in this subchapter shall apply to any business or enterprise on or near an Indian reservation with respect to any publicly announced employment practice of such business or enterprise under which a preferential treatment is given to any individual because he is an Indian living on or near a reservation.

Preferential treatment not to be granted on account of existing number of percentage imbalance

(j) Nothing contained in this subchapter shall be interpreted to require any employer, employment agency, labor organization, or joint labor-management committee subject to this subchapter to grant preferential treatment to any individual or to any group because of the race, color, religion, sex, or national origin of such individual or group on account of an imbalance which may exist with respect to the total number or percentage of persons of any race, color, religion, sex, or national origin employed by any employer, referred or classified for employment by any employment agency or labor organization, admitted to membership or classified by any labor organization, or admitted to, or employed in, any apprenticeship or other training program, in comparison with the total number or percentage of persons of such race, color, religion, sex, or national origin in any community, State, section, or other area, or in the available work force in any community, State, section, or other area.

Disparate impact as basis of practice

(k) (1) (A) An unlawful employment practice based on disparate impact is established under this subchapter only if —
  (i) a complaining party demonstrates that a respondent uses a particular employment practice that causes a disparate impact on the basis of race, color, religion, sex, or national origin and the respondent fails to demonstrate that the challenged practice is job related for the position in question and consistent with business necessity; or
  (ii) the complaining party makes the demonstration described in subparagraph (C) with respect to an alternative employment practice and the respondent refuses to adopt such alternative employment practice.

(B) (i) With respect to demonstrating that a particular employment practice causes a disparate impact as described in subparagraph (A)(i), the complaining party shall demonstrate that each particular challenged employment practice causes a disparate impact, except that if the complaining party can demonstrate to the court that the elements of a respondent's decision making process are not capable of separation for analysis, the decision making process may be analyzed as one employment practice.

(ii) If the respondent demonstrates that a specific employment practice does not cause the disparate impact, the respondent shall not be required to demonstrate that such practice is required by business necessity.

(C) The demonstration referred to by subparagraph (A)(ii) shall be in accordance with the law as it existed on June 4, 1989, with respect to the concept of "alternative employment practice."

(2) A demonstration that an employment practice is required by business necessity may not be used as a defense against a claim of intentional discrimination under this subchapter.

(3) Notwithstanding any other provision of this subchapter, a rule barring the employment of an individual who currently and knowingly uses or possesses a controlled substance, as defined in schedules I and II of section 102(6) of the Controlled Substances Act (21 U.S.C. § 802(6)), other than the use or possession of a drug taken under the supervision of a licensed health care professional, or any other use or possession authorized by the Controlled Substances Act or any other provision of Federal law, shall be considered an unlawful employment practice under this subchapter only if such rule is adopted or applied with an intent to discriminate because of race, color, religion, sex, or national origin.

Alteration of test results

(l) It shall be an unlawful employment practice for a respondent, in connection with the selection or referral of applicants or candidate for employment or promotion, to adjust the scores of, use different cutoff scores for, or otherwise alter the results of, employment related tests on the basis of race, color, religion, sex, or national origin.

Motivation for practice

(m) Except as otherwise provided in this subchapter, an unlawful employment practice is established when the complaining party demonstrates that race, color, religion, sex, or national origin was a motivating factor for any employment practice, even though other factors also motivated the practice.

Challenges to practices implementing litigated or consent judgments or orders

(n) (1) (A) Notwithstanding any other provision of law, and except as provided in paragraph (2), an employment practice that implements and is within the scope of a litigated or consent judgment or order that resolves a claim of employment discrimination under the Constitution or Federal civil rights laws may not be challenged under the circumstances described in subparagraph (B).

(B) A practice described in subparagraph (A) may not be challenged in a claim under the Constitution or Federal civil rights laws—

(i) by a person who, prior to the entry of the judgment or order described in subparagraph (a), had:

(I) actual notice of the proposed judgment or order sufficient to apprise such person that such judgment or order might adversely affect the interests and legal rights of such person and that an opportunity was available to present objections to such judgment or order by a future date certain; and

(II) a reasonable opportunity to present objections to such judgment or order; or

(ii) by a person whose interests were adequately represented by another person who had previously challenged the judgment or order on the same legal grounds and with a similar factual situation, unless there has been an intervening change in law or fact.

(2) Nothing in this subsection shall be construed to—

(A) alter the standards for intervention under rule 24 of the Federal Rules of Civil Procedure or apply to the rights or parties who have successfully intervened pursuant to such rule in the proceeding in which the parties intervened;

(B) apply to the rights of parties to the action in which a litigated or consent judgment or order was entered, or of members of a class represented or sought to be represented in such action, or of members of a group on whose behalf relief was sought in such action by the Federal Government;

(C) prevent challenges to a litigated or consent judgment or order on the ground that such judgment or order was obtained through collusion or fraud, or is transparently invalid or was entered by a court lacking subject matter jurisdiction; or

(D) authorize or permit the denial to any person of the due process of law required by the Constitution.

(3) Any action not precluded under this subsection that challenges an employment consent judgment or order described in paragraph (1) shall be brought in the court, and if possible before the judge, that entered such judgment or order. Nothing in this subsection shall preclude a transfer of such action pursuant to section 1404 of Title 28.

Appendix G

Religious Freedom Restoration Act of 1993
42 U.S.C. § 2000bb

An Act
To protect the free exercise of religion.

Be it enacted by the Senate and House of Representatives of the United States of America in Congress assembled,

Section 1. Short Title.

This Act may be cited as the "Religious Freedom Restoration Act of 1993".

Section 2. Congressional Findings and Declaration of Purposes.

(a) Findings.—The Congress finds that—
   (1) the framers of the Constitution, recognizing free exercise of religion as an unalienable right, secured its protection in the First Amendment to the Constitution;
   (2) laws "neutral" toward religion may burden religious exercise as surely as laws intended to interfere with religious exercise;
   (3) governments should not substantially burden religious exercise without compelling justification;
   (4) in Employment Division v. Smith, 494 U.S. 872 (1990) the Supreme Court virtually eliminated the requirement that the government justify burdens on religious exercise imposed by laws neutral toward religion; and
   (5) the compelling interest test as set forth in prior Federal court rulings is a workable test for striking sensible balances between religious liberty and competing prior governmental interests.

(b) Purposes.—The purposes of this Act are—

    (1) to restore the compelling interest test as set forth in Sherbert v. Verner, 374 U.S. 398 (1963) and Wisconsin v. Yoder, 406 U.S. 205 (1972) and to guarantee its application in all cases where free exercise of religion is substantially burdened; and

    (2) to provide a claim or defense to persons whose religious exercise is substantially burdened by government.

Section 3. Free Exercise of Religion Protected.

(a) In General.—Government shall not substantially burden a person's exercise of religion even if the burden results from a rule of general applicability, except as provided in subsection (b).

(b) Exception.—Government may substantially burden a person's exercise of religion only if it demonstrates that application of the burden to the person—

    (1) is in furtherance of a compelling governmental interest; and

    (2) is the least restrictive means of furthering that compelling governmental interest.

(c) Judicial Relief.—A person whose religious exercise has been burdened in violation of this section may assert that violation as a claim or defense in a judicial proceeding and obtain appropriate relief against a government. Standing to assert a claim or defense under this section shall be governed by the general rules of standing under article III of the Constitution.

Section 4. Attorneys Fees.

(a) Judicial Proceedings.—Section 722 of the Revised Statutes (42 U.S.C. 1988) is amended by inserting "the Religious Freedom Restoration Act of 1993," before "or title VI of the Civil Rights Act of 1964".

(b) Administrative Proceedings.—Section 504(b)(1)(C) of title 5, United States Code, is amended —

    (1) by striking "and" at the end of clause (ii);

    (2) by striking the semicolon at the end of clause (iii) and inserting ", and "; and

    (3) by inserting "(iv) the Religious Freedom Restoration Act of 1993;" after clause (iii).

Section 5. Definitions.

As used in this Act—

    (1) the term "government" includes a branch, department, agency, instrumentality, and official (or other person acting under color of law) of the United States, a State, or a subdivision of a State;

    (2) the term "State" includes the District of Columbia, the Commonwealth of Puerto Rico, and each territory and possession of the United States;

    (3) the term "demonstrates" means meets the burdens of going forward with the evidence and of persuasion; and

    (4) the term "exercise of religion" means the exercise of religion under the First Amendment to the Constitution.

Section 6. Applicability.

(a) In General.—This Act applies to all Federal and State law, and the implementation of that law, whether statutory or otherwise, and whether adopted before or after the enactment of this Act.
(b) Rule of Construction.—Federal statutory law adopted after the date of the enactment of this Act is subject to this Act unless such law explicitly excludes such application by reference to this Act.
(c) Religious Belief Unaffected.—Nothing in this Act shall be construed to authorize any government to burden any religious belief.

Section 7. Establishment Clause Unaffected.

Nothing in this Act shall be construed to affect, interpret, or in any way address that portion of the First Amendment prohibiting laws respecting the establishment of religion (referred to in this section as the "Establishment Clause"). Granting government funding, benefits, or exemptions, to the extent permissible under the Establishment Clause, shall not constitute a violation of this Act. As used in this section, the term "granting", used with respect to government funding, benefits, or exemptions, does not include the denial of government funding, benefits, or exemptions.

Approved November 16, 1993.

Appendix H

Freedom of Access to Clinic Entrances
18 U.S.C. § 248

Chapter 13 of title 18, United States Code, is amended by adding at the end thereof the following new section:

§ 248. Freedom of Access to Clinic Entrances.

(a) Prohibited Activities.—Whoever—

(1) by force or threat of force or by physical obstruction, intentionally injures, intimidates or interferes with or attempts to injure, intimidate or interfere with any person because that person is or has been, or in order to intimidate such person or any other person or any class of persons, from obtaining or providing reproductive health services;

(2) by force or threat of force or by physical obstruction, intentionally injures, intimidates or interferes with or attempts to injure, intimidate or interfere with any person lawfully exercising or seeking to exercise the First Amendment right of religious freedom at a place of religious worship; or

(3) intentionally damages or destroys the property of a facility, or attempts to do so, because such facility provides reproductive health services, or intentionally damages or destroys the property of a place of religious worship, shall be subject to the penalties provided in subsection (b) and the civil remedies provided in subsection (c), except that a parent or legal guardian of a minor shall not be subject to any penalties or civil remedies under this section for such activities insofar as they are directed exclusively at that minor.

(b) Penalties.—Whoever violates this section shall—

(1) in the case of a first offense, be fined in accordance with this title, or imprisoned not more than one year, or both; and

(2) in the case of a second or subsequent offense after a prior conviction under this section, be fined in accordance with this title, or imprisoned not more than three years, or both;

except that for an offense involving exclusively a nonviolent physical obstruction, the fine shall not be more than $10,000 and the length of imprisonment shall not be more than six months, or both, for the first offense; and the fine shall be not more than $25,000 and the length of imprisonment shall be not more than 18 months, or both, for a subsequent offense; and except that if bodily injury results, the length of imprisonment shall be not more than 10 years, and if death results, it shall be for any term of years or for life.

(c) Civil Remedies.—

    (1) Right of action.—

        (A) In general.—Any person aggrieved by reason of the conduct prohibited by subsection (a) may commence a civil action for the relief set forth in subparagraph (B), except that such an action may be brought under subsection (a)(1) only by a person involved in providing or seeking to provide, or obtaining or seeking to obtain, services in a facility that provides reproductive health services, and such an action may be brought under subsection (a)(2) only by a person lawfully exercising or seeking to exercise the First Amendment right of religious freedom at a place of religious worship or by the entity that owns or operates such place of religious worship.

        (B) Relief.—In any action under subparagraph (A), the court may award appropriate relief, including temporary, preliminary or permanent injunction relief and compensatory and punitive damages, as well as the costs of suit and reasonable fees for attorney and expert witnesses. With respect to compensatory damages, the plaintiff may elect, at any time prior to the rendering of final judgment, to recover, in lieu of actual damages, an award of statutory damages in the amount of $5,000 per violation.

    (2) Action by Attorney General of the United States.—

        (A) In general.—If the Attorney General of the United States has reasonable cause to believe than any person or group of persons is being, has been, or may be injured by conduct constituting a violation of this section, the Attorney General may commence a civil action in any appropriate United States District Court.

        (B) Relief.—In any action under subparagraph (a), the court may award appropriate relief, including temporary, preliminary or permanent injunctive relief, and compensatory damages to persons aggrieved as described in paragraph (1)(B). The court, to vindicate the public interest, may also asses a civil penalty against each respondent—

           (i)   in an amount not exceeding $10,000 for a nonviolent physical obstruction and $15,000 for other first violation; and

           (ii) in an amount not exceeding $15,000 for a nonviolent physical obstruction and $25,000 for any other subsequent violation.

    (3) Actions by state attorneys general.—

        (A) In general.—If the Attorney General of a State has reasonable cause to believe that any person or group of persons is being, has been, or may be injured by conduct constituting a violation of this section, such Attorney General may commence a civil action in the name of such State, as parens patriae on behalf of natural persons residing in such State, in any appropriate United States District Court.

(B) Relief.—In any action under subparagraph (A), the court may award appropriate relief, including temporary, preliminary or permanent injunctive relief, compensatory damages, and civil penalties as described in paragraph (2)(B).

(d) Rules of Construction.—Nothing in this section shall be construed—

    (1) to prohibit any expressive conduct (including peaceful picketing or other peaceful demonstration) protected from legal prohibition by the First Amendment to the Constitution;

    (2) to create new remedies for interference with activities protected by the free speech or free exercise clauses of the First Amendment to the Constitution, occurring outside a facility, regardless of the point of view expressed, or to limit any existing legal remedies for such interference;

    (3) to provide exclusive criminal penalties or civil remedies with respect to the conduct prohibited by this section, or to preempt State or local laws that may provide such penalties or remedies; or

    (4) to interfere with the enforcement of State or local laws regulating the performance of abortions or other reproductive health services.

(e) Definitions.—As used in this section:

    (1) Facility.—The term "facility" includes a hospital, clinic, physician's office, or other facility that provides reproductive health services, and includes the building or structure in which the facility is located.

    (2) Interfere with.— The term "interfere with" means to restrict a person's freedom of movement.

    (3) Intimidate.—The term "intimidate" means to place a person in reasonable apprehension of bodily harm to him- or herself or to another.

    (4) Physical obstruction.—The term "physical obstruction" means rendering impassable ingress to or egress from a facility that provides reproductive health services or to or from a place of religious worship, or rendering passage to or from such a facility or place of religious worship unreasonably difficult or hazardous.

    (5) Reproductive health services.—The term "reproductive health services" means reproductive health services provided in a hospital, clinic, physicians' office, or other facility, and includes a medical, surgical, counseling or referral services relating to the human reproductive system, including services relating to pregnancy or the termination of a pregnancy.

(6) State.—The term "State" includes a State of the United States, the District of Columbia, and any commonwealth, territory, or possession of the United States.

Table of Authorities

Cases

Table of Authorities

Books, Articles, and Other Sources

Table of Authorities

Constitutional and Statutory
Provisions and Other Rules

Index

About the Author

Mathew Staver is an attorney specializing in insurance litigation, nonprofit corporation and church law, appellate practice, free speech and religious liberty constitutional law. He is president and founder of Staver & Associates, a law firm based in Orlando and Tallahassee, Florida, but whose practice extends throughout the country. He is editor of the firm's monthly newsletter, *The Advocate*, a legal publication dealing with insurance litigation.

Mr. Staver is also president and founder of The Staver Group, a governmental consulting lobbying organization. In addition to lobbying on business, commercial and insurance related matters, The Staver Group lobbies on pro-family, religious liberty, and private education issues.

In 1989, Mr. Staver became founder and president of Liberty Counsel, a religious civil liberties education and legal defense organization established to preserve religious freedom. Based in Orlando, Liberty Counsel provides education and legal defense throughout the nation. As president, Mr. Staver has produced many informative brochures on religious liberty issues. He is also editor of *The Liberator*, a monthly newsletter devoted to religious liberty topics. He also produces a radio program called *Freedom's Call*, a daily commentary on religious freedom and church related issues.

In addition to receiving a doctorate of law degree, Mr. Staver graduated Summa Cum Laude with a Master of Arts degree in Religion, and while pursuing graduate study, he was an honorary guest lecturer at the American Society of Oriental Research at the University of Illinois.

He has numerous legal opinions credited to his work and has argued before the United States Supreme Court in the landmark case of *Madsen v. Women's Health Center, Inc.*, 114 S. Ct. 2516 (1994).

About Liberty Counsel

Liberty Counsel is a nonprofit religious civil liberties education and legal defense organization established to preserve religious freedom. Founded in 1989 by president and general counsel, Mathew D. Staver, Liberty Counsel accomplishes its purpose in a two-fold manner: through education and through legal defense.

Liberty Counsel produces many aids to educate in matters of religious liberty. *The Liberator* is a monthly newsletter reviewing various religious liberty issues throughout the nation. *Freedom's Call* is a two-minute weekday radio program produced by Liberty Counsel providing education in First Amendment religious liberties. Many brochures are continually being produced by Liberty Counsel outlining various aspects of religious liberty. Most of the cases in which Liberty Counsel is involved resolve through education, either by a telephone call, informative literature, or letters. Many individuals and public officials are ignorant of the First Amendment. Religious rights are often restricted or lost simply out of this ignorance.

Education will not solve all religious liberty issues. Some individuals are hostile and bigoted toward religion. In these cases, if education does not resolve the issue, Liberty Counsel aggressively fights for religious liberty in the courtroom. Liberty Counsel represents individuals whose religious liberties are infringed, and defends entities against those trying to restrict religious liberty.

Liberty Counsel is a nonprofit tax-exempt corporation dependent upon public financial support. Contributions to Liberty Counsel are tax-deductible. For information about Liberty Counsel, or to make tax-deductible contributions, please write or call:

> Liberty Counsel
> Post Office Box 540774
> Orlando, Florida 32854
> (407) 875-2100
> (800) 671-1776